WITH A SINGLE STEP

The Story of a Non-Motorized Circumnavigation of the Earth

Joe Oakes

Piano! Piano! Press
Portland, OR

Requests for permission to make copies of any part of the work should be emailed to alcatrazjoe@hotmail.com or mailed to PIANO! PIANO! PRESS, 3075 NW Montara Loop, Portland, OR 97229.

Library of Congress Cataloguing-in-Publication Data
LCCN: 2009927121
Oakes, Joe
With a Single Step: The Story of a Non-Motorized
Circumnavigation of the World/Joe Oakes—1ˢᵗ ed.
p. 269 cm.
ISBN: 0-9787627-1-1
1. Oakes, Joe: 1934- 2. Athletic Adventure—Nonfiction
3. Long-Distance Cycling 4. Ultrarunning 5. Open Ocean Swimming 6. Dog-mushing 7. Kayaking 8. Older Athletes I. Title

Text set in Adobe Garamond Pro
Cover and book design by John Morris-Reihl, www.artntech.com
Manufactured by Lightning Source, LLC

To Walter Stack, my role model, my mentor, my friend –

Old Bean, I hope you can read this in Heaven:
I MADE IT, BUDDY, and I'm still breathing.
Say hello to Arctic Joe for me. And don't you two guys get
God pissed off or you will get kicked out.

How's the beer up there?

Table of Contents

Preface

In my 70+ years of roaming this planet I have gotten good use out of my body, beating the hell out of it in the process, working it for all it is worth. As a result I have had five knee and shoulder surgeries, concussions, broken bones, a fractured skull, sprains, torn ligaments, hepatitis, giardiasis, shigellosis, melanoma, lymphoma, lingering diarrhea, road rash, skin ailments, injections, and prescriptions for an entire panoply of illnesses—some of them the results of exposing myself to evil bugs that lurk in strange places. My eyes and my ears need mechanical help. My poor *corpus* has long ago paid its dues.

How did I inflict all that damage on myself? By *being healthy*. In high school in 1948 I started competing in running events, and I never stopped. Over 60 years I have finished 130 marathons, 51 ultra-marathons and God knows how many shorter runs. Add 100-mile runs, Arctic and Antarctic marathons, the infamous Death Valley Ultramarathon, and a few multi-day runs, and eventually you wear your parts out. A recent review of my workout logbooks showed a lifetime running mileage that totaled five and a half times around the earth. That is a lot of sneaker wear. The folks at New Balance love me.

But I do *not* think of myself as a runner. Ocean swimming is more exciting, and I have done lots of that, too, including a few that scared the hell out of me. There was a solo swim across the jelly-fish laden Dardanelles; I was the first person ever to swim from Russia to Alaska in the frigid (37° F) Diomede Islands; I have done more than 40 swims from Alcatraz; etc. Even more fun were relay swims, when you get to share the fun with your friends and maybe a school of dolphins: the English Channel; Spain to Morocco; Channel Islands; Lake Tahoe; Maui Channel; the Croatian islands; and an attempt from Robben

Island, South Africa, which was rudely interrupted by a great white shark. I believe that I am the only person in the world who has both run a marathon and done a long swim on every continent.

Then there were six of the early Ironman Triathlons in Hawaii (hot and interminable); a bunch of shorter triathlons; long bike rides (hazardous), like Fairbanks to New York or Calais to Moscow;* the Iditarod Trail on a dog sled (bloody cold); Golden Gloves boxing (two wins, one spectacular loss and a bent beak); crossing the Atlantic in a sailboat (brilliant, especially at night, but no fun during the hurricane); kayaking the Yukon (incomparable); climbing a few high mountains (puff-puff). It has been my extremely good fortune to be able to do so very many wonderful things that a lot of people *want* to do but never get around to doing.

So here I am, this old guy who has been lucky enough to have logged a lot of adventures, and still doing what I can. No knowledgeable person would call me a great athlete—just persistent and maybe opportunistic. I could bullshit you about the awesomeness of it, but frankly, observing most endurance events is about as exciting as watching grass grow. But there *is* one chapter in my *curriculum vitae* that I hope might interest you, something that will never be repeated by anyone in quite the same way.

There has always been this urge in me to do something bigger, longer, more, but never quite enough. What, I asked myself, could put an end to this sick need to keep pushing myself further? There was only one thing on this planet that would satisfy me: *I had to circumnavigate the whole freaking earth, and do it without the use of motors.* Selfish: yes. Stupid: sometimes. And *that* is what I want to tell you about.

My journey took place in several distinct pieces over ten years. Nor was it a neat, connect-the-dots trip. The dots were offset in the Atlantic crossing; i.e., we finished the bike ride in New York but picked up the sailboat in the Caribbean. Siberia was chronologically out of place, but when I got a rare chance to go to Siberia, I jumped on it. Not perfect, but I'm satisfied with what I did and how I did it. That is what ultimately matters when a dream becomes reality.

Maybe the most important thing about the trip is this: There was always a friend along to share the fun and keep me going.

Some names have been changed to protect the innocent, including me.

Adolf Hitler said, "*Today Munich; Tomorrow the World!*"

The World? To quote Frank Sinatra, I did it my way, not Adolf's.

* Because of the way I seemed to wander freely in and out of the USSR, and later Russia, I have heard it said that I must have been with the CIA. Others have said, no, he must have been KGB or a double agent. While it is true that I served in a military intelligence unit many years ago, I can truly say that I have never been associated with the CIA or the KGB. (But wouldn't I say that anyway?)

Introduction

This is a story about a journey, the fulfillment of a dream. As a young boy I wanted to travel all the way around the world at my own pace. My dream stayed with me for a half century, but the day came, finally, when I could really do it. I had the time, the resources and good health. I decided to use whatever non-motorized mode of transport was appropriate to the varying terrain and conditions. And then I took the first step.

People of my generation have watched, sometimes helplessly, sometimes heedlessly, as large chunks of our planet have been badly damaged. I felt some guilt about being a part of that and decided that the theme of my journey would be giving mother earth a symbolic hug, going once around our Big Mama, taking a good look at her as I went.

The 20th century has witnessed some devastating wars, usually based on the idea that "my people are better than your people." My father was shot up badly in WW I. Four of my siblings served in the WW II, and two of us were in the Korean Conflict. I became something of an active anti-war person, but, alas, as with my tepid environmentalism, it has always lacked the fire in the belly that would have made me feel satisfied that I had done enough. My wife, Sylvia, is of Russian descent, Ronald Regan's "Evil Empire." I wanted to make this a joint Russian-American trip if I could find a Russian partner, which would also be a great advantage when crossing the USSR.

If there is a lesson in this story, it is that big dreams really can come true with persistence, flexibility, good humor and patience. And good friends are absolutely vital.

Maybe now I can trade in my sneakers for fuzzy slippers. No pipe, please.

Chapter I

THE GRAND PLAN: HUG YOUR MAMA

If it sounds too good to be true, it probably is.
        – My wife, Sylvia

The best laid plans of mice and men aft gang agley.
        – Robert Burns

A WINDOW OF OPPORTUNITY

I had a hard time believing the item in the April 1989 issue of *UltraRunning* magazine. It is a respected publication in its narrow field: the coverage of distance running events of fifty miles or longer. The article said there was going to be an extremely long running event across Siberia: "*The event is sponsored by the Director General for Transportation and Building for Siberia, who is interested in having Americans join in with teams from Poland, North Korea, the USSR, and other nations. All expenses for travel, support, food and accommodations will be taken care of by the race sponsor. Individuals must arrange, at their own expense, transportation to and from Moscow.*" It was to start June 15, 1989, and up to ten Americans would be welcome. It went on to give the telephone number of a contact person named Bob in Colorado.

I had to make that phone call. Bob answered and said that, yes, it was true. The Director General would, indeed, pay for support, food, transportation and housing within the USSR from the time we got off the airplane in Moscow until we were delivered back to our homebound flights. "They want to open up Siberia, expose it to the outside world. If you're interested and capable of doing this run across Siberia, we have room for you."

For years I had wanted to cross Siberia on foot, impossible during the decades-long Cold War. This looked like a unique opportunity. I had plenty of experience competing in "ultra-distance" running competitions, up to 100 miles, as well as multi-day runs. This run, as difficult as it might be, was within my capabilities. I jumped on that invitation like a praying mantis on a fat, juicy fly. Then I had to figure out how to tell my wife, Sylvia, that I was going to hightail it off to Siberia and that I'd be gone for a long time.

Sylvia took it very well. I had once again underestimated her. "Look at it this way, Joe. How many times have *you* said 'If it looks too good to be true, it probably is?'" But I was pumped up, my vision was blurred, I wasn't thinking clearly. "I read it in *UltraRunning*, and they never lie. I even called that guy in Colorado. If I don't grab this chance to get started now, I probably never will."

Get started referred to something much more important to me than a trip to Siberia. That was the zinger that got to her, waylaying her logic, going straight for her sympathy jugular. After some thought she said, "Maybe you're right. If this is real, it's an opportunity for you to do what you've always wanted to do. If it isn't, you can cut your losses and come home. You've been to Russia, you know the language and how to work within the system." She took a deep breath and continued, "You're a big boy; it's your decision. I'll back you." She did back me, and she always has, more than I deserve.

Why did I want to run a race across Siberia? Because crossing Russia would be a very significant part of a dream I had been nurturing for many years: *a circumnavigation of the entire earth, bit by bit, using only non-motorized transportation.* In 1984 I retired from a successful business career and all of a sudden I had the time, means, energy and desire to pursue my dream.

A non-motorized circumnavigation, unless you want to do it all in a sailboat, has to take place in the Northern Hemisphere. Geographically there are four big segments to that northerly route: the North American continent, the Eurasian landmass and the two bodies of water that separate them. Politically, physically and logistically, the longest and most difficult part would be crossing Ronald Reagan's "Evil Empire." The distance across the Soviet Union from the Baltic to the Bering Straits is about a quarter of the circumference of the earth. Getting permission and arranging logistics presented two huge sets of problems, and it was clear that I would need help from inside the USSR.

SEVEN YEARS EARLIER: "CAN BORIS COME OUT AND PLAY?"

On a typically cool, sunny San Francisco afternoon in 1982 I made a visit to the Soviet Consulate on Green Street in the upscale Pacific Heights neighborhood. I had just come from a business appointment and was wearing a suit and tie, carrying a briefcase. Parking close to the consulate was impossible, so I parked a few blocks away. The walk was pleasant, and I enjoyed looking at the multi-million dollar mansions along the way. I rang the doorbell outside the high, black iron gate that separated the entrance to the Russian Consulate from the USA. In those days there was often a crowd of demonstrators outside the building, but on this particular afternoon it was quiet.

A tiny peephole opened and a scratchy voice crackled through a speaker, "Pliz go to side entrance." I followed along the chipped, rusting fence to the side entrance, where I was buzzed through another iron gate and again through a heavy wooden door. The lobby was claustrophobic. It was about 14 feet square, with dark wood paneling dating from the time when the building had been someone's mansion. In racks around the walls were pamphlets extolling the virtues of the USSR. One described a glorious hydroelectric project; others told of the evil things that capitalism was doing to the oppressed peoples of the world. A few were travel brochures, cheaply done, not designed to appeal to American tastes.

An officious clerk with thick eyeglasses and a sallow complexion stared out at me through a thick window of what looked like bullet-proof glass. He addressed me in a heavily accented monotone. "I am Boris ("Bah-REES"). Khow can I khelp you?" I was prepared for his question. I had written an outline of my plan to cross Russia on foot and bicycle, half expecting that he would classify me with the many nutcases he must surely meet in dealing with the American public. I shoved my outline through the small slot in the bottom of the window. He looked at it for a few moments, then raised his dreary eyes up to me. In answer to my question of whether this crazy scheme was possible, he replied in a low drone: "Certainly. Vhy not?" He seemed to say that all things were possible in the USSR, the best of all possible worlds. He slid several pamphlets under the glass, a visa application along with complicated instructions, and a large-scale map of the USSR. I could imagine him sobbing as I left his stifling dungeon. I could feel his eyes burning in my back, and I thought of him thinking, *"Vhy should you be able to go free into the Kalifornia sunshine vhile I am trapped in this building day after day?"*

My little trip to the Soviet Consulate only got me a few pieces of paper and a teeny glimpse of how things were done in "Do-Nothing-grad." I was well aware that the papers he gave me were worthless and that almost all of the Soviet Union was off limits to me. But it was a start and I felt good. As I walked back to my car, I took the time to go the long way so I could see more of the beautiful neighborhood that Boris the Vole could only dream about exploring. That little walking detour back to my car is what got me into trouble, not with the Russians, but with our own American officialdom.

Six months after my visit to the Soviet Consulate I got a phone call. The caller identified himself as Agent So-And-So from the FBI and said that he wanted to come to my home to talk to me. In the early 1980s I was one of the few people who had finished the Ironman Triathlon in Hawaii, so people came to me for triathlon training advice, including a few FBI men and Secret Service agents. I assumed that agent So-And-So wanted to see me about triathlons. Being a big-hearted guy, I invited him to come right over. He showed up 15 minutes later. When he flashed his badge at me the way they do in the movies, I thought to myself that this was a funny way to say "Hi" to someone who is about to do a favor for you. I took note of his ponderous belly and sallow complexion and warning lights went on: "This fellow is not here to talk about training for a triathlon." Since I had no idea what it was he wanted, I invited him in to find out.

After some small talk, in which I made sure to let him know about my FBI acquaintances and what a good guy I was, he came to the point. "Mister Oakes, we know all of that. We have been investigating you for the past six months. We looked into your business, your personal life, and your family. We know, for example, that you drink beer with the Hash House Harriers on Monday nights and that you run with the DSE on Sunday mornings. What we are trying to find out is why you made a visit to the Soviet Consulate in San Francisco a few months back and if you have access to information related to national security. Please be frank with us." Was he going to read me my rights? I had almost forgotten about that visit to Boris at the Russian Embassy.

I explained to the agent that I made that visit because I was interested in a sports-related trip to the Soviet Union. I also told him that I had served as the Long Distance Running Chairman for the AAU, which he knew, and was a founding member of the Board of Governors of the Triathlon Federation, which he also knew. He pondered my explanation, made a few notes and asked why I had taken a circuitous route walking back to my car. "Did you have in your briefcase any information that might be of value to the Soviets?" My answers seemed to satisfy him. He made a few more notes, closed his folder, smiled, thanked me, shook my hand and waddled out the door.

I later learned that the investigation had cost the American taxpayers about $40,000. They could have saved 40 grand by asking me in the first place. Since then I have made it a habit to call the FBI whenever I am going to do anything they might want to spend tax dollars investigating. I tell them what I plan to do, and tell them to save the taxpayer's money. I am doing my part to reduce the federal deficit.

I put going to Russia on ice for a while; there would be time enough for that later. I needed to find out what it would actually be like to do a very long, non-motorized trip. It was time for an experiment.

TRIATHLON AMERICA

In early 1983 I contacted my son Chris, an engineering student at the University of Arizona, and asked him about his plans for the coming summer. "Nothing yet, Pop. What's up?" Would he like to take an interesting trip across the USA with me? Every day would be like training for a triathlon: cycling, running and swimming. Chris is a natural athlete. I thought that this would be a great thing for us to do together, and so did he. We talked about routes, and decided that since it would be summer, it would be best to stay as far north as possible. It might be fun to roughly follow the Lewis and Clark Trail east, then part of the route of the Voyageurs, and finish at one of the first places where white men set foot on the North American continent: Plymouth Rock.

Chris had a friend, Steve Smith, a bicycle mechanic. He wanted to go along. Wiry and intense, Steve brought with him a good attitude and useful skills. Word of our proposed trip reached Mike Russell, a juvenile probation officer in Spokane, Washington. If Steve was intense, Mike was unflappable. He had to be, working with troubled kids in the penal system. He was fair skinned, balding and gentle. His round eyeglasses and bright blue eyes gave him the look of a scientist, but physically, he was as hard as nails. Mike lived in Spokane with his wife and four lovely and active teenage daughters. He had never been east of Idaho and wanted to join us. We were lucky to have both of them.

Sylvia showed me a newspaper advertisement for a 21-foot camper/trailer with an old Lincoln Continental to pull it. I had a mechanic look it over and offered the owner $3,000 for both. It was collecting dust and running up storage bills, so we had a deal. We now had a four-man team, a support vehicle and a home on wheels. We were ready for our experiment, which we named *Triathlon America*.

In late April 1983 I baptized our venture with a swim across the Golden Gate, with my pal Peter Butler piloting for me in a rowboat. As I swam north in the 54-degree water, breathing on my right side to avoid swallowing the waves coming from my left, Peter gave me a big grin and shouted: "Joe, do *not* look to your left." Naturally, I turned to my left to find myself face to face with a half-ton bull sea lion with a black head as big as a prize-winning pumpkin and breath that made it very clear that he was a fish-eater. His eyes looked like bloodshot billiard balls. He sized me up, decided that this scrawny thing was not a rival for his harem, belched a gruff bark and dived for the bottom, soaking Peter with a great splash of his tail. It was a good omen; Mother Nature was on our team. I picked up my pace as I swam towards the north tower of the Golden Gate Bridge.

Mike, Steve, Chris and I got together two days later in Seaside, Oregon, the western end of the Lewis and Clark Trail. After a brief ritual dip in the frigid water of the Pacific Ocean, we turned eastward, three of us riding bicycles, one driving. That would be our *modus operandi* most of the time. Our goal was to cycle 100 miles a day, with each of us driving the trailer for a 25-mile stretch while the others pedaled. We did some running, but miles peel off much more rapidly on the bikes.

Whenever we came to a river we swam across it. We had a folding rowboat, and one of us would row while the others swam. In the Tri-Cities area of eastern Washington we swam across the confluence of the Columbia and Snake Rivers, heavy with early May snow melt. It was fast and cold but neither as fast nor as cold as the Kootenai River in Idaho a few days later. We crossed the Mississippi in three places, first where it is born as a dribble near Bimidji, Minnesota, and last at Lake Pepin, where it is big, wide and slow. By far the filthiest rivers were the Connecticut River and the Hudson, near Albany, where we swam through thousands of dead fish. The annual shad run had come to a screeching halt not far from the large GE facility, six-inch silvery fish bodies blanketing the surface. The stench was nauseating, but we came to swim, so we swam.

Generally, things went smoothly. We got along well: cooked, ate, rode, swam and slept together. It could have been stressful, but the four of us were cooperating to make it a successful journey. There was one day when we all got lost going in different directions entering Syracuse, New York. When we finally got back together in the camper, somebody had left the refrigerator door unlatched and its contents were all over the floor of the camper, including a gallon of milk and a Humpty-Dumpty-ed watermelon. All the king's horses and all the king's men would have been hard pressed to put our equanimity back together again on that day.

Our route was straightforward. We went from Seaside, Oregon, to Portland on Rte. 26, a forested road as pretty as any we would travel. On our first day a herd of elk crossed the road just in front of us. The big bull stood eight feet tall, his right of way uncontested. He stood his ground, head down, blocking us while his girlfriends sashayed across the road. Through the magnificent Columbia Gorge we had a strong wind at our backs. After a visit to Mike's family in Spokane we made a beeline east on US Highway 2, crossing the Continental Divide below Glacier National Park. We camped right on the Divide, near an obelisk dedicated by Teddy Roosevelt, locally known as Teddy's Last Erection.

Route 2 going east from Blackfoot was paved with road-kill prairie dogs, Montana's answer to the lemming. Through the flatlands of eastern Montana and North Dakota, we saw graceful and shy pronghorn antelope grazing peacefully, boing-boinging away when they thought we might be too interested. In the town of Wolf Point we met the meanest dogs anywhere. A dog attacking a bicycle can usually be sent packing by brandishing a bicycle pump, but these snarling curs would not be deterred. They kept coming back for more, and we were relieved to get out of there uninjured. Entering western Minnesota with the help of a strong tailwind, we clocked over 25 miles an hour most of a day. On occasion we'd tuck in behind a farm tractor or a slow truck for a few miles, drafting in its slipstream. It isn't a good practice, but we sometimes let making miles take precedence over good sense.

After a swim in frigid Lake Superior we headed south from Duluth, through Madison, to Chicago, where my sister-in-law Dorothy made an attempt to fatten us up in one day. As we moved eastward the roads got narrower and the traffic got heavier. Approaching the Blue Water Bridge into Canada from Michigan in a hailstorm, Chris and I had a close call. The road was heavy with truck traffic, and there was no shoulder. I was following Chris too closely, taking advantage of his draft, when my front wheel nudged his rear wheel.

He went down and I came down on top of him, both of us only a few inches from the wheels of a fast moving semi. That scared the heck out of us. We agreed that we would maintain a safer distance between bicycles.

That night we donated blood to starving Canadian mosquitoes on the shore of Lake Huron. After a much-needed rest in Toronto we crossed back into the US at Niagara Falls. We had swum in all five of the Great Lakes. From Niagara we continued east through Syracuse and Albany, across the Hudson and into Massachusetts and on to Plymouth Rock and Cape Cod on the first of July.

INDEPENDENCE DAY

We had made arrangements for 13 friends, representing the original 13 colonies, to meet on the Fourth of July at the bottom of Manhattan near the World Trade Center. Our Independence Day celebration consisted of a swim from Manhattan Island around the Statue of Liberty and on to New Jersey, followed by a bicycle ride across New Jersey to the Delaware River. Bill Freeborn had rented big rowboats for us to cross the Delaware River, a la George Washington, and we finished the day by running ten kilometers to the Liberty Bell in Philadelphia. We called our Fourth of July jaunt the *Liberty To Liberty Triathlon*. What a way to cap off our trip across the country!

Triathlon America was a successful experiment. I learned a lot about planning and executing a very long journey. The best part of the trip was meeting people. We were welcomed into the homes of the Russells in Spokane, the Beddors in Minnesota, and the Craners in Cohoes, New York. One evening while we were camped behind an Amoco gas station near Great Falls, North Dakota, a road worker came over to see what we were up to. After a chat, he returned to his camp and came back with a sack. He told us that he was a beekeeper when he was not working construction and that he wanted to help us with our journey. In the sack were several jars of honey. Through his energy-giving honey he went along with us. We met a lot of generous people like that beekeeper, and all of them went with us in one way or another.

Chris drove the trailer back to Arizona and lived in it during his senior year. We haven't heard from Steve in a long time. I visited with Mike Russell in Spokane while vacationing up that way a few years ago. He has retired and his girls are grown.

CHERNOBYL

Nothing ever came of my 1982 visit to the Soviet Consulate. In April of 1986 Sylvia and I were invited to go to the USSR with a San Francisco "citizen diplomats" group. The goal was to develop one-on-one relationships between citizens of the US and the USSR. I had hopes of meeting someone who was interested in my project.

The day we arrived in Russia, President Reagan ordered the bombing of Libya, once again straining US relations with the USSR. Several days later, while we were in Kiev, the Chernobyl Nuclear Plant blew up 75 miles away. We were evacuated to Armenia the next morning with no explanation whatsoever. It took a week to learn about Chernobyl.

I made another trip to Moscow in December 1986, this time as a governor of the U.S. Triathlon Federation, to promote the sport of triathlon to the Soviet Sports Committee as a potential Olympic event. In a series of frustrating meetings with Commissar Gramov, I made no progress, nor did I get any further in pursuit of my goal of getting permission to cross the USSR, or even finding an interested confederate.

AN OLD SIBERIAN

If I was going to cross the USSR, I needed to learn to speak Russian and to read and write in the Cyrillic alphabet. How hard could it be? Russian kids do it, don't they?

I enrolled in Russian language classes in the evening school at De Anza College in California. Doctor Nikolai Ivanovich Rokitiansky, a tall bull of a 75-year-old native Siberian, was an excellent teacher and a tough taskmaster. He gave rigorous assignments and expected them to be done on time. One evening, when I was not quite up to par with my preparations, he shot me an icy glare and asked: "Mister Oakes, are you really a student, or are you a bum from the KGB or CIA here to spy on me?" I got the feeling that if I were really a spy he would not have hesitated for one minute to feed me to the Siberian tigers he had encountered as a youth. From then on my nickname was Shpion, the Russian word for a spy.

I had the privilege of spending four semesters with Doctor Rokitiansky. His stern and demanding approach kept me on the ball, and his insights into the Russian people added spice to the classes. Thanks to the good professor, I acquired the Russian language skills that I needed. Without his help I would not have been able to function in Russia.

By 1989, when I saw the item in *UltraRunning* magazine, I was ready for my invasion of Russia.

Joe in training

CHAPTER II

PINOCCHIO GOES TO SIBERIA

"Sibir, zemlya bolshikh vosmoshenya." Siberia, land of great opportunities.

"At this third lie his nose grew so long that poor Pinocchio could not move in any direction." "The Adventures of Pinocchio," Carlo Collodi, Italy, 1882

A GATHERING OF EAGLES AND A FEW VULTURES

Colorado Bob asked the runners to gather at the Aeroflot gate at JFK for our flight to Moscow. We had not yet met each other, but people who run ultra-marathon races have a "lean and hungry look." I approached a tall, slim fellow, a bit younger than I, and asked him if he might be one of the runners going to Siberia. "That's me," he said with a broad smile, introducing himself as Ted Epstein. "I guess we are the senior citizens in this gang." Ted was an amiable fellow, and anxious to get started. We shared our concerns about what we might be getting into. As we talked others drifted toward us, drawn by the herd instinct that draws members of a common species together. Most were somewhat apprehensive but looking forward to doing what no one had done before.

One face was familiar: Jesse Dale Riley from Key West. I had met Jesse at the Washington State Centennial Run, where he finished first in his division. That footrace went clear across the state of Washington, from the Idaho border to the Pacific. It was run in stages of 60 miles a day, a run that might be comparable to our Siberia journey. "Howzit, Joey. Good to see you." Riley stood 6'3," cut his hair really short and wore thick eyeglasses. No one has a bigger smile than Riley, and he wasn't as edgy as the others. "This is a no-risk situation for me, man. They are gonna feed me, house me and take good care of me once I get to Russia. And my sponsor came up with my airfare. This is gonna be a big, free adventure."

What a great attitude! Really, all we had at risk were the airfare (not an inconsiderable amount), the time we were taking away from our lives at home . . . and maybe our lives if things turned sour. I didn't want to rain on Jesse's parade, but while all of us were whistling our happy tunes, there was real concern just below the surface.

Into our midst strode a short, chubby, unkempt fellow with a bad complexion problem, younger than Ted and I, but older than the others, clearly not a runner. "You must be my runners. I'm Bob. I know you have a lot of questions, but hold them until we get together with the sponsor in Moscow. They have all the details. In the meantime I want to assure you that everything is *completely* under control." So much for getting answers.

It was a long flight from San Francisco to New York and an even longer flight to Moscow, where it took forever getting through Soviet customs and immigration. We were dealing with bureaucrats who probably hadn't smiled in a decade. The atmosphere brightened when we got into the main terminal, where we were greeted by a group of upbeat Russian runners. They piled us into small Russian Ladas and took us in pairs to the apartments of several Russian hosts. Ted and I went to the home of the publisher of a running magazine. Before dropping us off, our driver told us, "Get quick nap. We make party for you tonight."

A HOT PARTY

It was *some* party. The organizer of the affair was a thirtyish Ukranian who introduced himself in good English as Alexei. He and his father were to be in charge of our group for our entire time in the USSR. Alexei hustled me off to the side, away from the others. "Listen, Joseph, it is illegal for me to change money but I want to help you. I'll give you a better deal than the official exchange rate. The government is screwing you." Big deal. Nobody in his right mind used the ridiculous official rate. What he offered was not bad, but it wasn't very good either. At his rate he could go into a subway underpass and make 50 percent profit in minutes reselling my dollars. I didn't want to offend my host on the first day of the trip, so I changed $20 with him. "Look, Joseph, this is illegal. Please don't tell my father, okay?" During the next half hour he made the rounds of our group, cozying up to them one by one. The younger runners believed that he was doing them a big favor, and they seemed to enjoy the cloak and dagger aspect of it. I watched him change about 1,000 good US greenback dollars for rubles that we would have to spend before we went home, because rubles were worthless outside Russia. They were not worth much in Russia either.

That one series of transactions made more money for Alexei than the average Russian made in a year. Every time he made a score, he implored his mark in his most sincere manner, "Please don't tell my father." We would get to know the ways of Alexei and his virtuous father all too well.

When Alexei was finished with his rounds a ferret-faced man, probably 55 years old, skulked quietly into the room and settled in next to him. It was Alexei's revered father, the fellow we were not to tell about the illegal currency exchanges. They chatted in hushed tones for a while, and after introducing his father, Ivan, to the runners, Alexei left the party. Ivan spoke almost no English, but it did not deter him from summoning me into the kitchen. He addressed me the way he would many times in the weeks to come, "Mine Dear Amerikan Frient. You vant change sahm mahney, yes? I give you good deal, but pliz not to tell Alexei."

That would not be the last time Alexei and Ivan would woo us with a one-two punch or conflicting stories or some other way to scam us. Eventually the runners realized that these guys were not to be trusted, and someone came up with the names of "Pinocchio" and "Pinocchio Junior" for them. We were among serpents. The Pinocchio Gang got no more money from me that day, but they weren't through. We would be together for a long time in Siberia. I probably should have abandoned the Pinocchio Gang and headed home immediately. But I have never been known for my good judgment.

Our hostess was Olga, an exotic looking Tatar, slightly built, dark eyes and hair, dressed simply but beautifully. A short, slim young man of about 30, with a full mane of black hair, bright black eyes, and an aquiline nose entered and brightened the room. There was no doubt that Nail (Nah-YEEL) Bairamgalin was among the best in the current crop of very talented Russian distance runners. After producing a couple of unlabeled bottles of a clear liquid from under his coat, he went from runner to runner introducing himself, not for a minute allowing the fact that he spoke nothing but Russian to be an impediment. Then Nail made his way over to the piano and started tickling out jazz and current pop American tunes. The party was on!

The Pinocchios had left, probably to haggle over the day's take. We were toasting each other with the stuff from Nail's bottles, cut with equal parts of water. I asked a fellow named Rashid about it. He explained that Gorbachev was trying to reduce alcoholism, so he had severely cut the production of vodka. Not to be deprived of something so basic to a way of life, Russians quickly turned to home brew, and the strongest of it was called *spirt,* reminiscent of Prohibition and bathtub gin, maybe 160 proof.

In the crowd was Gennady Schvets, a daily sports columnist for *Komsomolskaya Pravda*, with a circulation of 23 million, the biggest newspaper in the world. We talked for a while, and he showed more than a passing interest in my dream of an around the world journey. In fact, he seemed enthusiastic.

Nail was holding court in the bedroom, and he called us in. He wanted to show us just how potent his *spirt* really was. Filling a tumbler part way with the witches' brew, he lit a match to it, turning to show the flame. As he did so, he bumped into Olga, spilling some of the flaming liquid onto his own wrist. He instinctively dropped the glass and its contents onto our hostess's oriental carpet. There was a big blue puff. Before anyone else could move, Olga had ripped off her sweater and smothered the fire, slightly singeing her face and hair in the process. Somebody called the fire department, but the fire was extinguished quickly. The fire fighters never came anyway. Olga, in her most gracious hostess role, said that it was nothing, please go on with the party. She refused to have our team doctor look at her burns, saying that they were superficial, and she sure as hell would not go to a Russian doctor for treatment.

But the party was over. We were all exhausted from our long flight, and Nail's potion had set us up for some very necessary sleep. Ted and I spent the night together on a convertible sofa in the living room at Gennady Schvetz' apartment, while Gennady, his wife Irina and his teenaged son Alexander shared the bedroom. In the morning, over black bread, kasha (cereal) and tea, we talked more about my plan to go around the world and my need for a Russian counterpart. Gennady didn't say anything at that point, but I could sense that wheels were turning.

SIBERIA, AT LAST

The trip from Moscow to Siberia was an adventure in itself. We were at the mercy of Aeroflot, and it took four flights to get to our destination. Part of that had to do with our hosts, who had sought the very cheapest flights, but part also was due to the enormity of Siberia and the remoteness of our destination. We were also traveling illegally, courtesy of Pinocchio, using forged travel documents.

It is not enough to say that Siberia is much bigger than the entire USA, including Alaska. Starting at the Ural Mountains, the border between Europe and Asia, Siberia blankets the Middle East, Pakistan, India, China and Mongolia, and keeps on eastward past Japan, and stretches out to the Bering Strait, less than 100 miles from Alaska. Immense, gigantic, enormous, huge—all those words fit. Moving our feet along the ground, step by step, would give us a feel for it.

Americans know about the Trans-Siberian Railroad, but outside of Russia, few know about the *other* trans-Siberian railroad. The well-known route runs very close to the border with China, built when relations between Imperial China and Czarist Russia were amiable. At one time the Chinese city of Harbin was home to 300,000 Russians. In the late 20th century, relationships between Communist China and Communist Russia were strained. By the 1980s their common border along the Amur River was heavily fortified. The Trans-Siberian Railroad, close to the Chinese border, Russia's main link with the city of Vladivostok, her main Pacific port, was vulnerable to attack by the Chinese. So they built a parallel route, further north, away from the Chinese border. This second railroad line is called the *Baikal-Amur-Magistral*, known in Russia as "BAM." It was along the BAM railway right of way that Pinocchio started our long run.

To construct BAM, engineers had to build on permafrost, cross several large rivers, survive severe Siberian winters, and battle swarms of biting insects in the summer. In the end Russia had duplicated what they had in the first place: another Trans-Siberian Railroad, more secure, but not very useful. Before it was completed, hostilities between China and Russia thawed. A Russian friend, who was in the Soviet Army at the time, says that for years the troops of both nations bitterly faced each other daily across the wintry Amur River. Then one day the hostilities simply ended. The morning that troops on both sides were ordered to withdraw from their positions along the Amur, 10,000 Chinese troops in unison dropped their trousers and mooned their Russian adversaries. On command 10,000 Russians together returned their lunar salute. That comes to 40,000 smiling cheeks. My friend swears that this is true. There were 20,000 witnesses.

BAIKAL THE BEAUTIFUL

Lake Baikal is the sparkling gem of resource-rich Siberia. Our route would pass north and east of this magnificent body of water, following the idle BAM tracks. On a globe one can always find Lake Baikal, long and slender, running north from Irkutsk, near the Mongolian border. Russians sing of her staggering beauty. No lake anywhere compares with it in size and grandeur. One fifth of the liquid fresh water in the world is contained in this sweet inland sea, which descends to a depth of over 5,000 feet. 26 rivers that feed Baikal and only one, the Angarsk, drains it, starting at the southern end and turning north to the Arctic Ocean. Lake Baikal reminds one of California's Tahoe, surrounded on three sides by snow-covered peaks, but on a much grander scale and more pristine than the beautiful but over-developed Tahoe.

The southern Baikal region, known as the Autonomous People's Republic of Buryatiya, is lightly populated. The indigenous Buryats are Buddhists whose religion and culture migrated north from Tibet. It seemed odd to find prayer flags and Buddhist temples in the USSR. Not far from Baikal is Ulan Ude, the center of the Buryat culture.

In Siberia, where a dozen major rivers flow great distances into the Arctic Ocean, highways are unnecessary. In summer, freight and passenger traffic travel by boat. In winter, when rivers and lakes freeze solid, goods and people move over the ice by truck. The signal of springtime is the first truck falling through the ice.

SCAMMING ACROSS SIBERIA

We were running along the BAM route north and east of Baikal. Most of us ran more hours and more miles along the BAM route than we had ever run in a comparable period. But we were always wary of what the Pinocchio Gang might do next, and they never ran out of ways to scheme and to scam, targeting both us and the local people. Soon everyone had a Pinocchio story to tell. The Russian runners among us were referring to Bob, the American organizer, as *Durock*, a Russian word for stupid. The American runners called him Dickless, or D.L., because he wouldn't stand up to the Pinocchios. D.L. wasn't one of the bad guys, but he sure didn't rate any merit badges for heroism or intelligence. Of course, he did not speak Russian, allowing the Pinocchios to make all the decisions.

How did the Pinocchio Gang work their petty scams? In a hundred ways, with ingenious angles that still amaze me today, and many that I will never understand. Here's a typical one. The isolated villages along the desolate BAM route, built solely for the construction and maintenance of the railroad, were far from prosperous. The Pinocchios did not want to spend any of the money the sponsor had fronted them for our food and housing. As we runners approached a village, one of the Pinocchio Gang would go ahead in a truck to tell the villagers about the world-class runners, maybe even Olympic athletes, coming their way. A heavy hint would be dropped among these poor citizens that there were millionaires among us, executives from General Motors, producers from Hollywood, people who were looking for places to invest a ton of money making a film or building an auto plant. That would get the ear of the unsophisticated local politicos, and the red carpet would come rolling out. The scam was on, and we were the bait. I was the only American who spoke Russian, and at first we were all unaware of how we were being used. Our group was being housed, fed and entertained under false pretenses; we thought that they were just being good hosts. The sad part is that the deception was unnecessary, because the Siberians would have treated us just as well if we were strangers passing through. I'm sure that there was a bad taste left in the mouths of these generous people after they learned that they had been duped.

Towards the end of the trip we learned that "business magnate" D.L. was trying to negotiate contracts with local officials for exclusive rights to minerals in the area, as well as for tourism exclusives. That's hard to do when you can't read or write the language. I have my doubts that he ever had a chance. He wasn't smart enough, and the Pinocchios would never have let him walk off with anything they could take themselves.

Villages were far apart. The Director of BAM Construction lent the Pinocchio Gang a couple of trucks for transporting our gear as we ran. We ran along a dirt service road a few yards from the railroad tracks. Day after day the villages came and went, places with names like Chara, Taksimo, Muinsk, Tunnelnii, Angoya, Severo-Baikalsk, Neriungri and Yakutsk. Most of the villages had just a few hundred people, but they always found a way to make us feel welcome. The residents had been sent there, unwillingly, from the Ukraine, Belorussia and Azerbaijan to build the railroad.

One day we ran into the village of Taksimo. The villagers were waiting for us. Except for the Russian mayor, every person in the village had been transported from Azerbaijan in the south. Two young women accompanied the mayor as she ceremoniously greeted us with the traditional bread and salt. They ushered us to the village square where a fine meal was served, followed by music and traditional dancing. In Azerbaijan, men dance with men, and we were expected to participate, even though we had just run a marathon. Azerbaijani wine and cognac got us lubricated enough to dance in the afternoon sun. We went to bed exhausted and well fed.

I think it was in Kuanda that Pinocchio pulled his "hat trick." We had just run into the village when a local official took our American team doctor and me, the elder of our group, into the back room of a warehouse where we were presented with expensive gifts, hats made of sable fur. We offered money, but our host refused payment, saying that it was his honor to present them to us. Pinocchio was upset that the hats were given to us instead of to him. Two days later Pinocchio Junior and D.L. approached the doctor and me, saying that they needed to collect $40 from each of us for the hats, or we would be in trouble with the police. I told them to look for it where the sun does not shine.

On a typical day we would eat a small breakfast in our host village, start running around nine, and arrive at the next village in the late afternoon. When the next village was too far away, we would be transported there in the trucks, and next morning taken back to where we had stopped. We usually slept in a gymnasium or a *Pioneer* (Boy Scout) camp, in sleeping bags on the floor. Most days the food was poor but sufficient, heavy on potatoes and cabbage. Some of the villagers were shy, but the kids never were. They swarmed all over us. Ted would pop on a gorilla mask and balloons, sending them into a giggling fit. Barry, our token Canadian, wowed them with face paint and Canadian flag pins. We had brought tons of souvenirs for the kids, from pens and pencils to music tapes.

If seeing the children of Siberia was a high point of the trip, organization was not. Jess Stainbrook, a video pro from Philadelphia, called our series of fiascoes "a quest for disorganization." Arriving in the village of Kichara, five of our runners were missing, and the organizers had no clue as to where they might be. D.L. mouthed words we had heard too often, "Our only concern is for the runners." But he made no move to search for them. Stainbrook said that it was a good thing that we had all had lobotomies before leaving home. The five lost runners showed up eventually, bedraggled and too late for dinner. Riley and I looked at each other. "Par for the course."

The constant running was grueling, but there were sweet moments. When we could, we would cool off in a creek, a wonderful feeling of relief for our hot and beaten feet. Every village had a traditional *banya,* a Russian sauna, great for melting away our pains with soothing heat every night. The *banya* gave us an opportunity to relax and mix with the locals, to talk about the run and to joke about "the scam of the day." Often our hosts would offer a *programma* of entertainment for us, sometimes put on by the Pioneers. Once in a while there was a special *programma,* like the time we heard the Krasnoyarsk Opera Company's version of Carmen, sung in Russian. The star had a huge voice and a body to match. Another day our *programma* took us to a coal mine in Neryungrii. It was interesting if you are into ugliness. One of our runners, a Californian who constantly complained about being sex starved (Blue Balls), called the huge open pit mine "an ecological piss pot." Disneyland need not worry about competition for the tourist trade.

What wasn't fun was the "Siberian Air Force": hordes of carnivorous insects. They came in two varieties, mosquitoes and "helicopters." The nocturnal mosquitoes were bad, but we could hide from them. The daytime "helicopters" were more aggressive and delivered painful bites. Fortunately, they were completely predictable. These huge deerflies would circle their victim once, twice, and on the third circle land and bite instantly. Your only hope was to spot them on the first circle and swat them on the second. We got pretty good at it. One day I swatted a "helicopter" with my baseball cap on his second loop. He

24

got even—he was still in the cap when I put it back on my head.

The best runners were the Soviets, and there were a dozen of them. Their identity cards said that they were Russian, Tatar, Ukranian, Jewish and Estonian. Aside from the Americans there was one Australian, Graeme Woods, a professional runner; the Canadian, Barry Lewis; and an Irishman named Brendan O'Connell. The American runners were Epstein, Nunya, Riley, Brundle, a wandering physicist, Blue Balls, Pat Cooper, Thunder Woman, The Shadow, and me. We got along reasonably well in spite of poor food, marginal accommodations, atrocious planning, lies, route changes and scams because we really were having a memorable adventure together and because we knew that this insane event could never happen again. As bad as we felt the Pinocchio Gang was, I don't know if anyone could have done a better job under the circumstances. There is a place in this world for sleaze.

Thunder Woman was interesting. She got her name because when she talked, she yelled. She was an ex-marine, and there was a rumor among us that she had been discharged for being overly aggressive. Skinny as a rail, and as hard looking, she had the appearance of a raptor. Sentimentality and femininity were not her strong points. Her credentials included an extremely long run, but there was a lively debate in the running press about whether she had actually done what she claimed and doubters presented their arguments. Nonetheless, she ran well with us, as did her second, The Shadow. She showed little sensitivity to local mores. It is one thing to want equal rights for women, but when it comes to sharing village saunas, there are gender traditions that need to be respected.

MISTER WISE GUY

Don't get the impression that I was always Mister Nice Guy. I wear a hearing aid when necessity overcomes vanity. For me to understand them, Russians have to speak slowly and clearly. One day a Yakut villager asked me, in his difficult-to-understand version of Russian, what the thing in my ear was. I told him it was a brand new, highly sophisticated *Yaponski komputer perebodchik,* a Japanese computer that automatically translated Russian into English inside my ear, but *only* if he spoke slowly and clearly. From then on, he did.

Another time we arrived at a village that had been a restricted military area closed to foreigners. We arrived just as the restrictions were lifted. A team of American scientists, disarmament monitors, was due to arrive that very afternoon to witness the dismantling of ICBMs. They had been told that no Americans had ever been there. Not quite. Pinocchio Junior and I decided to play a joke on them, and we got the local officials to go along. I would pretend to be the Russian head of the greeting committee, and Pinocchio Jr. would be my interpreter, as I pretended to speak no English.

When the Americans stepped from the plane, I went forward to greet them. Local dignitaries and press were holding back their smiles, enjoying the joke along with us. Pinocchio Jr. formally asked in English for the American's identity and place of origin, which he translated into Russian for me. I made a welcoming speech in Russian, finishing with *Ochen priyatno poznakomitsye* (A pleasure to meet you.), all of which Pinocchio translated into English. It went back and forth like that for a while, and the Oregon scientist asked my name. "Dzhosef Oakes" I replied in a heavy Russian accent. I could see him thinking that was an unusual name for a Russian. "Where are you from, Mr. Oakes?" Pinocchio translated, trying not to giggle. "Sant Frantsiska, Kalifornia," I replied, with my biggest grin. He looked astonished. Everyone burst out laughing. "You leg-pulling S.O.B. Who in the hell are you? And what are you doing here?" Over a cold drink I told him that we were just passing through on foot. I don't know if he believed our crazy story.

ROMANCE AMONG THE SAVAGES

All good things eventually come to an end, and so did our footrace in eastern Siberia. Did I say race? It was supposed to be a race, but the "organizers" never bothered to time anyone. I doubt that they even had a stopwatch. Did anybody win? Who knows? My nomination for winner would be Ted Epstein, because he ran more hours than anyone. Not necessarily more miles, mind you, but he just kept going, and going, and going. He even ran extra miles after the run was done, while we were all temporarily lodged in a scammer's apartment in Irkutsk on the way home. During one of his runs he came across people in Irkutsk who helped him make a solo exit home. I should have gone with him.

Blue Balls and Brundle were feeling the burdens of celibacy, and someone (could it have been Pinocchio?) sent two bimbos to the apartment. Oksana and Olivia, "The Giggle Sisters," didn't speak English but had no trouble communicating with the needy. In fact, for two days they ministered non-stop to the needy. The newly deflowered Brundle had fallen deeply in love, and Blue Balls swore off sex for life. Oksana was a wild one, dark, slim, beautiful, Asian in appearance. She used flamboyant gestures, laughed loudly, and danced whenever she was not horizontal or guzzling vodka. Olivia, on the other hand, was pudgy and boring. She always appeared to be in need of a nap when not taking one. Oksana glommed onto Brundle like a fly on poop. When we finally left Irkutsk to go home, Oksana accompanied him all the roundabout way to Moscow, hoping to go to America with him. By that time she had developed a brilliant command of the English language, and it consisted of the following: "I lohff you, dahlink, I lohff you." Alas, this marriage was not made in heaven but in a dirty, overcrowded apartment in Irkutsk. It was not meant to be.

Before leaving Irkutsk a pair of seedy characters began to

frequent the apartment. They claimed to be friends of Pinocchio and wanted to buy our clothing, sell us things, barter and maybe steal from us. They gave us no peace. It took some heavy convincing before they finally got the message that they were not welcome in our fleabag.

The trip to Moscow from Irkutsk was a repeat of the flight to Siberia, cheap sleepers puddle jumping west. And guess what? *We did not go to Moscow*! We were taken to Kiev in the Ukraine, home den of the Pinocchios. In fact, we spent only one night in Kiev. That night several people slept in Pinocchio Junior's apartment. I was not invited, but this is how it was reported to me. It was a sentimental evening. Junior supplied plenty of vodka, and everyone went to bed smashed. While they slept, three people were robbed. Woodsy, the Australian, had $500 lifted from his wallet. Pinocchio Junior was *so surprised*! "How could such a thing happen in my own home while I slept?" How, while you slept indeed! Those guys were good at what they did, and they never ran out of ideas.

CAMP WHATCHA-GONNA-DO?

The next day we were moved en masse to a dilapidated former "sports camp" in Brovaree, some distance from Kiev. The building was falling apart. There were beds, but no linens. There was one toilet on each of two dormitory floors, and neither worked. "Dump" would be too nice a word for it. "Dumped" is what happened to us. Pinocchio did not want us in a position where we could cause him trouble with the KGB before our homebound flight, so he secreted us in this remote crap hole. The Pinocchios and D.L. did a disappearing act, abandoning us for several days. Were we kidnapped? Probably not, but we were certainly there against our will, and we sure as hell wanted out.

After a couple of days the rotund manager of the sports camp called me into her office. I was the only one with whom she could communicate. Were we really the U.S. Olympic squad, as she had been told? "You don't look like it!" I told her, no, actually we weren't. Well, she had not been paid one kopek for our room and board by our sponsor (Guess who!), so she stopped feeding us. We would have to leave. I pleaded with her to let us stay until our masters returned. We were able to buy apples from street vendors with the rubles so generously sold to us weeks before by Pinocchio, and in time I found a shop that was willing to sell food to foreigners.

At long last our benefactors, Junior and D.L. returned. They had arranged for us to have dinner in a restaurant. They each had a rather professional-looking lady in tow and would not sit at the same table with us. During dinner I had the temerity to leave my table and ask D.L. when we might be returning to Moscow because we were all concerned about missing our flight home. He said something to me that sounded like, "When we are damned good and ready." At that point I lost it. I wanted to lift him from his chair, turn him around, put my right foot against his fat butt and boot him out into the street. O'Connell, Woodsy and Barry Lewis prevented me from doing any damage. The four of us left, found a lovely bar where we could drink ourselves to death, and destroyed a great number of germs and brain cells. I was not proud of myself, but I felt much better.

SAVED BY THE KGB

The next day, hung over, I grabbed my duffel bag, determined to find my way to Moscow with or without papers. The Pinocchios had our passports and visas. I hitchhiked, took a bus and a Metro, dragging my worldly goods with me, and eventually got to the main Kiev railroad station. By some miracle and with a lot of help, I got a call through to Gennady Schvets in Moscow. I told him what had happened. He said that he would get the KGB after Pinocchio, and he would meet me at the train station in Moscow. With no travel documents it was difficult buying a ticket, but a small inducement for the clerk succeeded where pleading and groveling did not.

Schvets set things in motion. The cops were alerted, and the Pinocchios were called in. Within 48 hours our entire crew was in Moscow and staying with people unrelated to the Pinocchio Gang. While waiting for the others to arrive, Gennady and I made plans for the next stage of the around the world trip. *He wanted to be a part of my adventure.* He would join me in Alaska the next year, after he finished his work reporting for *Komsomolskaya Pravda* at the Good Will Games in Seattle.

Was I through with Pinocchio? Not quite. A couple of years later Ivan used my name as a reference applying for a visa to come to America. I suspect that he was going to enter the USA legally and just stay illegally forever. I hope that my reference shot the bastard down. No way was I going to help him come to America.

I have made eight trips over the years to Russia and her predecessor, the USSR. In 1990 I joined Gennady Schvets along with a group of Americans, Frenchmen and Russians to do 14 days of ultra-distance running in an area of Russia known as the *Zolotaya Koltso,* the Golden Circle. I have good memories of that trip. I can close my eyes and see Bill Beddor, Mike Modzelewski, Gary Hill and myself running down a country road. As we approach a farmhouse we can hear music coming from the hayloft, a toothless old man flashing us a broad smile as he pumps away on his accordion. His ancient *babushka* wife is operating a roadside hand pump to give us a drink of water. It is a scene right out of "Fiddler on the Roof."

Of course Pinocchio showed up when our group got to Moscow. He made every attempt to work his wondrous scams with his "dear Amerikan friends," and in fact did lure three of our innocent, non-Russian speaking Hawaiian friends to an apartment someplace. It took us half a day to find them. They were unharmed, chastened and a bit embarrassed. After all, they had been warned about Pinocchio.

Here's how I reflect, years later, on the Siberian episode with the Pinocchio gang. We did get in a good, long journey across eastern Siberia. I had an adventure, I didn't get hurt and it didn't cost me a lot of money. I guess that Jesse Dale Riley was right about that. But the big thing that came out of it was that my circumnavigation was now underway. I made some good friends, and two of them would join me for later segments of the journey.

I learned once again that Mom and Sylvia, as usual, were right—if it sounds too good to be true, it probably is.

But does that mean don't do it?

Runners at "banya" (Russian sauna) near Lake Baikal

Runners at rest

Remembrance of times past. We passed several gulags while crossing Siberia.

Welcome to the "Pioneer Camp." Like our Scouts, we were treated very well in the villages of Siberia.

*Siberian kids love
puppies, too.*

*Home, sweet home. Our BAM support vehicle. All of our belongings
were in the truck as we ran from village to village.*

The Americans, not afraid of the big dude, before the run in Tynda

An old wooden church built by Polish Catholic laborers in Irkutsk.

Runners spread out on a long, lonely road on BAM route.

CHAPTER III

THE NORTH COUNTRY

O Canada! Where pines and maples grow,
Great prairies spread and lordly rivers flow.
How dear to us thy broad domain,
From East to Western sea!
Thou land of hope for all who toil!
Thou True North strong and free
　　　　– Second verse, Canadian National Anthem

ALASKA

It was here that I became a criminal. There were three of us working our way south and east from College, Alaska, near Fairbanks. Our goal was to bicycle 100 miles a day to New York. Seymour Blinderman was our road manager, driver, psychiatrist, repairman, cook and mommy. Gennady Schvets and I pedaled together on a tandem bicycle.

Sylvia, Seymour and I had driven to Alaska via the Alaska Marine Highway and had spent a week seeing some of the high points. We saw first hand the damage the Exxon Valdez had done in Prince William Sound. We took a Park Service bus tour of incomparable Denali, where we saw caribou, moose, eagles and a massive blonde grizzly bear frolicking in a stream just below the road. At the end of a week Sylvia returned home. It was time for us to ride.

I had spent several months learning to ride a tandem bicycle, getting a lot of help from experienced riders. The Back Room Gnomes at the Bicycle Outfitter in Los Altos, California, rigged out a hybrid tandem bike for us, with interchangeable light racing wheels and hardy off-road wheels. They put in extra hours and even rode with me, no mean feat of bravery. After a while I got the feel of riding a tandem bike on both the rear and front seats, which are very different jobs. We named the tandem bicycle "Magenta Mama." But I still had not been on a bicycle with my Russian partner, Gennady.

And finally, we were in Alaska and moving. While Gennady and I were pumping away on the bicycle, Seymour drove his support vehicle, a motor home he called "Foxy Lady." Seymour and Foxy Lady enabled Gennady and me to travel light, with little more than water bottles and a pocket full of trail mix to carry. Not having to lug sleeping bags, tents, food and clothing up and down hills on the bike made life a lot easier. Even so, our package of bike and bodies weighed over 400 pounds.

Early on a cold rainy morning on August 8, 1990, we started our long ride in College, Alaska, to the roar of acclamation of a roaring throng of four (thank you, Don, Jane, Peter and Kelly Bostian, cub reporter with the Fairbanks *Miner*.) Aside from a brief practice session the day before, it was the first time Gennady and I had been on the tandem together. We were entering a long, steep learning curve, but aside from the chilling rain, we were doing okay. Gennady reminded me about a Russian saying that rain at the beginning of a long voyage is a good omen.

The road was smooth, traffic was light, and we were fresh. We had reason to believe that our plan was going to work out just fine. About ten miles out of town Simon, the Back Room Bicycle Gnome from All Weather Sports in Fairbanks, and his friend Jane joined us on their bikes all the way to the McDonald's in North Pole, Alaska, where we stopped for breakfast and a break from the rain. Simon and his co-worker Ian, in the true spirit of Bicycle Gnomes, had come in to work on their day off to inspect and adjust the bicycle for us.

The road was flat the first day, but the cold rain continued. We learned a trick to keep our feet from freezing in the cold rain. We got plastic bags from the vegetable counter at a supermarket and put them over our socks inside our shoes, with a rubber band to keep the top from flopping around. That kept our toes warm but not dry. Even with our yellow rain suits and plastic bags we were soaked when we reached Delta Junction, our resting-place for the night.

We logged slightly over 100 miles on day one, right on schedule. Day two brought new lessons. The learning curve included steep hills and brisk headwinds. The day was unusually warm, almost 70 degrees, and the scenery was superb. At Dot Lake we called it quits for the day. After asking us what we were doing in the boonies on bikes, the proprietor of the Dot Lake Lodge bought dinner for us. It was the first of many times that people would show us kindness.

Two grown men on the road on a magenta-colored tandem bicycle tends to arouse curiosity. People frequently stopped to ask us what was going on. We never hesitated to tell them about our project, two Don Quixotes, one Russian and one American, straining our rumps (literally) to test the principle that people from very different backgrounds could work well together under stressful conditions. We were not out there to preach to people, but neither did we hesitate to answer questions if they asked. We got responses of bewilderment and disbelief, but mostly of hearty approval.

ILLEGAL ENTRY NUMBER ONE

It was near the end of the second day that Gennady told me rather sheepishly that there was going to be a problem, and real soon. We were within 100 miles of the Alaska-Canada border, and we were going to cross into Canada the next day. "Joseph, in Moscow I applied for the wisa to enter Canada several months ago. It never came, so I am without papers to enter Canada. Is there something that we can do about this?" Holy shit! He came all the way to Alaska to ride for only three days? We three stooges put our heads together and we came up with a plan—not a great one, but it just might work.

Here's what we decided to do. On day three we would ride the final 100 miles of highway in Alaska and stop just short of the Canadian border. Very early the next morning Seymour would cross the border 15 minutes ahead us in his Foxy Lady. At the border he would tell the Canadian border guard that we were following behind him, very soon, and that we were trying to set a new bicycle speed record from Fairbanks to New York. Seymour was an honest man, and this monkey business did not go down well with him. But he was also a pragmatist and he knew that there was no reasonable alternative.

We hung back for 15 minutes while Foxy Lady crossed into Canada. I told Gennady to be very quiet and I would do all the talking. Americans didn't need Canadian visas, but his Russian accent would be a dead giveaway. Gennady's feelings were hurt. He had worked very hard at his English lessons, and he thought he had no accent. We rode towards the border structure and cruised right past the border guard at full speed. The guard jumped out of his booth, gave a loud blast on his whistle and shouted, "You guys come right back here." Between my teeth I hissed, "Don't open your mouth, Gennady!" When we got close enough the border guard asked, "You American?"

"Yup," I replied politely.

"From where?"

"California, San Francisco area."

"Got any drugs, firearms or liquor?

"Nope," I replied with a grin. Gennady mumbled "I also do not have."

"Get moving, then, and good luck on your ride, eh!"

And that is how I became a lawbreaker and border crasher. I'm sorry we had to do it, but I'm glad that it worked. I promise never to smuggle a Russian into Canada again. Gennady asked what kind of punishment we would receive if we were caught. I told him that we would probably be expelled from Canada, and there might be a stiff fine. There was very little likelihood that we would end up in jail. He thought about that. "I am Russian. Can Canadian jail be so bad?"

THE ALASKA HIGHWAY

In 1942 the Japanese invaded the Aleutians in Alaska, picking the lock on the back door of North America. In those days the only practical way to get to Alaska was by sea. There was no land route. The U.S. Navy was busy fighting a war on two fronts and couldn't defend Alaska. President Roosevelt ordered a road built, over 1,000 kilometers, through Northwest Canada, some of the most inhospitable territory in the world, and to have it done in within a year. Without bothering to wait for the permission of the Canadian parliament, the U.S. Army Corps of Engineers was told emphatically to "*Build the road!*"

The terrain was mountainous, boggy and uncharted. There was no solid foundation for a road in the wet places, so a roadbed had to be built up, hauling thousands of tons of gravel across long distances. Conditions were brutal, winter temperatures staying well below zero for weeks at a stretch. Working from both ends toward the middle, scouting and surveying as they went, the rugged road was finished ahead of schedule in nine months, one of the most remarkable engineering feats in modern history.

The Alaska Highway has undergone reconstruction several times. When our wandering trio arrived in Beaver Creek, Yukon Territory, on the Canadian side, construction was once again under way. That segment of the road had never been paved, and the Yukon Territory government was finally getting it done. For hundreds of miles we were on rough gravel road with no shoulder. The heavy August traffic consisted of huge construction vehicles and motor homes with road-weary drivers. Neither of these species seemed willing to share their piece of road with our bicycle. We were constantly pelted by kicked-up gravel, and the road dust was suffocating. When we weren't grinding up a big hill in a low gear, wet with perspiration, we were careening down the other side, our wheels pitching gravel back at the same people in the trucks and motor homes as we sped by them, their faces agape.

The Alaska Highway is flanked by some of the largest mountains on the continent: the Wrangels, the Saint Elias Range, the Big Salmons, The Pellys and the Cassiars. Canada's Kluane National Park, not far from the border with Alaska, has some of the most inspiring scenery in the world. The mountains, lakes and forests kept whispering to us, "Stay for a while," and we would have loved to. But every day we had to put in our 100 miles on the bike. That does not mean we didn't stop to smell the roses. After all, we had nothing to do but ride 100 miles, eat, sleep, work on the bike and look around us.

August is the best time of the year in the North Country. The short summer is almost over, and all of creation is putting its energy into making ready for the next generation before the snow calls a slowdown in the processes of life. An abundance of flowers is everywhere, and the colors want to make you want to sing. In late August the mosquitoes and black flies are gone, so one can relax unassailed in the grass, which we did frequently.

When we crossed the Yukon River Gennady recalled reading about it in Jack London: "I have always dreamed about this." It was a hot day. We looked at each other and smiled. In no time we stripped down and were paddling around *au natural* in the chilly water, a baptism of sorts. Gennady climbed up the bank, lay down on his clothing and closed his eyes. I was 20 yards away, adjusting the brakes, when a movement caught my eye. A large moose cow pushed through the brush and walked right up to the sleeping Gennady. She lowered her head to sniff the strange pinkish thing on the ground, found it uninteresting, and moved on. By the time I got my camera out, Ms. Moose had strolled out of sight. Gennady didn't believe a word of it when he awoke.

By the second week we were into a routine. We would get up early, have bread, jam and tea and get on the road. We were building a good working partnership on the bike, and Gennady proved to be a strong cyclist. After about 20 miles we would find Seymour waiting for us by the side of the road, another breakfast of cereal, fruit, bread and tea ready for us. The three of us would talk and rest, look over the map and the *Milepost* guidebook, and be off again. Seymour and Foxy Lady would hang back for an hour or so, then drive by us to make sure that everything was all right before setting up again a few miles down the road. A sandwich lunch brought another rest and chat session. We rode twice more each day: after lunch and after a mid-afternoon snack. We were burning a lot of calories, so heavy eating was mandatory to keep grinding out 100-mile days. We were usually finished by about four o'clock, so we had late afternoons free for the touristy part of the day.

One afternoon we stopped at the top of a hill at a broad meadow. It was a warm, sunny day, and the few clouds in the sky were moving so slowly that they might as well have been safety-pinned in their places in a canvas sky. The fragrance of clover was thick in the air, almost intoxicating. We removed our helmets, gloves and shoes and settled back into the grass, content for the moment to do nothing but breathe. "This is a superb moment, a unique one," Gennady said. "In this life you can always work or play, but there are only rare moments to sit back and enjoy the smell of a field of clover." He was quoting from *Odnoetazhnaya Amerika (Single Story America)* by Ilia Illf and Evgeny Petrov, Russians who traveled in America in the early 1900s. It was indeed a rare moment.

After a few days of gravelly roads, the Alaska Highway got better. Instead of dust and gravel it was well paved, and there was a shoulder to ride on instead of competing for space with motor vehicles. It was late in the season and most of the motor-home traffic was gone. The riding was so good that we decided to switch from our sturdy "dirt" tires to lighter and faster racing tires. We got a bit rambunctious on a long downhill stretch near Fort Saint John, cooperating fully with gravity, letting her rip at about 40 mph. At the bottom we came to a steel bridge. The open grillwork on the bridge had a little surprise for the puny tires. POP! POP! We blew out both racing tires and were lucky that there was a sharp uphill on the other side of the bridge to slow us down fast. We were carrying only one spare tire on the bike with us—and no patch kit.

Seymour had already passed us. We were stuck. We envisioned him sitting in his folding chair by the side of the road, waiting for us, reading and having a cup of tea, ten miles ahead. It would be hours before he realized that we were in trouble. We could wait, or we could do something about it. I left Gennady there with the bike, sunbathing, and hitchhiked to where I hoped to find Seymour some miles ahead.

Now I don't normally recommend hitchhiking, but if you *must*, here is a piece of advice. Stand by the side of the road, fully clad in bicycling gear, wearing a helmet (a sign of good judgement), with a limp inner tube dangling from your outstretched hand. Look forlorn. The message is, "I'm a bicyclist and I have a problem. Please help me. I'm harmless." The very first car to come along took me to Seymour, who was indeed sitting in his folding chair by the side of the road, reading and having a cup of tea, ten miles ahead of us. We scooted back to a sleeping Gennady and replaced the racing tires with rugged knobbies. The knobby tires stayed on all the way to New York without another flat.

The towns along the Alaska Highway were going by fast: Haines

Junction, Carmacks, Watson Lake, Summit Lake, Fort Nelson, Fort St. John, and, finally, Dawson Creek, the end of the Alaska Highway, 2395 km (1488 miles) from Fairbanks. Just above Dawson Creek the face of the land underwent a radical transformation. Behind us were vast forests, ranging through British Columbia, Yukon Territory and Alaska, millions of acres of forest rarely visited by people. The primary sign of man was this road. Despite more than half a century since the construction of the Alaska Highway, the wilderness was still largely unspoiled.

South and east of Dawson Creek we started to see horses, cattle and grain fields as we made the transition from northeastern British Columbia into northwestern Alberta. The rich black soil is like that of the Ukraine, the breadbasket of Europe. Over a hundred years ago, this part of Canada drew migrations from Eastern Europe, and Ukranian refugees came empty-handed, determined and willing to work hard. Their descendants are now prosperous ranchers, farmers and oilmen. As we moved on, the houses became newer, bigger and more ornate, with thoroughbred horses and Charolais cattle. Oilrigs and construction crews were everywhere, and the trail of prosperity led right into Edmonton.

The immigrant's dream is alive in Alberta. Gus, a Greek immigrant, said that he had "washed enough dishes in 16 years to build a bridge back to Athens." Despite his complaints about Canadian taxes, he had saved enough money to buy his own restaurant. One day he would retire and go back to his Greek island birthplace with a Canadian fortune. Frank, a Vietnamese boat person, came to Edmonton via Hong Kong, and after a few years opened his own auto parts business. We stayed at a motel run by a man named Ashok, an East Indian whose family had been driven from their home in Nairobi after three generations. "The True North strong and free" is as much a beacon of hope as the Statue of Liberty.

EDMONTON

Between Dawson Creek to Edmonton it was cold and wet. A raw wind smacked us in the face, driving the rain at us horizontally, fighting hard to find openings in our rain slickers. Visibility was limited for us and for the drivers straining to see the road past their windshield wipers. We were miserable and tense.

It was terrifying. Seymour suggested that we abort and drive into Edmonton, but Gennady and I were not about to give it up. Six miles out of Edmonton on busy Route 16 our valiant fight was halted when we hit a pothole the size of Rhode Island, pretzeled the front wheel and bent the brake arm. No one was hurt and, fortunately, Seymour was right behind us to gather up the pieces.

In Edmonton we located a shop aptly named "The Hardcore Mountain Bike Store" where a wonderful Back Room Bicycle Gnome, Jim Moulden, made quick work of the repairs and had us on our way in no time.

Edmonton was the end of the line for Gennady. He had to return Moscow to earn a living. He had made arrangements for his replacement on the bicycle, his son Alexander, "Sasha," to meet us in Edmonton.

We got rained on during our first day of cycling— a good omen in Russian culture

Pepsi break in the Yukon—Joe and Gennady Schvets

Gennady, Seymour and Joe

CHAPTER IV

MISS LIBERTY

"Keep, ancient lands, your storied pomp!" cries she,
With silent lips. "Give me your tired, your poor,
Your huddled masses yearning to be free,
The wretched refuse of your teeming shore,
Send these, the homeless, tempest-tost to me,
I lift my lamp beside the golden door."
     – Emma Lazarus, November 2, 1883

SWITCHEROO IN EDMONTON

Gennady was in Canada illegally, having sneaked over the border from Alaska, and Seymour and I had abetted his heinous crime. But what kind of a trick would we have to pull to get him out of Canada? It was a question we . . . no, *he* . . . would have to face at some point.

In the meantime we were in the international arrivals area of Edmonton Airport, waiting for Gennady's 17-year-old son, Alexander (Sasha), who was making his way to Edmonton from Moscow by way of New York and Salt Lake City. He had never been out of Russia and spoke little English. Sasha's airplane had been on the ground in Edmonton for two hours, and there was no sign of him. The flow of passengers from Canadian Customs into the terminal slowed to a trickle, then stopped completely. I tried to poke my head through the open door but was told to stay out of the security area. Gennady was upset. His son was missing someplace in North America, God knew where, and he was illegally in Canada, unable to help.

49

A uniformed man came through the door. "Does anybody out there speak Russian? There's a problem with a kid in here and we need help." I inquired as to whether it might be Alexander Schvets. He said yes, it was, and took me into the inner sanctum. "We found a can of beef from China in his luggage. You can't bring beef into Canada. Hoof and mouth disease, eh? Regulations, you know, and he won't surrender it." "Is that the only problem?" Yes, that was the only problem. I explained to the officer that giving up a can of meat was a big thing for a Russian, and that Sasha was fatigued from a long, hard journey. I convinced Sasha to surrender the illegal beef, and he was reunited with his illegal alien father.

The reunion lasted two days, during which time we took a break from cycling to see Edmonton. We went to a street fair celebrating the city's ethnic diversity, sampled a variety of national dishes and watched street performers. Seymour took us to the world's largest shopping mall in West Edmonton, with everything from luxury shops and fast food joints, to a full-sized hockey rink, an indoor surfing pool and an amusement park. Sasha and Gennady took great interest in used car lots and got a big kick out of a car with the license plate, "MONEY." That evening they watched Canadian television, amazed that there were so many channels available at the click of a button.

The next day we deposited Gennady at the Edmonton airport. He told us not to be concerned because he was very resourceful. He would exit Canada using his press credentials. Gennady and I had become a good team on the bicycle. We had started as two individuals trying to work together and ended up functioning as a unit. Now he was gone, and I had this kid to break in. I was going to miss Gennady real soon.

After two days on the road with Alexander, I was ready to write a letter to Gennady:

Dear Gennady,

Your son is a pain in the 'zh**pa'. If he were my son he would be wearing my number ten shoe where the bicycle seat goes. Thank you for inflicting him on me.

When it is time for bed he wants to wander around whatever town we are in. You and I went to bed early and got up early when we were cycling together. Sasha never wants to go to bed before midnight. While he is skulking around town, I worry about him and I can't sleep. In the morning he doesn't want to get up, and when he finally does, he is a zombie, unfit for the bicycle for at least an hour. While he is figuring out how to get dressed, Seymour and I have to do everything. He is as useful as a rubber crutch.

On the bicycle it feels like I am carrying a load of bricks for the first hour and the last two hours of every day. When we stop for a five-minute break he manages to stretch it into a half hour. As soon as the bicycle stops, off come his shoes, helmet, gloves and shirt. While I am doing a quick visit to the bush, he gets horizontal. After five minutes, when I'm ready to get back onto the bike, THEN he decides to visit the bush. After a prolonged pee he drags himself back, slowly puts on his shoes, managing to weave an intricate pattern of 37 knots in the process. He will then peer into his helmet, study it for a while, put it on, buckle it very deliberately, then take it off again. He forgot to put on his sunglasses first! He ALWAYS forgets to put on his sunglasses first. Off comes the helmet. On go the glasses. On goes the helmet. He adjusts the glasses meticulously, examining himself in a mirror that isn't there, and with the blazing speed of a slug dons his cycling gloves. All the while I am straddling the bicycle, waiting for him to get going. When we finally get started it takes 20 minutes before his legs remember what they are supposed to do. More than once I've thought about asking him to lie down so I can lay flowers on his dead carcass.

51

Every day seems like drudgery to him, Gennady, and getting him enthused about the day's cycling is like getting the Motor Vehicle Bureau interested in shortening the lines. The good news is that I'm sending him home a week early. When he changed planes in New York his entry visa was stamped, so his stay in the United States started then, not when he re-enters the US from Canada. He will be going home October 8, not October 15.

> *Your friend,*
> *Joe Oakes (address unknown)*

Stop! Stop! Stop! I didn't really mean that, and I never sent it. It was how I *felt* when I was overheated, tired, thirsty and grouchy as hell, which was too often. Okay, the kid wasn't perfect, but I had to keep in mind that he was only 17, and a rather inexperienced 17, at that. Second, he is in an alien environment, undergoing culture shock, trying to be like the cool American kids he sees on TV. For the first few days he was jet-lagged. His English is poor, and he is thrown in with two old farts 24 hours a day, camping in a different place every night. This may be his only chance to see America and he surely wants to see something other than the white line down the middle of highway. I should have been aware of this when I accepted him as a partner, so I will try to be more patient with him.

JUST ANOTHER TEENAGER

The nickname for Alexander in Russia is "Sasha." In America he wanted to be Alex, an American sounding name. He also wanted to be known as 18 years old, although he had just turned 17. Sounds like a normal teenager to me. He was taller and slimmer than his father, but with the same dark eyes and hair, and he was very athletic. Overall, a pleasant young man, a bit on the quiet side. In the previous year he had played water polo for the Soviet junior national team, serving as goal tender, but he had no experience cycling. Seymour and I were going to have to get Alex up to speed in many ways.

Alex's biggest problem was his almost non-existent English. He would need to remedy that to function effectively in America. Lack of language skills had already caused him problems in Canadian customs. Seymour, a retired educator, devised a plan to have Alex learn six new words per day. We would not accept sign language, grunts, nods or pointing, and I was not allowed to speak to him in Russian. He didn't like the idea of "homework," but he needed to learn to communicate.

We headed east from Edmonton on Canada's Yellowhead Highway. Alex actually turned out to be a quick study on the bike, even more so than Gennady. It took only a few days of cycling for him to get into the rhythm of it, and I came to appreciate his strength and stamina. Alex was working hard, but he wasn't having much fun. We saw him perk up one day in a campground in Alberta when the park ranger, an 18 year old of Ukranian heritage, took Alex for a ride around the campground in his jeep, letting Alex drive, something he had never done.

The other time Alex loosened up was in North Battleford, Saskatchewan. He saw a motel sign that said "Waterslide." "What is waterslide?" The only way to explain it was to do it. The folks at the Tropicana Inn generously allowed Alex to use their waterslide gratis, and he was overjoyed. We had to tear him away for one of Seymour's special dinners, although Alex would have been content to stay on the waterslide all evening, with a *Beeg Meck* at McDonald's for dinner.

That evening, walking around barefoot in the grass at our campground, I stepped on a yellow jacket. The stinger didn't come out, and when we bicycled into Saskatoon the next afternoon my right foot was swollen and painful. I went to a clinic where they anesthetized the foot, cut out the stinger, bandaged me and gave me an antibiotic and a painkiller. The total cost was $21 plus $8 for the medication. *Canadian* dollars!

Along the Alaska Highway we had seen large animals: deer, moose, bear and elk. By Edmonton they were gone. Farms and towns replaced the forests. Other than the occasional road-kill skunk, rabbit or squirrel, there was no more wildlife. It felt like there were too many people, too much civilization, after that immense wilderness.

One Sunday morning we came upon a Ukranian church. Alex wanted to attend services. As an infant in Odessa he had been baptized in the Ukranian Catholic Church, different from Russian Orthodox. The congregation welcomed us, though we were inappropriately dressed in our bicycle regalia. After church we continued east on the Yellowhead. At the Manitoba border we came face to face with a 1,000-foot downhill. Alex and I looked at each other mischievously. Seymour had just driven by. I don't know how fast we were going when we passed an apoplectic Seymour, but when he caught up with us on the other side, he gave us a lecture for exceeding the speed limit.

A FLOWERY WELCOME TO THE USA

Straddling the border between Manitoba and North Dakota is the International Peace Park, run jointly by communities on both sides of the border. A profusion of late summer flowers greeted us as we entered the gardens. What a bright, colorful, happy and fitting way to mark our transit between Canada and the USA! Even the border guards were pleasant. South of the Peace Park is the town of Rugby, North Dakota, the geographical center of North America, with an obelisk in front of the town diner to mark the spot.

Rugby is also smack-dab in the center of a large group of Americans who migrated to the USA from the Ukraine and Russia long ago. At the diner we met Dan Hornstein, who said that all four of his grandparents had come to North Dakota from Russia. They were part of a large group of German pacifists who had been invited to farm in the Volga area centuries before. Eventually conditions in Russia became as bad as they had been in Germany, so they made the difficult decision to move again, this time to America, ending up in North Dakota. Though Dan was not Russian and was 100 years removed from Russia, there was a feeling of kinship between Dan Hornstein and Alex.

Alex was becoming a strong cyclist and a team player. I could feel the strength of his powerful legs as we stroked together towards the Minnesota border. There was a strong wind pushing us along and it was carrying a storm, so we quit early to find a good camping spot. After an early dinner Alex and I retired to the tent to read and rest and Seymour got into the camper.

At ten p.m. the fireworks started. It was an incredible storm with continuous lightning and crashing thunder, but no rain, and very little movement of the air. The noise had a soothing effect on city kid Alex, and he was asleep in short order. At midnight the rain started, and it got heavier and heavier. Then the wind picked up, tearing loose the rain-fly from the tent. I climbed out, got soaked replacing it, climbed back in and dried off.

Alex woke up dazed, looked at the strobe-lit scene and seemed about to panic. We looked at each other and broke out in hilarious laughter, curled up again and ignored the storm. In another half-hour the rain let up. Our goose-down sleeping bags were damp, but we were able to get a few more hours of slumber.

If Alex was getting stronger, Seymour was not holding up very well. He had a painful back condition and was on medication. At 65, sitting in the car hour after hour every day was taking its toll on him. He went to bed early every night, and sometimes we found him napping at the side of the road when we caught up with the van. Working as a support person, alone most of the day, is draining, psychologically as well as physically. Alex and I could have been more considerate of him since he was doing so much for us. Managing to keep us healthy and in good spirits under varying and stressful conditions was not an easy job.

When we got to Minneapolis just after my 56th birthday, I had been on the road for more than a month. I was homesick and called Sylvia, but that wasn't as good as being home. Seymour's daughter, Annette Ozer, invited us to dinner and to stay for the night. She surprised me with an after-birthday party, inviting the Croiturus, relatives I had not seen in years. The next day my friend Bill Beddor thrilled Alex by taking him out on Lake Minnetonka in a speedboat. We were feeling much better when we headed south and east from the Twin Cities.

EAST OF THE MISSISSIPPI

We had a big decision to make, but there was a difference of opinion. There are several routes east from Minneapolis, and most of them lead right through a chain of big cities to New York. The shortest route led through Madison, Chicago, Gary, Detroit, Cleveland, Pittsburgh, Philadelphia and New Jersey, and all the suburbs in between. That would put us in hazardous, heavy traffic, day after long day. It would also have us crossing Pennsylvania against the grain of the mountains, a series of difficult climbs. Alex wanted to see the fabled cities of America, especially Chicago. Seymour argued for safety, and I agreed. We decided on a southerly route, going east through southern Illinois, Indiana and Ohio, into West Virginia. We would ride parallel to the grain of the Appalachians from Hagerstown, Maryland, through Harrisburg and Allentown, Pennsylvania, to New Jersey.

If anyone tells you that Illinois is flat, show him the northwestern corner of the state. The hills are not huge, but they are big enough and steep. They start in Iowa, across the Mississippi River, and continue eastward. The terrain flattens near Indianapolis but becomes hilly again in Southern Ohio, the start of the Appalachians. We rode on back roads where possible, but the main routes had better shoulders to go with the heavy traffic. What we hadn't expected were the ubiquitous road construction projects, calling for nerves of steel.

From Edmonton to Dayton we were in farm country, a rich cornucopia of much of the world's food supply. We rode through stretches of wheat as far as the eye could see, then potatoes, corn, soybeans and livestock.

The air in Middle America was thick with odors. On a muggy day the pungent aroma of a barn would hit us like a wall. We could smell families cooking dinner. Most of the odors were pleasant, like the smell of freshly turned black earth in Ohio. A rainy day or a field being mowed offered their own fragrances. The hot, heavy, stench of a passing diesel truck was offensive. Once in a while the remains of an unfortunate skunk would remind us that he had lived and died. A particularly offensive stink assaulted us from a factory making plastic camper tops. The concentration of the malodorous solvent in the air was almost explosive. But when Midwestern air was fresh and clean, you could almost drink it.

Bugs. How many caterpillars crawled across our path, and how many did we squash? Thousands of grasshoppers leaped to safety in front of us. Broken butterflies at the side of the road said "Sorry, too slow." In one place we saw a dozen barn swallows killed by passing cars, even as 100 more persisted in their aerobatic daredevil act.

From Dayton east the farms got smaller and scrubbier. Stretches of hardwood forests were holding their own, and oak, curly maple, birds-eye maple, catawba, cherry and walnut had thus far escaped the furniture factories.

Hardwoods and hard lives. Appalachia has long been home to some of America's poorest. We were in United Mine Workers country. Strikebreakers here have been shot. Jobs were scarce and had to be defended. The mine was the only place to work and the UMW was their salvation. I remember flying over the hills of West Virginia 30 years ago. The tops of the hills had been bulldozed into the valleys below. Hundreds of flattened hills, scalped to get at a thin stratum of coal, left looking forever ugly, leaching muck and pollution into the valleys and rivers. For a couple of decades, authorities put a stop to the topping of hills, but coal interests in West Virginia, with the help of state legislators, were once more mounting a furious assault on the state's patrimony.

We found nothing flat in Appalachia, only hundreds of knobby mountains hard against one another. Cycling was difficult, either sweating on a steep climb or freezing on the next steep drop. But the whole thing is only a few days ride across, and by western standards these aren't really mountains, just a clutch of medium hills. The highest point on our route through Appalachia was Negro Mountain, in Maryland, which rises only 2,980 feet. But that same day we climbed seven other hills of 1,500 feet or more.

In Parkersburg, West Virginia, I mentioned to a hotel clerk that I would probably never be in that area again. "You're damn lucky," was his quick reply. On the other hand one fellow said he was "a pure heel-billy, and dang proud huv it." I noticed that many people had problems with tooth development, complexion and weight, probably diet-related. It wasn't easy to explain to a Russian kid, who knew nothing but communism, why pockets of poverty existed in so rich a country.

That Russian kid, by the way, was getting stronger every day. We sure as heck weren't impoverished, and Alex loved to eat. His typical day's intake included two or three slices of bread and honey on waking up. After riding an hour he would consume a big bowl of cereal with fruit and honey along with two or three more slices of honey bread, and tea with honey. The mid-morning snack might include a couple of jellyrolls or donuts (Seymour always had a surprise "goodie" for us.), tea and honey. Lunch might be two sandwiches, fruit, pastry and tea. We frequently found "all you can eat" restaurants for dinner, and Alex did just that. Before dinner he would down a quart of milk and a half loaf of bread (with honey.) On the bike during the day he snacked on trail mix and Coke. I suspect that he gained ten pounds in the time he was with us, and his Moscow pallor became a healthy outdoor tan. Seymour loved to feed him, and he loved to be fed.

Twelve-year-old Susannah Botko-Yovino came to see us on the rainy day that we came north from Maryland into Pennsylvania. Her dad, Doctor Steve, drove from Altoona to Chambersburg so we could have breakfast together. Susannah had won first prize in National Geographic's Geography Bee, a $25,000 scholarship. At that time it would have been 20 years salary for a well-paid Russian. Alex got his nose a little out of joint with all the fuss Seymour and I were making over Susannah. Later he remarked, "What, so she is good only in geography?" It took compassion and tact not to tell him that she had also placed third in mathematics in Pennsylvania.

A POWER BREAK

On the eastern bank of the Susquehanna River, just below the state capital of Harrisburg, is Middletown, Pennsylvania. In the middle of the river sits Three Mile Island and the nuclear power plant that made it famous. Not long after the Chernobyl disaster in the Ukraine, the General Public Utilities plant at "TMI" spewed enough nuclear material into the atmosphere to cause major concerns among the local people. We visited an information center run by GPU, and the trained professionals had a canned answer for every question, sounding a lot like the hucksters who telephone my home at dinnertime.

Looking southwest from Middletown we saw four massive parabolic cooling towers. Clouds of steam were rising from two of them. The other two, no longer cooling the downed reactors, rose like dead monsters. I asked the PR guy what would happen to that now-abandoned part of the island. "Well, it's our island and we will probably never build there." Never is right. It is permanently contaminated, as are the sites of dozens of decommissioned nuclear plants throughout the US. Plutonium has a half-life of 25,000 years. That means that if you wait 25,000 years you will still have half of the poison, a quarter in another 25,000 years, etc. In human terms, that is forever. How long is recorded human history? For how many centuries can they fence and guard a chunk of poisoned real estate?

Alex looked at the plant and sighed. He turned his camera instead across the river to the northwest, where there were a couple of pretty islands. "Is better view in this direction."

MISS LIBERTY

All of a sudden teeny New Jersey was all that remained of our trek across North America. But bicycling in New Jersey wasn't easy. The roads were built a long time ago and shoulders were non-existent. Drivers in New Jersey were among the rudest and meanest we had encountered in our trek anywhere. The best thing about New Jersey was that it was small and over soon. Seymour, whose home was in New Jersey, was terrified that we would be killed on our last day.

But we weren't killed. We made it to our goal, Liberty Park, facing the Statue of Liberty. She was a wonderful sight on a sunny day, standing tall and proud, guarding New York Harbor. Alex gazed at Miss Liberty for a long time. He took in a lungful of fresh Atlantic air. "It is just like pictures I have seen, but stronger, more feeling."

We could go home now, feeling good about a job well done. It had taken 50 days from Fairbanks to New York, averaging 100 miles a day. One major continent was behind us, 5,000 miles of it. Gennady could be proud of himself and of his rapidly maturing son. Seymour had been wonderful, as solid as a rock. I proudly took Alex to meet my in-laws in Long Island, then to stay with friends of his father in Brooklyn for a well-deserved Big Apple holiday before returning to Moscow. I packed my gear and went home.

There was the Atlantic Ocean to think about.

Joe and Sasha Schvets

Rainy day in Chambersburg, PA

62

CHAPTER V

CROSSING THE ATLANTIC

Oh, we sail the ocean blue,
And our saucy ship's a beauty;
We're sober men and true,
And attentive to our duty.
　　　– H.M.S. PINAFORE, Gilbert and Sullivan

SAILING SCHOOL

The plan for 1991 was to cross the Atlantic in a sailboat and travel by bicycle to Moscow. I spent the winter of 1990-1991 at home, planning. I wasn't a sailor, and I didn't have a boat. That gave me two major tasks for the winter. A trans-Atlantic crossing is serious business, so I had to learn to sail. And I had to find a boat to cross the Atlantic.

I wanted to sail from New York, where we ended our bicycle trip. I called the New York Yacht Club and a polite gentleman told me, "Young man, you are going about this in entirely the wrong way. What you must do," he said, full of New York sarcasm, "is to go to a marina and hang around until you find someone looking for a crew." Also, he added, most spring sailboat traffic across the Atlantic was not from New York, but from the Caribbean. I suspected that Sylvia would just love having me hang out in a marina someplace in the tropics, hitch-hiking a ride across the Atlantic, maybe with drug dealers. Or not.

Nearby was a good sailing school. My instructor was an amiable Frenchman who had arrived in America by sailboat. He taught me about attaching sails, rigging, winches, raising sails, tacking, jibing, reaching, docking the boat and trimming the sails. We had sessions on safety, hypothermia and seasickness. We did man-overboard drills. There were trips to plan and execute, knots to tie, and anchors and dock lines to deal with. I felt I might eventually be of some use as a sailor, after all. After many wet winter days on San Francisco Bay, I got a piece of paper from the American Sailing Association that certified me as a sailor.

MURPHSKY'S LAW

In December I got a midnight telephone call from my Russian partner, Gennady. He had wonderful news. We would cross the Atlantic in a Russian sailboat. It would be shipped as deck cargo on a freighter from Odessa on the Black Sea to New York, off-loaded in the Hudson River. It was a complex arrangement, and it would be a major triumph for Gorbachev's *perestroika*.

Let me tell you about Murphsky's Law. No, not Murphy's Law: *Murphsky* is definitely a Russian. The primary precept of Murphsky's Law is this: "If we *can* foul things up, we *will* foul things up." An important corollary is, "And we will do it at the very last minute, when we have little time to make alternate plans." Murphsky's Law was part of Soviet life, governing the way everything was done or, more often, not done. I heard one Russian comedian describing the system to an American audience. "Think what it would be like if everything in the country was run by the postal service."

Red tape was the rule, wrapped up in ambiguous regulations, surrounded by petty functionaries, bureaucrats whose only joy in life, was the slow mouthing of the four-letter word, "*n y e t*." Worse yet was when papers got lost or buried, or sat on a desk collecting dust, and you never even got the courtesy of a *nyet*. People waited years hoping for permission from these bureaucrats to travel, buy a car or to get an apartment.

Murphsky's Law caught Gennady and me in a predictable way,

walloping us upside the head. We were scheduled to depart from New York on our Russian sailboat on April 1. (Is there something significant about that date?) In mid March, when the boat was supposed to have already been loaded on the freighter and on its way across the Atlantic, Gennady got a phone call in Moscow from the shipper in Odessa. "Voops! They forgot to load the boat. Sorry." #!$%*!! Predictably, they slammed us with a *nyet*. The timing was perfect—at the last minute when it was hardest to deal with.

The word that Russians turn to in a situation like this is *normalno*. Maybe the best way to translate it is, "Normal. What did you expect?" taken with a belt of vodka and a deep, long-suffering, melancholic Russian acceptance of the fact that the powers that be will inevitably dump all over you. That's Murphsky's Law.

WHERE THERE'S A WILL . . .

No Russian boat! Now what? I put through a call to Mary Crowley at Ocean Voyages, who invited me to Sausalito, California, to talk about it. Over lunch she explained to me that every autumn a large number of wealthy boat owners, Americans and Europeans, move their luxurious yachts from the Mediterranean to the Caribbean, where winters are milder. Some of the boats are used for racing, some are chartered, and some are the *pied a mer* scene of the jet set. When spring returns to the Mediterranean, these same sailing ships make the return trip across the Atlantic. Owners rarely make the crossing themselves, depending on hired captains and crews to sail the vessel to its destination. The timing of the spring crossing fit in with my schedule. Mary found an 85-foot aluminum sloop scheduled to "cross the pond" to Europe, leaving Antigua on April 16. I presented my sailing papers, admitted my limited experience and was accepted as crew.

Starting in Antigua created a route discontinuity for me. I did some calculations and discovered that our actual route would be longer than a crossing from New York to Europe. Anyway, I didn't have much choice. In a flash of inspiration I decided to think of it as a reverse-direction crossing of Christopher Columbus' first sailing to America. The next year, 1992, would be the 500th anniversary of that 1492 journey of discovery. Besides, it was better than hanging out on the waterfront, holding up a sign that said, "*Ride needed to Europe. Will share driving.*"

And we wouldn't have to worry about being shot down again by a bunch of Soviet *nyet-niks.* WRONG! At the last minute the USSR refused Gennady his exit visa. He would not be joining me for the Trans-Atlantic leg of the around-the-world journey. Murphsky strikes again! Gennady was saddened by the turn of events. *"Normalno,"* he said. We would meet in Europe for the next leg of the journey (if Murphsky didn't interfere again.)

I had a lot of things to do, and only a couple of weeks to get everything done. I would not be able to transport the tandem bicycle with me on the sailboat. There was no room for it. I decided to ship it to England, where I would join it in May. I had to make arrangements to get to Antigua. Have you ever tried to buy a one-way ticket to anywhere? It costs as much as a round trip. I also had to get visas for Poland and Russia and permits for any vehicles we might be using in Russia.

Sylvia was planning to join me in Europe. She would drive a support vehicle to Moscow, where we planned to end the 1991 trip. And we had to get a support vehicle.

KRISMI II

"I am the captain of the Pinafore! And a right good captain too"
...And be it understood, I command a right good crew!"
    – Gilbert and Sullivan

Notable date: Sylvia's birthday is April 15. That's the day I had to be in Antigua to board the *Krismi II*. Sylvia got up at four a.m. to drive me to the airport. There are better times to skulk away from home than on your wife's birthday.

The *Krismi II* was scheduled to leave Nelson's Dockyard on April 16, bound for Gibraltar, under the command of Captain Gerhard Lomnitz. Our schedule called for two and a half weeks of sailing to Gibraltar, with a short stop in the Azores, Portugal, reaching Gibraltar May 5. The good captain met my flight to whisk me through Antigua's customs. Technically I was not in Antigua, but a sailor in transit, so he took me directly to *Krismi II*. He seemed to be under the influence of either alcohol or some more exotic substance, and I wondered about putting my life in this man's hands. In retrospect I can say that I never saw him overindulge in anything but work, which he seemed to do 24 hours a day. There was no two-hour period when he didn't make an entry in the ship's log.

Krismi II was a well-appointed 85-foot aluminum-hulled sailing sloop, a rare melding of a high performance sailboat and a luxury yacht. The owner was a British consortium, and the sloop was used as a high-priced charter. With six spacious, two-bunk cabins, there was plenty of room for our crew of ten. She had a beam of 19', and a mast 108' tall towered over a beautiful teak deck. In an emergency she could draw on two 93-horsepower diesel engines. Fuel capacity was 880 gallons, and she carried 1,300 gallons of water.

The crew consisted of a German captain, a Zimbabwean sailor and two Americans. The rest of the crew of ten were English, all experienced young sailors. They would be interesting and enjoyable shipmates.

Antigua is located at about 16 degrees above the Equator, below the Tropic of Cancer in the Lesser Antilles. A sea breeze keeps the oppressive heat at bay along the waterfront. Leading up to the pier, one runs a gauntlet of T-shirt and souvenir hawkers, mostly portly black women with rich sing-song voices, lined up in front of a row of bars. Nelson's Dockyard is a ghetto for the millionaires who arrive on luxury yachts. Many of them never venture from the boats. I wasn't in Antigua long enough to buy a T-shirt.

PROVISIONING

Tuesday, April 16, 1992, eight a.m. The water tanks were full. All we had to do was fill the tank for the auxiliary diesel engine at the fuel dock 50 yards away. Unfortunately the good captain was short of funds, so they refused to sell us fuel, suggesting that we buy fuel at St. Bart's or St. Maarten's, a day's sail to the north. We also had to buy our provisions there, enough for ten persons for three weeks at sea. Obviously, this should have been done before leaving port, but according to the captain, the owners had not sent funds. If they wanted their boat in Europe on time, funds had better be waiting at the next port.

Von Murphy's Law: If you are depending on someone to send you money at a critical time, forget it. It won't be there.

Krismi II sailed directly to St. Maarten's. With good facilities for repair and supply, this half-Dutch and half-French island is a haven for sailors. But before loading up we had to wait two days for funds to arrive. Next time you drive the SUV into the Safeway, think about this: Our bill for fuel and groceries in St. Maartens was over $ 3,000. What did we buy besides 880 gallons of diesel fuel? Start with fruit . . . lots of fresh fruit: oranges, grapefruit, apples and bananas. Bottled water. The water tanks were not clean enough for potable water, so we put in liters and liters of water. French bread, chicken, ground beef, cheese and eggs. How much food did we buy? Example: 720 eggs!

It was a big chore lugging all of that on board and stowing it properly. We were at anchor out in the harbor, not at dockside, so everything had to be transported in the dinghy, requiring several trips back and forth. Most of our provisions were put into a huge walk-in refrigerator. Everything had to be stowed securely because at sea anything not properly tied down becomes a missile when the sea gets rough.

While Captain Lomnitz was shopping I donned a snorkel and swam to the reef at the mouth of the harbor. The water was warm and the air was warmer. The swells were gentle and the currents light. In an hour of snorkeling I made friends with a large green turtle, several spiny lobsters, a moray eel and a whole aquarium of very colorful fish. The bottom was remarkably clear of bottles, cans and old tires. I told myself that I'd come back someday to smell the roses.

"AND NEVER, NEVER SICK AT SEA"

Krismi II now had full larders, fuel and water tanks. We were ready to go to sea. After motoring out of the harbor, Captain Lomnitz gave the order to raise the mainsail and the genoa. The sails stayed up until . . . but I'll tell you about that later. We sailed 24 hours a day, every day. To get from Antigua to Horta in the Azores we would have to travel north through 25 degrees of latitude, and east some 30 degrees of longitude. We sailed north first to find the westerlies, which move to a higher latitude in the spring. Our total mileage would be in excess of 3,000 nautical miles, and we hoped to sail at a steady twelve to fifteen knots.

Von Murphy's Corollaries:
1. The wind is always someplace else.
2. When it is in your vicinity, it is in the wrong direction.
3. Sometimes there is too much wind.

Our northward journey was rigorous. Light and wrong winds meant a lot of tacking, making us work at changing sails. When your masthead is 108' above the deck, the sails are very big, and the work is hard and dangerous. Our backs bared to the warm sun, we played at being sailors and moved *Krismi II* steadily northward 24 hours a day.

Everyone but the captain and the cook took two watches at the wheel for a total of six hours a day. There were always two persons on watch, one handling the wheel and a lookout nearby. My steady watches were two to four in the afternoon at the wheel, four to six standby, and three to five in the morning at the wheel. Once out of sight of land we became intimate with the sea and the sky. The sighting of another vessel was rare.

We relaxed. All of the reading material I brought on board was quickly devoured. After I finished something, the others grabbed it. To keep fit I did pushups and sit-ups, and I jogged in place in my cabin. I had an eight-foot length of surgical rubber tubing, and by looping it around the mast I made a mini-gymnasium. Roger, one of the English sailors, had a large repertoire of sea songs. They ranged from bawdy ballads to songs of the loneliness of the sea, and he always had an appropriate ditty.

We fished. There were usually two lines trolling during the day. Gifts from the sea included tuna, dorado and king mackerel, immediate table fare. Catching a nice fish was as much fun as eating it. Even the captain took a turn at the rod. When we had enough fish for the day, the lines came in.

We ate. I had my usual cereal and fruit breakfast. "Cookie" wanted us to eat more of those 720 eggs, so she made custards, French toast, omelets, anything to help empty the bulging fridge. Lunch might be a sandwich or pizza, made from scratch. The real masterpiece of the day would come at dinner, when a beef Bourguignon, a curry or chicken Majorca would grace the table. It was intriguing to watch her prepare complicated meals in heavy seas on *Krismi's* small, double-gimbled stove-top. No matter how the boat rocked and rolled, that stove stayed level. The meals were excellent and copious. This cook was accustomed to catering to wealthy clients.

We slept. I got five hours of sleep between dinner and my night watch, and another three before breakfast. The boat was constantly in motion. As we sat, stood or lay horizontal, it was always rolling left or right, pitching forward and back, and going up and down. I just let the ocean rock me to sleep, albeit with a line around my midsection to keep me from getting dumped from my bunk.

During my night watches there was plenty of time to study the sky. At the new moon, when the sky is darkest, the stars take on an added brilliance. At first we had the Southern Cross low in the sky to our stern. Forward and slightly to port was Polaris, the Pole or North Star, easy to find from the edge of the cup of the Big Dipper. It was interesting to watch Polaris sit perfectly still in the sky while all the other stars did a slow rotation around it. The compass in front of me read 18 degrees declension from true north, so we adjusted for that in setting our course. When steering at night I preferred to use the Pole Star instead of the compass. Sometimes we used a sextant, more out of sentimentality than necessity.

Most nights were clear, and I saw countless meteorites. I wondered about these space travelers, wandering aimlessly around the universe for millions of years. The only time they even fleetingly enter our consciousness is during a blazing death-plunge to earth, a bright streak in the sky, rarely lasting more than a second, then gone forever.

While still in the lower latitudes we were visited by whales. We watched them playing a few hundred yards from the boat. They seemed to be watching us, performing for us. We also had the company of schools of dolphins. They would swim and leap a few feet away from us, racing alongside the boat. I remember them silver in the moonlight and their backs black and bellies white in the daylight.

There was one very calm day when the Captain ordered the sails dropped so we could swim in clear, warm water, miles deep. Our young, brash Zimbabwean climbed to the first spreader on the mast and swan dived into the ocean, 30' below. I decided to give it a try. Going up the mast wasn't hard, but getting out onto the end of the spreader as the boat rolled, three stories above the deck, made my gut tense up. It took me a while to gather the courage to jump, feet first. The trick was to watch the rolling of the ship, and when the mast leaned out over the water on your side of the boat, jump fast. If you waited, you might be a pancake on the deck. I leapt, hit the water and backstroked triumphantly back to the boat.

Then that bloody Zimbabwean gave a great big grin and climbed to the second spreader, 60' above the deck. He confidently edged his way out to the end, waited, and gracefully dropped in. No, thanks. It is all yours, Tarzan. I'm a spectator.

Slowly, as we moved north the temperature dropped. The days of bare chests and shorts were behind us. On deck we felt a northern chill that had joined us, and we had to dress for it.

"AND I'M NEVER KNOWN TO QUAIL AT THE FURY OF A GALE . . ."

A storm caught us as we neared the Azores, Portugal's offshore islands, coming on suddenly during my afternoon watch. One minute the sun was shining, the next a black curtain came down, assaulting us from the rear. In minutes the water transformed from a placid, blue-green to a black sea covered by churning white froth.

We were headed east of northeast, and a strong wind from the west was putting up some very big following waves. Our stern would be lifted high, causing us to surf down the front of the wave. Seconds later the bow was raised high and we dropped backwards, stern down, with the next wave coming at us fast from behind. All the time we were rolling left and right. Again and again waves rolled our bow up, then down, with the stern slamming hard, rattling everything in the boat.

The captain, who had been trying to ignore the storm, called for all hands on deck in foul weather gear. Waves were crashing over the deck. We secured the hatches and everyone tied himself into a lifeline, lest he be washed overboard. With a tremendous effort we pulled the mainsail part way down to lessen the battering effect of the ferocious wind. It looked like we might be in for a long storm.

Off watch, I managed to get horizontal for a while, but there was no sleeping. It was still bad when I was called again for my watch at three a.m. The wind was now coming from the north. As I took the wheel it tried to pull away from me, trying to tear my arms from their sockets. The waves were running big, coming from our port side. The captain ordered a change of heading to due north, directly into the wind, to avoid being swamped. It was dawn before the weather eased off enough to turn east again. I was very glad to be relieved of that watch. Finally, after 18 hours the wind let up a bit. The storm had given us a push in the right direction, and we had logged extra mileage.

WATER, WATER EVERYWHERE, AND NOT A DRINK TO DROP

We were still three days sail out of Horta, and we were nearly out of drinking water, but there was still a good supply of beer. (Von Murphy's Law?) We could survive on that for three days to celebrate the end of storm.

But the letup was not to last. After a respite of a few hours the storm hit us again, this time with a vengeance. It stayed with us three more days. We had gotten off easy so far. We were constantly cold, wet and tired. Cookie had managed to keep us fed, but not her usual hot fare. We were on emergency rations: biscuits, bread, whatever she could dig up. The main thing was to get calories into us. As tired as we were, we were too afraid to spend much time below decks. The boat needed all the help we could give her.

On the third day the wind picked up to a crescendo at mid day. The din of the steel lines clattering against the aluminum mast, the howling of the wind and the crashing of the sea made it impossible to hear. Above that cacophony came a great roar, a deafening ripping sound as the heavy canvas mainsail split along the second reef, rendering it useless. Three men worked their way forward through the waves along the treacherously slippery, pitching deck. They struggled against the gale for control of the torn mainsail, attempting to reef it down to where it would no longer catch the full force of the wind. It took over an hour of extremely hazardous work to get it tied down. Without lifelines we would have lost all three men.

Almost immediately came a loud popping sound, then another and another, like gunfire. The jib was snapping away from its hanks, the eyelets that bind it to the lines. As one hank let loose, more pressure was put on the remaining ones. Before we could do anything about it, the jib was destroyed. We were now without jib and mainsail, and the storm had not yet finished with us.

The engines were intact and we had plenty of fuel in the tank, but we were still a full day's sail from Horta. If we were going to get there, it wasn't going to be under sail. Captain Lemnitz fired up the diesel engines. But this storm was going to have one last stab at us. A big wave overtook us from the rear. The stern went up as the wave struck, then slammed down like a sledgehammer as we plummeted down the back of the wave. Instantly we heard a high-pitched squeal from below. The propeller shaft was bent, and was putting a heavy load on the bearing, overheating it.

The captain devised a way to keep us going. To keep the bearing cool he had to send someone down into the congested engine compartment, to dribble the last of our fresh drinking water onto the hot bearing, gambling that the cooling water would keep the bearing from burning out.

I won the honor. Below, I opened the hatch into the dark stinking engine compartment and dropped in, sitting with my legs and back wedged against the bulkheads to keep the rolling of the boat from barbecuing my parts as I straddled the hot engine block. The compartment was less than three feet square, with no ventilation. The smell of diesel fuel and the burning bearing made me nauseous. The roar of the engine up close drowned out the raging of the storm and the sizzling sound of my vomit on the hot engine block. As we rolled, filthy bilge water rushed back and forth over my waterlogged feet. I was in an oven, but after so many hours on the cold, windy and wet deck, it was a relief. I stripped down and started dribbling the water as slowly as I could to make it last. The water hissed and steamed. The bearing was making an ear-piercing screech, but the engine kept running. I don't know how long I was crammed in there, but when I was finally relieved I needed help straightening up.

The storm finally released its grip on us. The ailing diesel engine got us limping into port. When we tied up at the dock, I was the first to jump off and kiss beloved terra firma. The captain had led us out of a very bad situation. He had enlisted the best efforts of a very harried crew performing under extreme conditions, and he had gotten the most out his crew and his boat. To celebrate our successful voyage, the captain broke out the remainder of the beer.

I left *Krismi II* knowing these things: I never want to go through a storm at sea again and I'm not cut out to be a sailor.

I do not know how long *Krismi II* was laid up for repairs. I was long gone, on the first flight to the continent, where I had a date with a tandem bicycle.

I had seen enough of sailboats to last me a lifetime.

Some days were blue skies – Joe at the helm

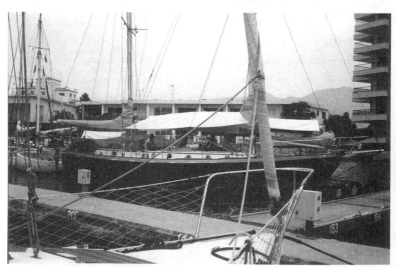

Krismi II in port

CHAPTER VI

OH, TO BE IN ENGLAND!

Oh, to be in England,
Now that April's there.
    – Robert Browning

Having concluded my illustrious career as a sailor, it was time to get on with the journey.

Here is what was *supposed* to happen next: I would fly to Germany to pick up a support vehicle, which I would then drive to England. Gennady would meet me at Heathrow Airport. The tandem bicycle had been shipped to London. Alan and Mary Firth, friends living near London, would put us up until we got started. Then they would accompany us as far as Berlin while Gennady and I cycled. Then we would meet Sylvia at Charles de Gaulle Airport in Paris, and she would drive the support vehicle as Gennady and I rode the bicycle from Berlin to Moscow.

WHEELS AND WHEELS

Let me tell you first about the support vehicle. We needed a vehicle to haul our gear, and in which we could eat and sleep: a camper. Renting was impossible. Because of hazardous conditions, unsuitable fuel and no insurance, none of the rental companies would let us take their vehicle "behind the Iron Curtain." Several weeks before sailing on *Krismi II* Sylvia and I visited a Volkswagen dealer and there we learned about a good deal. If we were to buy a vehicle through that dealership, we could pick it up at the VW factory in Germany. It would be built to meet California pollution standards, but the catalytic converter would be temporarily removed so we could use the leaded fuel that was available in Eastern Europe and Russia. After our return from Moscow we would return the vehicle to the factory, to be refitted to California standards and then shipped home at no extra cost. We'd save money three ways. First, as a factory pickup, we got a very good purchase price. Second, because we would have the car out of the country for over three months it would enter California as a non-taxable used vehicle, saving 7% of the purchase price. Third, we would not have to pay the huge cost of auto rental in Europe. The savings would be big, and we would end up owning a cool new VW camper.

The vehicle we bought had a two-burner gas range, running water, two double beds, a built-in table and chairs, automatic transmission and cruise control. It was economical at 20 mpg. There was plenty of time, we were told, for the factory in Germany to get our camper ready for us. *"Trust me!"* the car salesman said. We trusted him. I gave him my old car and wrote a check for the difference.

Travel from the *Krismi II* to the VW factory in Germany was restful following the last few days of raging storms on the Atlantic. I spent a night in Lisbon, had a good meal, slept in a big bed, caught a Lufthansa flight to Germany and a fast train to the VW plant. The hostess who took care of me at VW was a stern woman with military bearing: tall, straight-backed and direct. Riveting me with her cold blue eyes, she told me in crisp English that although my arrival was "precisely on schedule, there is a small problem." The exact camper that I had ordered was not ready, and would not be ready for two weeks. She insisted that there had been a procedural error that had *not* been made in Germany. If I did not mind waiting overnight, she said, they could get me a similar vehicle, but it would not have an automatic transmission nor would it have cruise control. And the color would be silver instead of white. Ranting and raving would have done me no good. I said *ya*, by all means. *Danke, Frau.* We agreed on the amount to be refunded to me "at some later date" by the lying dealer back home. In the morning I picked up the car. After getting detailed instructions on its care and feeding, I drove my new camper off the factory grounds. It was a nice enough vehicle, but Sylvia was going to have to learn to drive a stick shift.

I called Gennady in Moscow and found him in his office. I didn't like the way he sounded. Bad vibes were coming through the wire. "Joseph," he said at last, "I have some very bad news about our trip. I cannot come to London to meet you." He told me about his problems. There was a complicated explanation about the fall of the Berlin Wall, chaos at his employer, *Komsomolskaya Pravda,* and finances. "You must continue without me," he said. "I will meet you when you enter the USSR at Brest," a city in Byelorussia near the border with Poland. *Damn!* First he misses the Atlantic crossing, now he bails out on crossing Europe. I knew that it was beyond his control, but that didn't make me feel better. Freaking Murphsky's Law again!

A telephone call home got a sympathetic reception from Sylvia. She could live with a stick shift, she said. It would work out. We would meet Gennady in Brest. Sylvia would meet me soon in Paris. She offered to see if she could come up with a replacement rider on the tandem. Another call to the Firths in England assured me that all was in order there. I had to get there with the camper, pick up the bicycle at Heathrow, and we could be off. But who would ride with me across England?

It was a two-day drive to the Firth's from the VW plant in Germany, so I called Ger Wijenberg in Tilburg, Holland, halfway to the ferry in Calais. Ger is a wiry, red-haired Dutchman. We had been roommates during a super-marathon (26 miles a day for ten days) running race in Russia in 1990, and we had got on well. Having spent time in Russia, he understood the difficulties faced by those unfortunate people. He invited me to stay at his place and talk about my problem.

A FINGER IN THE DIKE

I found Tilburg easily enough but got lost when I got off the highway. I drove through a gate into a park-like setting surrounded by a very high iron fence. I couldn't understand the Dutch signs, but I did find an administration building. I parked the VW and went in. The fellow at the desk spoke no English, but he understood when I asked for the use of a phone. I reached Ger and turned him over to the man at the desk, who told him how to come down to rescue me. Ger later explained to me that I had called him from inside a supposedly locked mental institution. Maybe, I mused, I belonged inside.

We went to Ger's apartment and had a few beers and dinner. He helped me find a bicycle rack and a chemical toilet for the camper. We had a few more beers, and Ger patiently listened to me moaning about my bad luck. After a while and said, "Joe, I have a few vacation days coming. I will help you with your problem. I will go with you to England to ride with you for the first part of the trip. Just stop your damned whining, please." We had a few more beers, and I went to bed happy. In the morning Ger made some phone calls to let people know he was leaving town, and we were off for England. Just like that. Where does one find friends like Ger?

We had a rough ferry crossing of the English Channel from Calais to Dover. I thought about what it might be like in a couple of weeks when we would be crossing it in kayaks. Mick Carpenter, recently retired from the British Army, was making the arrangements for our kayak crossing. Mick was tough and reliable, a good man to have on any team.

THE VIEW FROM THE CASTLE

Alan and Mary Firth are special people. We had met several years before at Arctic Joe Womersley's double marathon race on Baffin Island, Canada. (You will meet Joe Womersley later.) Alan is an Englishman, a retired insurance executive, generous of his time and energy, insightful and intelligent. Mary is a genteel North Carolina lady with a big smile and an even bigger heart. Add to that a twinkle in her eye and good looks.

In 1992 they were living in Farnham, in the south of England in what they called their "cottage." There are no such "cottages" in California. Two stories of solid stone with skillful and intricate masonry, it looked like something out of a fairy tale. On the grounds was an arboretum with trees from around the world, including tall California redwoods. A short walk up the hill was the South Downs Way, a public footpath that runs mile after beautiful mile across southern England.

Alan, Mary, Ger and I drove west to our starting point, Land's End, at the extreme southwestern point in England, in two campers, my VW and the Firth's. Our goal was to cycle across the country to Dover. Every day Alan and Mary would each drive one of the campers, while Ger and I rode the tandem. Alan had spent many hours laying out a route that kept us biking on quiet country lanes and accessing beautiful camping spots.

We spent our first night camped among sheep on a foggy Cornwall hillside. The next morning, cool and damp, we started cycling from Land's End, logging 100 kilometers. From Alaska to New York we averaged about 150 kilometers per day, but in Europe we wanted to go at a more leisurely pace.

We had Cornish pasties in a pub in Penzance. At times we dined in pubs, and sometimes Mary prepared dinner for us. Although she claimed to be a poor cook, her meals were filling and tasty. Typically she prepared something like turkey burgers, mashed potatoes and a salad, with a scrumptious lemon curd for dessert. A pub dinner would be similar to the one we had at the White Stag in Mortonhampstead, Devon: steak and kidney pie, chips (french fries) and a pint of ale. Our routine was to rise early, have tea and a sandwich, and get going. Breakfast would be at the camper after an hour of riding, typically cereal, juice and tea. Then we were off again. We would usually finish around five, after a lunch break and a snack in the afternoon.

Southern England is hilly. The hills are steep but, thankfully, short. It took Ger only a day to get into the rhythm of riding. Holland is flat, but Ger is from the hilly Limburg area, jokingly called the Dutch Alps. He is a strong cyclist and opted for the stoker position, the rear seat, where he could hammer away without thinking, hour after hour. My job was to pedal, to shift gears, to pay attention and to aim the missile.

We were headed through Bristol, Farnham and Maidstone towards Dover, through lovely hamlets with names like Abinger Hammer, where a statue in the town clock clouts the bell with a big hammer every hour. People go there just to watch the bell get whacked. We were ahead of the tourist season, so the traffic was light. Our campsites were well situated and reasonably priced. We crossed two rivers by ferry, a restful change of pace. The weather was pleasant, not much wind, no precipitation.

BAD PONY!

One day, after taking the ferry at Plymouth, we stopped for lunch in Dartmoor National Park. Mary set out a hungry man lunch: pork pies, sausage rolls and sandwiches. As soon as the food came out, wild ponies converged on us from every direction, at least 20 of them. Compared to horses, ponies are small; compared to people they are big, and they are unmannerly. These wild ponies were favorites of English tourists, who loved to feed them. They are dependent on handouts. They were cute, but we wanted to eat, and we were not about to share our lunch. One pot-bellied old stallion with foul, wet breath kept poking his drooling snout into my face as I repeatedly turned myself and my lunch away from him. Ger climbed onto a rock to get away from them. They stopped being cute. Mary produced a package of butter cookies and some apples for the ponies, letting us finish our lunch in peace as she entertained her equine guests. Alan pointed out another local attraction, Dartmoor Prison, home to England's hard-core bad guys. Couldn't they put the ponies behind that fence, too?

Large areas of England are in the hands of the British National Trust, a private group akin to the U.S. Park Service. They have preserved much of Great Britain's national heritage, and we passed several of their properties along our route. The English are keen lovers of nature. Flower gardens are plentiful and well tended, and the most prominent shop outside most villages is a large garden supply center. Besides a few wild deer and the feral ponies, there were hedgehogs, foxes, squirrels and millions of rabbits.

And the birds! Outside of the tropics I had never seen so many of them: blackbirds, sparrows, magpies, crows, wrens, finches, pheasants, partridges, hawks and cuckoos. The large wood pigeons were the size of chickens. Birds sang to us when we made camp in the evening, and they woke us in the morning. Alan introduced me to an English superstition. When you see a magpie in the morning, it is proper to greet it with, "Good morning, Mister Magpie." Failure to address these large black and white birds correctly could result in a bad day. We saluted a lot of magpies in England. I still do.

From Cornwall in the west to Kent in the east everything was green. California gets green only in the winter, when we get our precious rain. In Britain, blessed with the warmth and moisture of the Gulf Stream, the countryside is green most of the year, especially in the south.

I was impressed by the traditional building craftsmanship along our route. Masonry was done in imaginative patterns on homes, barns and commercial buildings. (Winston Churchill was an amateur mason.) Some of the homes had thatched roofs, the more elaborate of them with graceful, sweeping curves. We watched a thatcher doing his careful work, as it has been done for centuries. The crafts of masonry, thatching, slating and joinery are being lost as older artisans find no market for their skills, with no hope for the young people who might otherwise apprentice to them.

A picture often returns to my mind. We were crossing an old wood-planked suspension bridge coming into Bristol. It hung hundreds of feet above a gorge where the Severn River cuts a path to the sea. The boards clattered and the nails creaked as we bumped our way across. The toll was only tuppence. When Ger and I explained to the toll taker that we did not have any money with us, he threw in his own tuppence and waved the American and Dutchman on with a smile. The steep climb up Old Bristol Road from Wookey Hole put a strain on every fiber of our quadriceps. This hill was peppered with four letter words in Dutch and English.

ANOTHER BACK ROOM BIKE TROLL

Then came the day when Ger had to return to Holland. He would not be able to finish crossing England with us. We sent him home and returned to the Firth's home to conjure up a plan. The tandem needed adjusting, so we took it to the Acorn Bike Shop in Godalming, near Farnham. In the back room was a Bicycle Troll named Dave, which he pronounced *Dyve*. We watched him as he enthusiastically tuned up *Magenta Mama*, and we listening to chortled exclamations of "mmm, luverly, luverly" as he tightened spokes and adjusted brake cables. While he worked I told him my sad tale about Gennady not getting out of Russia to join us ("That's them Rooshins for yer"), and about Ger having to go home to Holland ("That's them Dootch for yer"). Might he know of a local cyclist who could ride the tandem with me for a few days? "I don't. But whyn'tcher just get yerself a cheap mountain bike and go on by yerself? You can pack the tandem onter the back o' the camper and meet up with yer Rooshin myte later on in Roosher."

Dyve was right, of course, and he had just the right bike for me, a blue off-brand from Taiwan, inexpensive and as sturdy as a mule. If I couldn't ride the tandem, I would ride that mule. He set it up for me that night.

Back at the Firth's I got a fax from Gennady, confirming that he would definitely meet me in Brest, just inside the USSR-Polish border. He would be there on June 15 for sure. Sylvia called in a half panic. Our visas to enter the Soviet Union had not yet arrived. "Patience," I counseled. "The papers will come before you leave for Paris," I assured her with my fingers crossed. There was a knot forming in my stomach. Was Murphsky's Law going to stick it to us again?

I called Mick Carpenter about the kayak trip across the English Channel, coming up in a few days. So far, he said, no problems.

THE ENGLISH CHANNEL

We moved on, with me on the new mountain bike and Alan and Mary leapfrogging me in the camper. Sometimes Alan would get far enough ahead, park the camper, and ride his own bike back to join me. The Firths were upbeat and enthusiastic, and they made the trip a joy. We got into a routine, and before long we were homing in on Dover. On our last night we camped by a duck pond. A raucous peacock, even louder guinea fowl and a pair of Canadian geese with a gang of goslings serenaded us.

The next day we rendezvoused with Mick Carpenter. He wasn't happy. After months of preparations for our kayak crossing of the English Channel, the Coast Guard had turned him down at the last minute. He was dejected. "We just can't go. They know all about us, and they'll be looking for us. If they catch us we will be in big trouble."

That was that. There would be no kayak crossing of the Channel. Mick rode his bicycle with me for most of the day, then went home. Alan, Mary and I rode on to Dover to catch the ferry to Calais. The roads were a mess because one of the biggest construction projects in the history of Europe was going on. They were building the "Chunnel" from Dover to France. Wouldn't it have been nice to ride the bikes through that wormhole to France? Too bad it wasn't ready for us.

(I eventually filled in my missing non-motorized English Channel crossing. In August of 2000, just shy of age 66, I was one of six swimmers on a team crossing the Channel, *with* the blessing of the authorities. That is a tale for another time.)

Traffic jam

A wild pony at Dartmoor wanted my sandwich

Arrived at Dover where the Channel Tunnel was under construction

CHAPTER VII

WESTERN EUROPE: GOOD LIVING

Immer mit der ruhe! German: "Always go peacefully."
(Smell the roses?)

VIVE LE FRANCE!

We crossed the English Channel on May 20, 1991. The P & O *Pride of Calais* left Dover on time, and we were in Calais in just over an hour. The sea was calm and the day was sunny and cool. It would have been a fine day for kayaking across the Channel.

As soon as the auto traffic exiting the ferry at Calais let up a little, I hopped onto my brand new mountain bike and started pedaling northeast, with Alan and Mary Firth driving alongside. We wanted to get out of Calais, find a nice place to camp and have dinner. Our route called for one night in France, and this was it. We wanted to make the most of our one shot at fabled French cuisine, but we were in unfamiliar territory and didn't know where to find a good local eatery or a campground.

I am so very, very lucky to have friends like Alan and Mary Firth. Without them Western Europe would have been much more difficult. Now I found an added asset in Alan: he spoke both French and German. He also had all the maps and guidebooks we might need. Even a simple thing like reading a sign indicating a campground nearby requires the ability to read the language, and Alan was up to the challenge.

Our night in France was spent in the town of Bergues, and by early evening there was a chill in the spring air. Alan found a *Ferme Auberge,* a farmhouse restaurant not far from our campground.

Annie, our hostess, sat us near a massive stone fireplace where we could get toasty warm. The building was centuries old, remodeled just enough for comfort, with heavy oak furnishings. We were the only customers.

This was Annie's farm and her restaurant. Because it was so early in the season, she had not yet hired any help, so Annie was our waitress, our bus boy and our chef. She and Alan discussed the possibilities, and off she went to the kitchen. Dinner was superb. We started with tomato-based fresh vegetable soup, all ingredients from her farm. The two large, hot loaves of bread could have nourished us by smell alone, but we slathered it with freshly churned butter. The main course was a succulent *coq au vin* with potatoes and carrots, again all from the farm. (My mouth is watering as I write this, years later.) A cheese tray was loaded with Dutch cheddar, local goat cheese and a gelatinous semi-brie, followed by ice cream, cookies and coffee. Of course we enjoyed local wines, red and white. My only regret was that Sylvia was not there to share this memorable meal.

IF THIS IS TUESDAY THIS MUST BE . . .

The next day we were in Belgium. Restaurants were featuring spargel, the delicate white asparagus available only in the spring. We savored it with roast pork and potatoes in Belgium and a few days later in Germany. We spent one night in the Netherlands before entering Germany. Our dinner was eaten at restaurants, where wholesome local cuisine always took care of ravenous appetites. Mary prepared hearty lunches, typically a big loaf of French bread with pate, chicken, cheeses and cookies.

We were floating across rich farmland dotted with dairy and truck farms, pleasant on the eyes when you are confined to a bicycle all day. My progress was about 60 miles a day at 10 to 15 mph, but the towns seem to whiz by too swiftly. Place names became a blur:

Bergues, Bourbourg, Brouckerque, Trelt, Dienze, Gavere, Oude-naarde. Sometimes we followed flat roads along canals. Here and there a fisherman sat on the bank of the canal, but I did not see a single fish giving up his freedom. There were many bicycles on the road—not tourists like me, but people using their bikes for transportation. Two-wheeled vehicles far outnumbered cars. No one seemed to be in a hurry. I could put the hammer down and maybe get there a little earlier, wherever "there" was, but I just wanted to enjoy the scenery and the day, taking it just a bit easier.

HOW TO NOT GET LOST

Every evening Alan, Mary and I would pore over the maps and the guidebooks, reviewing the plan for the following day. An important part of the plan was "What do we do should we become separated?" Each day we selected a place to regroup, and Alan wrote it down for me to tuck into my jersey pocket. This was a necessary precaution. We were using back roads in very old towns, where they would narrow, twist, branch and turn several times before spitting you out on the far side of town. It would have been very easy for us to go off in different directions and not realize it. So many towns! Dendermorde, Willebroeck, Mechelen. Frequently the road through town was made of ancient cobblestones, and I'd get a not so gentle massage from my bike seat.

Alan had a good way of dealing with confusing towns. He would drive through in the camper, following signs that only he could read. On the far side he would haul out his bike and head back to meet me. Not once did we get badly separated. I can still see him in the center of Mechelen, across the town square, waving energetically to get my attention so he could guide me through the maze.

Venlo, Strailen, Geldern, Wesel, Borkenberge. Whizzz. Gone! My body was holding up well, except for a slight pain in my right knee. We had no bad weather. Late one evening I called Sylvia. It was early morning in California. Everything was okay at home, she said, but still no visas for Russia. Fear not, I counseled, the papers will appear. I said a silent prayer for the repeal of Murphsky's Law.

THE GOOD LIFE

Germans know how to live. The windows of the butcher shops and green grocers were filled with quality products. The smells wafting from the bakeries were like grappling hooks, dragging us in by our nostrils. It was too easy to contrast this bounty with the paucity I had seen in Russia. What might it be like for an ordinary Russian to be turned loose amid this abundance? "How does it come to pass," he would say, "that these people have so much and we have so very little? Didn't we win the Great War?" Ahead, soon enough, we would be entering that other world again.

All over Germany there are vast stretches of forestland, reaching right up to the towns. At times the bike path went directly through these manicured woods. I never saw trash in the forests or along the roads.

At an intersection headed towards Braunschweig, I didn't know which way to go. Alan was not in sight, so, selecting a likely looking bystander, I made an attempt at asking for directions. After a while in a country you *think* you know the language. *"Bitte, Ich ben ein Americaknisch turister. Wo ist Braunschweig?"* After some puzzlement, he got the idea. The answer was an elongated version of "go straight ahead," with a finger pointing the way. Naturally, Alan was waiting a few blocks ahead.

We took the easier route across Western Europe. We didn't cross the Alps or anything like them. In fact, if you drew a straight line from Calais to Berlin, then arched it to the northeast, you would have a good approximation of our route. We avoided big cities and most of the hills of Germany. Our hilly route across England had been much tougher than on the continent. By using byways we avoided high speed Mercedes, BMWs, Porsches and Volvo trucks.

I have no complaint with the way European drivers treat bicyclists: they share the road. They understand that bicycles need space and are accustomed to hetero-vehicular cohabitation. It's not just the drivers. Many of the roads are built to accommodate bicycles, and there is an extensive network of bicycle paths.

Campgrounds in Western Europe were a welcome surprise. With no reservations and no idea where we might spend the night, we always found pleasant accommodations. It was early in the season, so there was plenty of room for us. The toilets were clean, with lots of hot water. Sometimes there would be a laundry and a mini-shop where we could stock up on essentials. Locations varied from way out in the countryside to inside the city limits of Berlin. Some of the spots were semi-permanent, being second homes or summer places rented by the season, often improved by the renters with picket fences, goldfish ponds, barbecue pits and wishing wells.

The names of some of the places we passed through recalled great WWII battles from my childhood in the 1940s, and from World War I, when my father was at war in Europe. But there were no bomb craters, and no signs of the horrible destruction that had rained down on those battlefields. We saw only prosperity and happy, healthy-looking people going about their business. Houses were neat and brightly painted, and flower-filled window boxes were everywhere. Businesses, from banks to butcher shops, were clean, colorful and well lit. Farms, factories and shops were all contributing to the general welfare. I marveled at the ability of mankind and nature to recover in a few years from such terrible blows.

We were nearing Berlin, the end of this segment of my journey. Behind were three ridges that had intersected the path, running perpendicular to my route, but they had not been difficult climbs. It was late morning before the land flattened out again. I had not seen the Firths for hours, so I stopped to look at the map that Alan had made for me that morning. I needn't have bothered because coming around the next bend was Alan. "Good morning, Joe. I thought you might be worried." That night we made it to the outskirts of Berlin.

BERLIN

Alan and I could have been the Allied Forces, Brits and Yanks, taking Germany in WWII. We were five decades late, but it was nevertheless a historic time to be entering Berlin: the Berlin Wall had just been breached. East and West Germany were reuniting after almost half a century. Communism had been routed, not by a war, but by the will of the people.

On May 29 we stayed in a public campground two miles from the center of Berlin, near a subway that made it easy for us to get around. The Western Europe leg of the journey was over. It was time for us to be tourists. We rode the subway downtown and walked to the Brandenburg Gate, an immense structure that marked the division of Germany as much as the wall itself. To the east everything was gray and drab, in need of scrubbing, paint, repair and modernization. The bright colors and the spotlessness of the west faded in the space of one block. It was clear that bringing East Germany up to par with the west would be an immense task.

We decided to drive over to the other side to see the wall that had divided this country for so many decades. Not far from the Brandenburg Gate we came to the place where the main road goes through the wall. There were guard towers on the eastern side. We saw machine gun emplacements. Across a narrow ditch was a field of barbed wire that would have had to be crossed by anyone desperate enough to try to escape, and many died trying. I could imagine Doberman pinschers

94

straining at their chains, a soldier shouting a single warning before he shot to kill. It was a place inhabited by ghosts of an evil past.

RUDY'S TOWER

Back on the western side there was a stone tower, very old, on a rise in clear sight of that terrible dividing wall 100 meters away. I carefully climbed 40 stone steps to the top of the tower. A middle-aged man was at the top, gazing toward the east. He was short, slender, neatly dressed and formal. I said hello in German and he responded in good English. He introduced himself as Rudolf Schlager. Rudy was born just across the line in 1939, when there was one Germany, in a small village that no longer existed. Both his parents died in 1943, leaving him and his brother Emil, a year younger. Three-year-old Emil was taken in by one relative and Rudolf went with others in the next village.

As fate would have it, the partition of Germany also became the parting of Rudy and Emil. Emil's village was on the east side of the wall and Rudolf's in the west. They were no longer able to visit each other, phone each other or even, at first, write letters to one another. But they remembered this old tower and another tower on the other side of the wall. Rudy and Emil would climb the towers and wave to each other. That was all, just wave. It was dangerous for Emil, but he never got caught. Once a week, on Tuesday afternoon, they waved. Year after year they visited across the void. They faithfully went weekly to the towers through the fifties, the sixties, the seventies and the eighties.

Just as things were starting to ease up, when people could move back and forth with a little more freedom, Emil fell ill. Rudolf thinks it was tuberculosis or emphysema, but he will never really know. Emil came to the tower a few more times, but it was too much for him. He was hospitalized and soon passed away. He never knew that the wall had come down. And Rudy never got to say goodbye to his brother, but after a half century, Rudy continued his weekly vigil at the tower.

He heard that there were plans to tear down the old stone towers, though they had nothing to do with the infamous wall. But as long as the tower stood he would continue coming. The ritual had become too much a part of him to give up. Before I left, Rudy said something else: "We were just children; there was nothing we could do. You know, the institutions we human beings build can cause terrible suffering, too often falling upon the helpless and the innocent. But I still believe that people are essentially good, and there is always a great hope, especially in the hearts of children."

The wall dividing East Germany from the west is gone. I do not know if the stone towers are still standing. If they are, maybe Rudy Schlager still goes to his tower every week to visit with Emil.

THE AUTOBAHN

Alan and Mary got into their camper van for the long drive back to England. It would be several days before Sylvia arrived, so I got behind the wheel of my new VW, with Magenta Mama on the bike rack, and drove to Brittany to run in a super-marathon race with Ger and some other friends.

It was odd to be behind the wheel of a car again after so long on a bicycle. I was on the main Autobahn going west from Berlin, and the traffic was terrifying. My Volkswagen camper was outclassed by orders of magnitude. The BMWs and Mercedes that ruled the road were not happy sharing it with a camper. The slow lane was moving along at 75 mph, and the fast lane was over 100. My new VW had never moved so fast, but it had to in order to keep up. If I drove too slowly, insistent tailgating with a light and sound show was considered acceptable encouragement by pursuing drivers.

On a long downhill about 50 miles west of Berlin, traffic came to a standstill because of an accident 300 yards ahead. One truck was sitting diagonally across the westbound lanes of traffic, and another had its nose up against the midsection of the first. The driver of the Mercedes behind me walked to the accident scene and came back with the report from the front. An Englishman in a car nearby translated for me. It seems that a Polish truck driver had collided with a Dutch truck. Herr Mercedes made it clear that this would never have happened if the drivers and trucks were German. It took over an hour to clean up the mess. A few hours later I picked up Ger Wijenberg in Tilburg, Holland, to go to *le Grande Course de Bretagne* super-marathon run.

LA GRANDE COURSE DE BRETAGNE

Americans are unfamiliar with super-marathon running races. There are no such races in North America. A standard marathon race is 26.2 miles long; the world record is just over two hours. Most runners take between three and four hours. In a super-marathon the runners run a full 26.2-miles *every day* for the duration of the race, usually seven to fourteen days. I know of super-marathon races in France, Russia, Siberia, the Czech Republic and Morocco, but no place else. There was, in fact, the Golden West Super-Marathon in California and Nevada, but it was held only once.

The way it is done in Brittany is interesting. You start in the morning in a village, after a small breakfast, *petit dejeuner,* and then race to a second village 13.1 miles away, a half marathon. At the destination village town officials greet the runners as they arrive. There is a ceremony and the lead runner is presented with flowers and an award. The runners are then fed a big midday meal, after which they rest. At two p.m. they get up and run another 13.1 miles to a third village, where another mayor greets them and they are fed dinner and housed. The next day they do it again to another couple of villages, then again each day for ten days. The team or individual winner will have the lowest total time when all of the individual segment times are added together. You must complete every segment of the race to qualify.

Running a marathon is difficult. Running two half-marathons in one day, even with a rest, is harder. You stiffen up. Running like that every day is extremely demanding. Do people do that? Yes, some do. With the right training and attitude it can be like taking a nice, long hike followed by a fantastic meal … again and again and again.

I had organized the American team in *le Grande Course de Bretagne* before I left home. We had a good team and the course was splendid, starting at the castle at Mt. St. Michel on the Normandy coast, with much of the running along canals and through forests. The French organizers did a marvelous job. Teams from Russia, Czechoslovakia, Hungary, Poland, Germany, France, Canada, Holland and the USA competed. The Russians were the strongest and the most willing to accept pain hour after hour and day after day. Our American team didn't fare badly.

Sylvia came directly to Brittany from Paris. She had two surprises for me. The first was that she had finally received our visas for Russia. The other was a new American bicycle partner who would ride the tandem with me as far as the Soviet border. He came from a magazine ad.

CHAPTER VIII

EASTERN EUROPE

"From Stettin in the Baltic to Trieste in the Adriatic an iron curtain has descended across the Continent."
— Winston Churchill, June 1, 1946
Independence, Missouri

In the early days of the theater an iron curtain was often lowered between the stage and the audience for the protection of the cast from unruly spectators. Sir Winston, with his theatrical background, made an apt analogy to an Iron Curtain separating the Communist East from the West. He would have been amused to be bicycling with us when the wall crumbled.

HUEY

After the super-marathon in Brittany, Sylvia and I drove to the French city of Tours to pick up Surprise Number Two. Sylvia had indeed found a bicycle partner for me. I will refer to him as Huey, not his real name. Prior to the Atlantic sailing I had requested information about a bicycle tour from an ad in a sports magazine. I spoke with the owner of the tour company, and I told him about my upcoming bicycle trip across Europe to Moscow. "Now, isn't that a coincidence," he said, "I have a son in college. He is an expert bicyclist, a fine bike mechanic, and he's fluent in Russian. He isn't doing anything this summer. Maybe you would consider having him join you?" It was tempting. A bike mechanic would be handy. His language skills might be useful in Russia, and he could share the driving with Sylvia.

Pop sent Huey's resume, along with a photo. He was a big, good-looking kid. On paper he looked a little too good. I wondered why his father, who worked hard at putting together bicycling tours in Europe every summer, would prefer to have Huey travel with me, rather than work in the family bike tour business. Huey and I exchanged letters and phone calls. I offered to pay his airfare and all of his living expenses if he came. He said that my offer was not enough. He wanted to be paid a full salary, so we did not come to an agreement. I sensed that he was overjoyed about that, and I later learned why.

All of that was long before I left home, before the fiasco with Gennady not showing up for the Atlantic crossing or the bicycle ride across Western Europe and before I drafted Ger Wijenberg in Holland by whining in his beer. Sylvia had said that she would try to find me a cycling partner. She did. Sylvia the Efficient, Sylvia the Problem-Solver, reactivated the Huey file while I was whining in Europe. She spoke to him, came to an agreement, helped him with his Russian visa and airplane tickets, and had him on board a plane before I knew about it.

Huey had spent a semester in France. He spoke French but did not like French people. He said that they never bathed. "They smell bad" was his explanation for the existence of the perfume industry in France. He said they were cheapskates and that we would be robbed in France. His experiences in France had been bad, except for the family he roomed with. In France Sylvia and I had experiences that were quite the opposite. We had been treated well, despite not speaking much French. Even in Paris, where the people are reputed to be as rude as New Yorkers, we were never treated poorly.

When we picked him up in Tours, Huey was like three of the seven dwarves: Mopey, Grumpy and Un-Happy. Sylvia kindly ascribed it to jet lag. The three of us went to the Mammouth Hypermarche, the biggest supermarket I had ever seen, to stock up on food

100

and supplies. We were not sure what we would find in Eastern Europe, and we knew that there might be little available in Russia. We bought pots and pans, Brillo pads, cutlery and everything we might need to be at home in the camper, keeping in mind the space limitations of the VW. Sylvia bought food, from canned peas to oatmeal, enough to keep us reasonably comfortable on the road. What we bought that day would sustain us for weeks to come.

As soon as he got into the camper, Huey fell asleep. He snoozed all day. He chose to stay in the camper while we shopped. He was very good at napping. When awake he was grumpy and argumentative. This guy was going to be fun to travel with!

We were on our way to pick up where I had left off in Berlin. After a night in Troyes it was a short drive along the *peage* toll road to the German border. The Autobahn was great, but suddenly the texture of the super-highway changed. There were cracks and potholes everywhere. The ugly towers we had just passed were part of the long border between the East and the West. We had entered the southwestern corner of East Germany.

AN AERIE WITH A VIEW

Our first stop was in the East German city of Eisenach. It had been only a few weeks since East Germany had liberated itself from communism. It was now part of the free world, but the systems that had been in place over the previous decades were all they knew. We looked for a campground and found none. Stopping in a drab little food store, we asked about a hotel. No one in the shop spoke English, but we made ourselves understood. Yes, there was a hotel, a helpful woman patron told us, and if we would follow her car, a rickety Trabant, she would lead us to it.

At the beat-up hotel we were told that there were rooms available, but there was no parking for the Volkswagen. Anyway, they couldn't yet accept credit cards or foreign currency, and we did not have Deutschmarks. The hotel clerk suggested that we go to a nicer inn nearby, a place called Der Wartburg. We would love it, he said, and they would be able to accommodate us. He gave us very precise driving instructions.

The drive to Der Wartburg was on a narrow road that snaked its way up a mountain overlooking the city. At the top we found ourselves at the gates of a *schloss,* a castle. The camper could not get through the ancient, narrow archway, but an attendant assured us that it would be very safe to leave it in the guarded parking area. The last few yards to the reception area were along a manicured garden path. The massive stone walls of the castle soared straight up toward the sky, while a steep cliff dropped off precipitously on all sides. The views in every direction were spectacular. We were well above Eisenach, miniaturized far below us. In the distance, toy train tracks scratched their way through the surrounding forest. I could imagine myself as the Lord of the Castle, surveying my domain of farms and forest. From up here lookouts could easily spot enemies approaching.

Inside, Der Wartburg was just as impressive. Décor was early twentieth century, but the castle was much older. The rooms had ten-foot ceilings and were spacious, with large windows overlooking the spectacular panorama. Under the windows were immense steam radiators in intricately decorated cast iron. Sticking one's head out the window afforded an opportunity to examine the castle's ornate exterior architecture, including gargoyles. Toilets were at the end of the hall, but inside each room was a voluminous bathtub that begged to be enjoyed.

The cost of the room, including dinner and breakfast, was embarrassingly low. We were the first western tourists to stay there, and they were uncertain about pricing. The price for that room a year later was ten times higher. Dinner that night was roast boar, potatoes, sauerkraut and a torte. At dinner I asked about the history of the castle. The hostess was shocked that I was ignorant of such a very important place. Pointedly, she informed me that Der Wartburg had been the residence of Martin Luther. It was in this very place that he had translated the Bible into German. (Huey asked me if this guy was related to Martin Luther King. I don't think he was kidding.)

Sylvia tried to bring Huey out of his doldrums. She had taught English at a university in Pennsylvania, and she loves to discuss literature. Huey was an English major. She thought that he might enjoy talking about what he had read. He was offended when Sylvia asked him about it. "I get enough academic crap at school. This is my vacation." He was a literary blank, having read the minimum, remembering and understanding almost nothing. English majors get a bad rap, and Huey was a good example of why.

The poorly maintained East German version of the Autobahn took us into Berlin, and we camped where Alan and Mary Firth and I had recently stayed. Sylvia, Huey and I went to see the Brandenburg Gate. It was early June, and the tourist season was starting to pick up. Peddlers were all over the place, mostly Turks and Yugoslavs. You could buy a chunk of the Berlin Wall from them, or a DDR military uniform. Maybe, I was told, even some interesting chemical substances. It was a short trip to Kufurstendamstrasse, "Ku Street," the entertainment and business street, Times Square with a German accent. Young people from all over Europe were getting publicly stoned in mid day as music blasted from a dozen speakers. Where was the conservative Germany we expected?

CLEARING THE AIR

Dinner that night was at a Yugoslavian restaurant. Huey started spouting anti-religious opinions, declaring that anyone who believed in God must be a damned fool. (Interesting choice of words, "damned.") He was shouting, drawing looks of disapproval from other tables. This kid was full of anger. Whatever his problem, he was pissing me off. I had enough to do on this trip without having to babysit a surly adolescent.

Sylvia took him aside and finally found out what was bothering him. He didn't want to be with us. He was in love and he wanted to be with his girl friend, planting trees in Canada, instead of with a pair of old farts on bicycles in Europe. He was worried about her up there in the North Woods with other guys. The only reason he had come with us, he said, was that his father, who didn't like his relationship with this young lady, had insisted. It would test the relationship, Dad had said. If it were real love it would survive the test. Huey's attitude was, "Bullshit, Pop," but his father was paying the bills.

It was out on the table. I told him that I regretted his problem, but it was his, not mine. He would have to deal with it. If he didn't want to be with us, he could take his ticket and go home. We would get along without him. If he decided to stay, he had better cut the crap and get wholeheartedly into the program. Our trip wasn't going to be easy, but it might be fun if he let it. Huey sulked as he thought it over and said that he wanted to go with us, and he would get his head on straight.

EAST GERMANY

The differences between East and West Germany were vivid and pronounced. Once we got east of Berlin, we dropped 50 years back into the past. Everything was colorless, and even the people were gray and joyless. Smiles were few and complexions were sallow. Secondary roads were paved in some places with ancient cobblestones, each stone jolting us through the bicycle seats. The air was foul. Pollution belched from smokestacks and from diesel trucks. Smelliest of all were the tiny, cheap Trabant autos.

We did not take long cycling across East Germany. We went through Muncheburg and on to Frankfort-am-Oder, the *other* Frankfurt. This Frankfort sits on the Oder River, the border with Poland. So far we had not experienced any problems with borders. Going from East Germany to Poland was a different matter. Neither the Poles nor the Germans were going to make it easy. First we had to make a 10 km detour to go through customs, driving directly away from the border. The customs agents, accustomed to dealing only with Poles, Russians and Germans, were surprised to see Americans. Our papers were in order. After an incredulous "Why are you here?" we were allowed to pass into Poland.

Before crossing into Poland Huey and I were riding the tandem along a byroad, headed for the border. The driver of a passing Trabant stopped and hailed us. He was a young Russian Army officer in full uniform. Inside the car were crammed his mother-in-law, wife and little girl, and whatever he could pack inside and on top of the car. In a heavy Russian accent he asked in bad German for directions to the Polish border. I responded in my best Russian with an American accent. I told him that we were headed the same way, and that we were also confused.

He got a laugh out of meeting his first Americans in Germany at the Polish border. He, along with thousands of Russians, was being kicked out of Germany. "When I get home to Moscow I will tell them that the Americans can't wait for us to leave. They are already here on purple bicycles and speaking Russian." I told him that I might see him in Moscow, *"Do Moskve," until Moscow.* As he went off chuckling, he was trying to explain the situation to his wife.

We entered Poland. All we knew was that we had to keep going east, but we had no idea of exactly what we would do next. Adventure was upon us, ready or not.

Huey was strong on the bicycle, and very knowledgeable. Two keys to cycling long distances are efficiency and technique, and he had both. He didn't have tandem cycling experience, but he learned fast. Riding a tandem is like dancing: the two riders must act as one, often anticipating what their partner is going to do. Huey made a good partner.

THEY TOLD US THAT

They had told us that food would be scarce in Poland. They told us that the roads would be antiquated and full of potholes, and that bicycling would be miserable. They told us that we would encounter thieves and that the Polish people would be unfriendly. They told Sylvia that with Huey and me on the tandem and her driving the VW support vehicle, we would become hopelessly and miserably separated in some remote and hostile place where no one spoke English. They told us that campgrounds or hotels would be non-existent, and that if we did find any, they would be of very poor quality and very expensive. They told us that there would be no motor fuel for sale. They tried to talk us out of going "Behind the Iron Curtain."

They didn't know what they were talking about. Poland was a wonderful place. But consider the location. To the east was the USSR, and to the west, Germany. During the 20th century both of these military behemoths had run roughshod over Poland. Caught in this vise, she had lost large pieces of territory and population. Now, for the first time in more than half a century, Poland was free of both the USSR and Germany. It was a good time for the Polish people.

In Poland we had a language problem. Between us we could speak a little German, French, Russian and Spanish. Over the years the Polish people had been forced to learn the languages of their German and Russian oppressors. Now speaking German was advantageous for them: German tourists had money; Russians didn't. Our first night in Poland was spent at a farmhouse in the small town of Torzym, near the German border. There was a hand-printed sign out on the highway, "ZIMMER," the German word for a room to rent. We followed arrows to a farmhouse, where we were given two clean bedrooms and breakfast for a total of $15. We had not yet changed money to Polish currency, but our dollars and deutschmarks were fine with the landlord.

Do you want to be a millionaire? Go to Poland. The unit of currency is the *zloty*, plural *zlotich*. The exchange rate was 11,300 zlotich to a dollar, so $100 would be 1,130,000 *zlotich*. There were both 100,000 and 500,000 zlotich bills in circulation. Our rooms that night would have cost us 169,500 zees, if we had had any.

A neo-capitalist named Tomas had set up a restaurant along the main road. He had cousins living in Chicago and Buffalo and wondered if maybe we knew them. Dinner consisted of beer for the men folk, fresh lemonade for Sylvia, borscht, cutlets, potatoes, cabbage, beets, pickles, cucumbers and lettuce. The total for the three of us was, again, $15. It would have been painfully difficult to shell out 169,500 Zlotich.

Sylvia has a "banana theory." It goes something like this. Where imported bananas are available, there is a developed economy and likely to be a decent level of culture. We found bananas in the cities of Poznan and Warsaw, the only two large Polish cities along our route. Bananas, imported via Germany, had recently hit Polish markets. They were filling pent-up desire, along with so many other signs of an economic system engaged in rebirth.

The situation in the rural towns and villages was different. Free enterprise had not quite arrived. The people in the agricultural areas were still tied in to the collective way of doing things. Half way to Poznan we stopped in a village to inquire about buying food. There was a man playing a fiddle in the upstairs window of a farmhouse. With a two-toothed smile he directed us to the farm collective's shop, where local families got everything from bread to tractor grease.

When we asked the girl behind the counter about the price of bread, jam and milk (*khlep, dzhem, moloko*) she became flustered. The young lady didn't know what to do, or even if she could sell to us. She called for the manager, who spoke some English. When we introduced ourselves and told him we were Americans, he was over-joyed. "You are our first tourists. And from America! Please excuse us. The girl does not know how to help you. Tell us what you need." He gave us our bread, jam and milk for about half a dollar. Word gets around fast in small towns. The whole village was out to get a look at the American tourists with our marvelous machines. We were trying to look nonchalant, but it's hard to be inconspicuous when you are wearing colorful bicycle togs and riding a magenta tandem bicycle.

One form of wildlife that was abundant were storks. They were everywhere–in trees, on chimneys and in fields. I hadn't thought about it before, but storks are hunters. Storks stalk. They stalk small animals. We would see them standing catlike in a field, patiently waiting at a mouse hole. They followed mowing machines, hoping to bag flushed animals or mower-munched tidbits.

The road was a beeline from Berlin to Warsaw. In East Germany roads had been rough with no shoulder for bikes. In Poland our route along the main highway had wide shoulders. There was no shortage of truck traffic, but there were also horse-drawn carts, and horses were pulling plows in the fields. The highway was smooth and flat and had few potholes, and that meant easy riding. Huey and I were clicking off the kilometers fast while Sylvia drove the van, hopscotching us, stopping every ten miles. When we cycled past her we would slow briefly to check in. After we passed the camper she would wait a while, let us get a few miles ahead, then look for her next stop. We saw each other every five miles or so. I was concerned about Sylvia parking alone along the road in a country where none of us knew the language, but nothing ever happened to give us cause for concern.

The city of Poznan has a population of over a half million. Since 1922 it has hosted an international industrial fair. Unknown to us, we were headed into town at the time of the fair. The hotels were full, and there was no campground. A few miles before Poznan we stopped at a roadside stand for a snack. As we rested a middle-aged man in a suit and tie approached us. He introduced himself as Stanislaus, a professor of mechanical engineering at the Polytechnic Institute of Warsaw. He was hitchhiking home from his moonlighting job as a guide on a German tour bus. Sylvia said she would not mind his company in the van for a while. In return for the ride he got us into the Garrison Military Hotel in Poznan.

It was a Sunday. After checking in at the hotel we went to a street fair. There were thousands of kids milling around, decked out in their Sunday best. An Oom-Pa-Pa band was turning out polka music, next to food kiosks and flea market stalls. One of the stalls had a display of antiques, being shown for the first time since the change in government. I noticed two very old-looking silver menorahs for sale and was told that they were artifacts from the Warsaw Jewish Ghetto. I would love to have purchased them, but we couldn't take them into Russia. Artifacts bring big problems when crossing borders.

The morning we left Poznan it was raining, and the road was slick. Huey and I were thoroughly soaked from the splash of passing vehicles. The sun returned before noon, and by the end of the afternoon we had logged a good 130 kilometers. In the small town of Koto we bought dinner and breakfast supplies: two loaves of bread, three sweet rolls and a jar of jam, $.90. We asked about a campground or a hotel. The shop woman tried to help us, but communicating with us was difficult. She locked the shop, took her small daughter and climbed into our camper, directing us about a half mile to an inexpensive B & B. She would not accept a ride back to the shop. Like so many of the Polish people, she was willing to go out of her way to help us.

WARSAW

The following day we were blessed with mild temperatures and a good following wind. With an early start and some hard pedaling we made it into Warsaw, a little more than a hundred miles. Near the city center, on a hill high above the Vistula River, we found an excellent campground with clean showers, a shop and a laundry. The location was good for touring the city, near public transportation.

In the campground we got to observe international camping in action. First a busload of Swedish youths rolled in, active, fun-loving cutups. Next to them was a group of French car campers, who had arrived in Peugeots and were sleeping in tents. They had set up a communal kitchen, and the odors were compelling. Then the hi-tech marvel of the camping world lumbered in. It was a huge Mercedes bus pulling a trailer as big as the bus, a hotel on wheels. The bus doors opened and 50 middle-aged Germans popped out. They fell to their chores like a disciplined platoon. Quickly they erected a military-style dining tent with chairs, tables, linen and silverware. A hot meal was produced from the engine compartment at the back of the trailer. They ate, took down the tent and got ready for bed. All 50 of them managed to sleep in the trailer.

One of the Frenchmen remarked, "I'll bet they have a spare engine in case the engine dies." His partner said, "Yes, and they have a spare German in case one of them dies." Old wounds heal slowly. But the Swedish kids got a kick out of the German invasion. A tall Swedish lad, about 19 years old, hauled out his guitar, strolled over to the German group, and with the help of his buddies serenaded the Germans. He started with a German beer hall song that they all knew. It was Octoberfest in Warsaw.

Professor Stanislaus, who had hitchhiked with us, came to the campground. He offered to assist us and helped us to call the Warsaw office of *Komsomolskaya Pravda*, Gennady's employer in

Moscow. He also made an appointment for us to visit the Warsaw Velo Club, Poland's 100-year-old bicycle club. The club was located in the basement of an apartment building, and they called a special meeting in our honor. The club president gave us mementos of Warsaw. We were privileged to meet octogenarian Kazimir Wladislavski, a former world record holder who had competed in Hitler's 1936 Berlin Olympic Games. The medal he won by beating the German cyclists got him two years in Dachau when the Wermacht rolled over Poland a couple of years later. But Kazimir outlived his Nazi tormentors and was still cycling many years later. After tea and chocolates at the bicycle club the professor took us to be interviewed on Polish National Television, aired across the country that night.

The Professor's daughter, Justinka, had a day off from her job as a dentist and took us on a guided tour of the city. We started with a visit to the palace of the old kings, then on to Belvedere, the presidential mansion. It was depressing to visit the old Jewish Ghetto. Fifty years after the war no Jews lived there. The high point of our tour was *Stari Mesta,* the old town square. The buildings around the broad square were centuries-old architectural gems. In adjacent side alleys were beautiful churches and historic buildings, the very heart of Poland. We had a relaxed lunch sitting in the sun in the *Stari Mesta* and sent post cards to ourselves at home.

There was one more thing to do before leaving Warsaw. The rear wheel on the tandem was going out of round. The pounding away of 400 pounds of meat and machine for long hours every day was taking its toll, and Huey did not have the tools to fix it. We had a spare, but it needed work, too. The people at the Warsaw Velo Club recommended a shop across the Vistula River in Warsawa-Brodno, where we found Pan Sztompka, a true Back Room Bicycle Gnome. He gave the wheels a quick examination, put them on his truing bench and brought both of them into round in a short time. When he was finished he refused to accept any money for his services: "It is my contribution to help you on your journey around the world. One cyclist is helping another. Think of me from time to time."

We continued east from Warsaw. There would be only two more days of cycling before entering the Soviet Union. With every kilometer we rode east, conditions became more primitive. Western Poland, near Germany, had decent places to stay. Sometimes we had a choice of eating establishments, and food markets could be found. Here, restaurants and markets were rare. On the farms work was still done by animal power, human and horse. All along the route we saw men and women in the fields doing the kind of hard manual labor that we in the west abandoned 50 years ago. Life seemed harsh.

Wild flowers were growing at the side of the road, blood-red poppies and blue, yellow and violet flowers. Often there was a cow or a goat tethered at the side of the road where the grass was thickest. At times we would see a farmer walking along the road, his cow on a rope trailing behind. Almost no one rode in a car. People moved about on foot or in small, sometimes ornately decorated horse carts with which we shared the shoulder of the road. An encounter with a pedestrian or a cart was always accompanied by a hello, *"Djen dobray, Pan."* and a big smile that needed no words.

Some of the people recognized us from our television interview. We heard frequent shouts of "good luck," and "to Moscow." In one town a group of 20 schoolboys on bicycles was waiting for us. They knew we would be passing through their town. We slowed down to let them ride with us. That was a bad idea, because they surrounded us, spilling out into the lanes of traffic. Somebody was going to be hit by a truck if we didn't break it up fast. Huey and I said goodbye and put the hammer down to pull away. One by one they fell back. One kid with curly blond hair stayed with us for over a mile. We hit a small rise and we could hear him gasping for air. Then he slowly slid back, having bested his mates by staying with the golden warriors from America longer than the rest.

We spent our next-to-last night in Poland at a motel. Not *in* the motel, *at* it. We paid the $10 rent before seeing the room, a big mistake. When Sylvia got a look at the room, she balked. She has always been fastidious about the cleanliness of toilet facilities. This was not the Ritz. "I am not going to sleep in this hovel," she said flatly. After taking a shower, during which Sylvia levitated two inches above the grimy floor, we traded places with Huey, who had been planning to stay in the camper. He was happy to get the room. Dinner at the motel, the best (and only) place in town, was big, cheap and greasy: a bowl of tomato-macaroni soup, black bread, mashed potatoes, cucumber salad, schnitzel with an egg on top, and soda and tea. The tab for three came to 88,000 Zl. You figure it out.

Around eleven p.m. we were awakened by a thunderstorm. With the heavy rain, wind and lightning, trucks were leaving the highway. Guess where they all headed! We had barely dozed off when the headlights of a dozen semis beamed in on us as they wheeled in. The grinding of gears and the shouts from truck to truck by tired men with deep, guttural voices in an unknown language did not help us sleep.

A NIGHT TO REMEMBER

Our final day of cycling in Poland was short and easy. It was, however, wet. The rain from the night before had left puddles, and we got well splashed. We reached the border town of Terespol just after noon. We would be crossing into the USSR the next morning. After lunch at the railroad station we asked the only town taxi driver if there was a place where we might stay. He directed us a half mile out of town, to a sign that read "PRIVAT KAPITALIST HOTEL MME. EMILIA WOLWODOWSKA." It looked okay, so we knocked.

Mme. Wolwodowska was out of town, the girl said, and the hotel was closed all week.

The tourist map I had purchased in Berlin showed a campground just east of town, close to the border. We drove out to take a look. There was indeed a campground, and we drove in. As soon as we entered the gate we were surrounded. From tents and lean-tos came a swarm of shouting, crying Gypsy women and children, their hands out, clutching at anything they could grab. They were miserable looking, dirty and emaciated. We felt threatened and had to get out of there fast. I leaned on the horn and carefully backed out onto the main road. Back in town the taxi driver told us that they were refugees from the bloody revolution in Romania. They had fled Romania and had been hounded north through Hungary and Czeckoslovakia into Poland. This band of Gypsies had gotten as far as the Soviet border and could go no further. Nobody wanted them and they were stranded at the campground, waiting for help from aid agencies.

Our taxi driver friend told us that there was one other place we might try. It was dinnertime when we found it, and we went right into the dining room. The food was plentiful and tasty. It seemed a little odd that the only other people in the restaurant were young, heavily made-up women. Sylvia and I took a small room that overlooked the parking lot. Huey stayed in the van. The place just didn't seem to be a hotel. As the evening wore on I noticed through the window that men were coming in, one at a time. That went on for a while, and I didn't want to say anything to Sylvia. At about eleven she remarked that there was a lot of laughing and commotion coming from the rooms to the left and right of us. What really confirmed our suspicions was a deeply satisfied customer loudly moaning, "Oh, Zoshia, Zoshia." He was not Zoshia's first friend that night, nor her last. We drifted off to sleep giggling. How would I tell the grandkids that grandma and I had spent a night in a whorehouse?

We had an early hearty breakfast at the brothel and headed for the border, stopping very briefly to drop off a food bag at the Gypsy camp. There was a long line entering the USSR, moving very slowly. We had left the "hotel" at 7:30, and we did not cross the Polish border station until 11:30. An even longer line was ahead on the Russian side. After seven hours of sitting, we were only about half-way through the line. I got out of the camper to take a walk to the front. Maybe I would be able to see Gennady and let him know that we were really coming. When I got near the front I asked a border guard how much longer he thought it might be. He looked me over and said, "You are American? Please come to the front." The line, of course, was for Russians. Different rules applied to tourists with money to spend. The others in line would be there for another five or six hours.

Poland was behind us. As we crossed into the USSR I thought I could see Gennady waiting in the crowd.

CHAPTER IX

TO RUSSIA WITH GLOVES

"Oh, East is East, and West is West, and never the twain shall meet,
Till Earth and Sky stand presently at God's great Judgment Seat;
But there is neither East nor West, border, nor breed, nor birth,
When two strong men stand face to face, though they come from the ends
of the earth."
— Rudyard Kipling: *The Ballad of East and West* (1889)

"So you've been over into Russia?" said Bernard Baruch, and I answered
very literally, "I have been into the future, and it works."
— Lincoln Steffans: *Autobiography* (1931)

BACK IN THE USSR

We entered the USSR on June 15, 1991. The line at the border was horrendously long, but because we had a special invitation from Gennady's employer, *Komsomolskaya Pravda*, we were "rushed" through the immigration process in only seven hours. We didn't even have to use any of the packs of Marlboros we had brought, the standard bribe for dealing with police and petty bureaucrats in Russia.

The USSR! Little did anyone realize then, including the CIA and the FBI, that the USSR, the largest country in the world, would soon cease to exist. Certainly we three Americans entering the country did not have a clue about the impending death of our cold war adversary of so many years. Nor, I am sure, did Gennady.

THE WELCOMING COMMITTEE

Ah, yes, Gennady! There he was, watching for us, a few yards inside the border, in the crowd waiting to welcome friends and loved ones. He spotted us and jumped up and down, waving like a happy boy, a big smile on his face. We had not seen each other since parting in Edmonton. What kind of shape was he in? Gennady was a fine athlete, but not always meticulous with his training. He looked like he had put on a few pounds since Edmonton.

He was standing with two other men, strangers. One was a pudgy, jovial-looking fellow, in his late 40s, wearing a gray suit and a crumpled necktie, with the unkempt look of a high school math teacher. The other man, about 40, was short, dark and intense. He looked like a coiled spring—tight, muscular and ready to erupt into action. His head was buried under a big mop of black, uncombed hair. He had a very large nose and darting eyes that scanned everything. I had never seen anyone quite like him. He could have been an assassin, a folk singer, or the reincarnation of Rasputin.

I pulled the camper to the side of the road as the three men approached. Gennady gave big Russian bear hugs to Sylvia, then to me. "Joseph, Joseph, Joseph! You look very good, fit like violin. Welcome to Byelorussia." He turned to the other two men and said, "I want you to meet my very good friends. This is Professor Gyorgy Gribov. Call him George. He is professor of philosophy at the University of Brest. We will be staying in his home tonight. And here is my very special friend Arkady Samuelovich Sarlik, known as "Sarlik the Mongol." Arkady is well-known poet in Russia. He speaks no English, but is very fast learner." A philosopher and a poet! Philosophers and poets have always held high places in Russia, where intellect and the arts were valued for their own sake, even in the utilitarian USSR. I introduced Sylvia and Huey, who received more bear hugs and multiple cheek kisses. Gennady suggested, "Let us go now to apartment of George. We have dinner waiting. You must be starving."

George Gribov and his wife Irina were professors of philosophy at the University of Brest, in the largest city in western Byelorussia. Their home was in a typical multistory concrete apartment block, identical to thousands of poorly constructed others. The inside was pleasant but like all Soviet apartments, quite small: one bedroom, a living room and a kitchen. Unlike many Soviet citizens, they had two children, a thirteen-year-old daughter, Veronika, and an eleven-year-old son Vladik. Grandmother lived with them. The walls were lined with books and hung with oriental carpets and the ubiquitous picture of Lenin. Sheer curtains let in the spring sunshine.

Irina prepared a tasty and filling lunch for us. We were aware of the difficulty of getting food in the USSR, with long lines, small allotments and poor quality. Sylvia expressed our deep thanks to Irina for the wonderful meal. Things were easier for them, she said, because they had joined a collective farm in the countryside near Brest. They raised their own poultry, eggs, dairy products and vegetables, and traded extra production for hard-to-find consumer goods. It meant long hours on the farm in addition to fulltime teaching jobs, but it gave them a secure supply of good food. Proximity to the Polish border made it easier to get imported items.

VILLAGE LIFE

We were encouraged to "Eat, eat!" until we could eat no more. "And now, our American friends" said Irena, "We will spend the night at our farm." We all crammed into the camper and George's tiny Lada automobile, the four Gribovs, Gennady, Sarlik, Sylvia, Huey and I, nine of us. We drove to the farm on unpaved roads, arriving at the village of Mlini in 45 minutes. The collective consisted of 20 homes and a few outbuildings. The Gribov home was an ancient one-room wooden building. To one side of the 20-foot-square room sat an old, cast-iron wood stove, for cooking and heating. Opposite was a sitting and eating area. In between a raised platform with many pillows and blankets dominated the center of the room. This was the sleeping platform where everyone huddled together to share body heat on cold winter nights. The cottage had a "homey" feel to it.

There was electricity but no plumbing. Water came from a hand pump outside. The toilet was a communal outhouse 50 yards away. The "honey bucket" product, caught in a pail, was used to fertilize the fields. It was an old village with ancient oak trees shading the cottages. At the end of two rows of houses was a large field, partly planted in wheat, the rest in vegetables. It was late in the day, but men and women were bent over, tending their crops. Two horses grazed lazily at one end of the field. Scattered about were cows, hogs, sheep, ducks, turkeys and chickens. A creek flowed on the opposite side of the field. I felt as if I had stepped into the middle of the 19th century.

Most of the people in Mlini were fulltime farmers who were born there, but part-timers like the Gribovs were a growing minority. The young people of Mlini had opted for city life, as in our own dying Midwest farming communities. "This is how our ancestors lived. It is in the blood of the Russian people," explained Irina. "It is a hard and simple life, but here we escape the stresses of modern civilization. By investing labor we get a small but very satisfying return. It is a good way to live."

The village of Mlini brought to mind an interesting Russian word, *Mir*. We Americans know *Mir* as a Russian spacecraft, but the word has three meanings deeply rooted in the Russian psyche. It is most commonly translated as meaning "peace," but it also means "the world." In old Russia, the word *mir* also meant one's own village. It must be comforting to use the same word to signify one's home, the world and peace. It was little comfort to the people of Brest and Mlini when the Nazis crossed into the USSR from Poland. Mlini was one of the first places they occupied on their bloody drive to Moscow, and the last to be liberated when the Nazis were forced to retreat.

George introduced us to Valodya, a professor of engineering at Brest University. We went to Valodya's cottage, where we met his wife, Larissa, and his son, Maxim. He asked me if I knew about the Russian tradition of *banya,* the Russian version of sauna. When I said yes, he offered to show me his inexpensive, quick and easy *banya.* We followed him to the creek, where I saw nothing but a bonfire burning down. Valodya sprinkled some water on the embers and pushed them aside. Underneath was a bed of hot stones. He quickly erected a teepee of three eight-foot poles over the hot stones and draped a sheet of plastic around the poles. We squatted inside, careful to avoid contact with the stones. Valodya sprinkled water onto the stones. Steam rose, and with it the temperature in our makeshift sauna. When we worked up a good sweat, we jumped into the chilly creek. I wondered if I could get a patent in the United States, where Americans might like a cheap portable sauna.

Sylvia and I opted to sleep in the camper. In the morning our breakfast started with raw milk, straight from the cow. From the Russians I learned to suck just-laid eggs. When in Rome," they say. Never again, say I. I had visions of salmonella and tuberculosis. Russians usually eat a small breakfast, maybe some black bread with butter or jam and tea. We got a chance to try swinging a scythe, mowing a snack for the cow in return for her milk. There is a knack to handling a scythe, and I did not have it. Tomorrow we would be getting back on the bike again, but today we would be farmers.

In the evening we went to a clearing on a high bank above the creek for a barbecue. The moon was big and high and backlit a stork's nest in a tree. "You know that a stork is good luck," said George. "So we are now sure that you will have good cycling." Over an open fire we cooked skewers of *shashlik,* cubes of beef, with onions and peppers. Valodya and Sarlik played guitars. Russians love their music and they love to sing. We were at it until about one in the morning. To fortify ourselves against the mosquitoes we were advised to eat a lot of salami and wash it down with copious amounts of vodka. "Vodka is good for everything."

It struck me that Huey was not using his Russian at all. Was he shy, or didn't he have the command of the language his father had promised?

SARLIK THE MONGOL

In the morning we got ready to ride. As I donned my cycling togs I noticed that Gennady was helping Sarlik to dress in his own cycling gear as Gennady remained in street clothes, and I asked Gennady about it. "Didn't you get my fax?" he asked. "Sarlik will take my place on the bicycle. I must return to Mosow, but I will stay with you until Minsk." There was no point arguing, nor pointing out that I had not been near my fax machine at home for a month, nor mentioning that I had telephoned him only recently. He couldn't go. Period. But at least he had found a replacement. "Sarlik is very fast learner. Quickly he will be good bicycle rider." Uh, oh! We had to start from scratch again! Of course I had an option. If Sarlik proved to be useless on the bike I could always stow him in the camper. Huey was champing at the bit anyway. He did not want to be confined to the van while Sarlik and I had fun on the bike.

I took a good look at my new cycling partner. Arkady Sarlik was a powerful man, and he worked at staying strong. In the past couple of days I'd noticed that he never sat still. He was constantly exercising his muscles with a length of rubber tubing. He had long, oily black hair and a full, shiny black beard. There was determination in his face. I asked him in Russian why he was called Sarlik the Mongol. "I am half Jew and half Mongol. I have inherited great intellect from one and ferocity from the other. Most of my life has been spent in remotest parts of Soviet Union, working as fisherman in the Kuriles, trapper in the Komi Republic, gold miner and reindeer herder in Chukotka. I am expert at hand-to-hand combat." This guy would be interesting once we got to know each other.

Our biggest problem was going to be language. My Russian was limited. His English was zip. We were going to have to quickly learn to communicate, because we were starting on the bike that very morning. We agreed on a few working phrases, half Russian and half English, and a few hand signals. The main object was to ride safely. Because Sarlik did not have the slightest idea of what he was doing, I made sure that I rode in the front seat, where I could steer and shift gears. Sarlik would be the stoker. In a few days he might get a shot at the front seat.

We drove back to the main road near the border crossing. Sylvia, Huey and Gennady sat in the camper as I showed Sarlik how we would get started. We must be in unison, I told him. *Da.* Ready? *Da.* "Okay, one, two, three, *Raz, dva, tree.*" We were off on *Magenta Mama*, headed for Moscow, 1,000 kilometers and ten days away.

I've known many muscular, powerful men. In general they have little endurance. Cycling all day long, like marathon running, requires more endurance than brute strength. Sarlik had the strength. The trick would be to teach him to make his energy last all day. He didn't know the basics that most cyclists take for granted. He refused to wear a helmet, gloves or any kind of a shirt when riding. "I will not fall and I will not get cold." He did not want to carry a water bottle. "I can drink before and after." As soon as he became confident of his balance, he started hammering hard on the pedals. *"Potikhonko,"* I told him, "Take it easy." He was slamming the pedals hard on the down stroke, making for a jerky, inefficient ride, instead of churning out smooth circles. To put a stop to that, I shifted to a higher gear, making him spin a bit faster. He would learn, but it was going to take time. We had ten days to become a team.

THE ZUBR

On the first day we stopped to see a national park, *Belovezhskaya Pushcha,* the White Tower Forest, a wildlife haven unknown outside of the USSR. We wandered among 700-year-old oaks and lichen-covered spruces, blueberries and wildflowers. The ruler of this domain is the *zubr* (pronounced "ZOO-brr). When I saw the *zubrs* I thought that they were American bison, kidnapped and claimed by the Russians as their own. No, Gennady assured me, this is an ancient animal native to this part of the world. A closer look revealed that the bull *zubr* was not as shaggy as a bison. They were larger, with a more curved face. They share the White Tower Forest with deer, elk, bear, wild boar, lynx and an assortment of small mammals and birds. "Gennady," I asked, "If a cowboy takes care of cows, who takes care of *zubrs*?" He looked puzzled. "Zubr-man!"

We cycled 100 kilometers to the town of Baranovich on that first day. Sarlik was putting on a brave face, but he was walking with difficulty. He admitted to having a very sore *zhopa*. I told him that it was not unusual to have a sore bottom the first day of a long trip, or even for a few days. I promised him that he would be riding painlessly soon. He looked at me dubiously. I dug around in my gear bag and pulled out a fleece seat cushion. His bright, dark eyes beamed with appreciation. Sylvia offered Sarlik a couple of aspirins, unknown in the USSR. He had never had an aspirin, nor any painkiller but vodka. Sylvia became his Florence Nightingale.

The third day I let The Mongol ride in front for a while. He went steer-and-gear happy. The shifting of gears must be done smoothly, used primarily for climbing hills or to change speed. Sarlik was shifting up and down simply because he could: he had a new toy to play with. If a partnership on a tandem bicycle is like a dancing partnership, riding with The Mongol was like doing the cha-cha-cha with a grizzly bear.

Huey was functioning as our bicycle mechanic and relief auto driver. Every evening he inspected, cleaned and lubricated the tandem and checked the wheels and tire pressure. After our third day of riding in the USSR he showed me what he thought was a serious problem. Fatigue cracks were developing inside the rims of both wheels. They would get worse. The problem was the road, which was even worse than the roads in East Germany. We had spare rims, but they were not much better. Because Magenta Mama was a tandem mountain bicycle, a new concept at the time, the rims were not a standard size. We had seven more days of cycling ahead of us. Would they last?

By the end of the day we were in Minsk, capital of Byelorussia. As a long-standing member of the Communist Party and as a journalist, Gennady was able to exercise a few privileges. He got us complimentary rooms at the Communist Party's big shot hotel, the *Oktyaberskaya*. There were a lot of bad hotels in Russia, a few of them barely acceptable for foreign tourists. As expensive as the tourist hotels were, there were always irritating little problems: no toilet paper, sink stopper, hot water or shower curtains. A stay at The *Oktyaberskaya* convinced me that Communist Party members took very good care of themselves. Every detail was attended to, right down to imported soap and an attractive floral arrangement. Even the hotel restaurant was good, and they actually *had* what was on the menu.

NAPOLEON SLEPT HERE

We crossed the Berezina River and stopped to look around. Napoleon's army entered Russia along this road in 1812. Along this same

124

road Hitler's army made its advance towards Moscow 130 years later, and it was again along this road that much smaller numbers of French and Germans fled homeward. There is a monument to mark the place where 20,000 French corpses were stacked like cordwood until they could be buried in the spring. Bright red poppies were everywhere. Kids were wading in the slow-moving Berezina on this warm June day, oblivious to memories of Napoleon or Hitler.

The four of us were advancing on Moscow, Sarlik and I on the tandem, and Sylvia and Huey in the camper. Beyond Minsk were rural areas. Sarlik suggested that it might not be safe at night for Sylvia and me to sleep in the camper. Huey and Sarlik would sleep in the camper and he would find hotel space for Sylvia and me. Just before reaching the town of Borisov there were two incidents that became problems because of language difficulties. First, Huey got a traffic ticket. It cost ten rubles, paid on the spot, directly to the policeman. Huey was very upset because he didn't know what he had done wrong.

The other situation seemed, at first, to be more serious. As they were parked at the side of the road waiting for us to arrive on the bicycle, a man approached Huey and Sylvia. He reached into his coat and pulled out a big knife. They thought that they were being robbed, and there was a moment of panic. Just then Sarlik and I came wheeling up on the bicycle. From the look on Sylvia's face I knew that she was upset. Sarlik shot some rapid fire Russian at the man, who now looked more frightened than Sylvia. The Mongol smiled and said that it was a misunderstanding. The man was just trying to sell these obviously rich foreigners a beautiful knife that he had hand-crafted. That was when I was certain that Huey did not understand Russian, despite what his father thought.

The hotel in Borisov was what we expected: terrible. No toilet seat or paper, no hot water and an abundance of wild life. But the bed was comfortable. Sarlik parked the camper in the yard of the police station, the safest place in town. He gave the night commander a pack of Marlboros to be allowed to park there.

Sarlik was our guide, our negotiator and our protector as we got further into the USSR. His English was improving. He always had his Russian-English dictionary handy, and he referred to it constantly. Our cycling wasn't great, but it was getting better.

RUSSIAN TOLL BOOTHS

Sarlik explained Huey's traffic fine. "You broke no law. It was a shakedown, a normal occurrence." It was a part of the culture. The police were grossly underpaid and they supplemented their meager incomes by setting up their own "toll booths." The standard bribe on the highway was ten rubles. A pack of Marlboros would be much better.

The next day we had another police incident. A cop stopped the camper outside of Borisov. He was wearing a uniform that looked as though he had slept in it for a month. Sylvia was ready for him. "No speaky Russky," she said. Whatever he said or shouted, she gave him blank looks, shrugged shoulders and eyebrows raised in feigned ignorance, playing the part of a dumb foreigner who didn't have a clue about Russian. He wrote "10 R" on a scrap of paper. She gave a knowing "Ohhhhh," winked, and handed over the "toll." Encouraged by his success, the entrepreneurial policeman attempted to sell Sylvia his uniform. If he had a gun, he might have tried to sell that, too. The toll booth scam became standing joke in the camper. If we wanted, we could have equipped a small police force with cheap, rumpled uniforms.

What did ten rubles amount to? It depended. On the *official* market in Moscow one ruble was worth about $1.60 US, so ten rubles came to $16. Tourists were required by law to buy rubles from official money exchanges, such as the banks. Nobody did so, because you could duck into any street underpass in Moscow and get 20 rubles for a dollar, so a ruble was about a nickel to a savvy tourist. If you were a good bargainer you could do better. To a rural cop, whose salary was unbelievably low, ten rubles might be a week's pay. A large loaf of bread cost eight kopeks, and 100 kopeks equaled one ruble. Because of this great disparity the cop's unofficial toll station was worth more to him than his salary. He undoubtedly had to pass some of it up the line to his superiors to keep his post. But to us ten rubles was insignificant.

Traveling in rural Russia brought to mind an earlier conversation with a Russian friend. We were having lunch in a restaurant in Moscow. It seemed that the waitress, although polite, did not want to sell us food. It took perseverance on his part to get her to serve us. I told him that I could not understand why a restaurant would not want to sell a meal. Wasn't that why they were in business? He laughed. "It is very logical for us. If they sell you the food, they won't have it any more. They take home what is left over."

Eating with Sarlik was always an experience. He ordered for everyone without bothering to consult us. His rationale was that he ordered the best of what was available. He always ordered an extra portion, and he personally made sure there were no leftovers. With great gusto, he filled the room with "mmms," "ahhhs" and appreciative shakes of his head.

Disaster struck! The rear wheel finally broke for good towards the end of the next day as we approached Orsha. There was no fixing it or getting a replacement. Please, let the spare hold up for the rest of the trip! We were about half way to Moscow. The hotel in Orsha made the dump in Borisov look good in comparison. Whenever we could, we ate in restaurants. When there were no restaurants we would dig into our cache of canned French food. Riding all day creates a big appetite, but we never suffered from lack of food. In the restaurant in Orsha we had a pig-out meal: borsht, salad, beef stew, potatoes, cookies, three glasses of grape juice, bread and an Uzbek meat pie.

Except for a few rain showers the weather was perfect during the first five days. The scenery was pleasant, with trees lining most of our route. We averaged 140 kilometers per day and were ahead of schedule. Maybe we were pushing a little too hard. We finished each day tired. Sarlik was getting better, but he was still jumping around on the bike like a flea.

The last major city on our route to Moscow was Smolensk, our first city in the Russian Republic. Byelorussia was now behind us. Sylvia was raised in the Russian Orthodox faith, so Gennady made arrangements for her to visit the Smolensk Orthodox cathedral. Metropolitan Nikolai himself gave us a half hour personal tour. An invading Polish army had destroyed the original of this magnificent cathedral 300 years before. In 1812 Napoleon stole a revered icon and ancient tapestries. But in one of the few acts of humanity ever performed by Adolf Hitler, he ordered his invading troops to spare the cathedral. He was not as kind to the Russian people. We spent a day seeing this lovely city, touring its old Kremlin and museums, and attended a fair in the city park.

That night we stayed in a children's camp in Smolensk, a delightful wooded place. In the middle of the night I came down with a severe case of diarrhea and I was throwing up. In the morning a Russian doctor prescribed vodka (what else?) because that was all he had. The next morning my bug was miraculously gone. No one else had gotten it, whatever it was. I told Sarlik that I was ready to ride, but I wasn't feeling strong.

DISASTER AND RESCUE

We had gone about 100 kilometers on our eighth day when the spare rear wheel gave out in the town of Vyazma. Sarlik and I sat on the sidewalk to wait for the camper to catch up, feeling sorry for ourselves. We were discussing stashing the bike in the camper and driving into Moscow when a city policeman came by. We explained our situation. After telling us "Good Russian bicycle not break like that," he went off to get the mayor.

It was a Sunday afternoon and we didn't expect the mayor or anyone else to help us, but the mayor arrived in a few minutes. I explained our problem, and told him about the around-the-world journey. He said that he considered *our* problem to be *Vyazma's* problem because we had come to grief in his town. He went off to fetch the head of the Spartak Sports Club. The head of Spartak quickly arrived with Viktor, the coach of Vyazma's bicycle team. We loaded the tandem onto the camper and drove across town to the Spartak bicycle club. Viktor and the club mechanics tried to fix the rims, but they couldn't. No one could have. Wheels that size just were not available in Russia, not even in Moscow, 200 kilometers ahead, two more days of cycling.

While Sarlik, Huey and I were at the bike shop, Olga, Victor's wife took Sylvia to her home for tea and a snack. Everyone was trying to help us, strangers in their town. The head of Spartak and his coach held a conference, and came up with a solution. It would be only two days ride to Moscow. When we finished in Moscow we would have to return home on the same road through Vyazma. They decided that they would lend us two of the club's new racing bikes. We would return them on the way home. I was astonished at their generosity. A racing bicycle was worth a year's wages, and they had no idea who we were. They just trusted us. They never even asked us to sign receipts.

In the morning Sarlik and I left Vyazma on two spanking new racing bikes. Four members of the bicycle club rode along with us for a few miles before turning back. It was easy riding. The bikes were as light as a feather and handled well. The six of us formed a pace line, each drafting off the rider in front. We were thrilled to be moving, and very appreciative of the generosity of the people of Vyazma. Both of us took great care to avoid the many potholes. We were going to take very good care of our fine new borrowed bicycles.

That night we stayed in the town of Mozhaisk, one day's ride from Moscow. The hotel in Mozhaisk made even the hotel in Orsha look good. Sarlik had to argue to get us rooms. When we saw them, they weren't worth the fight. We were on the second floor. The toilet was a filthy communal affair down a long, smelly hall.

At ten thirty that evening there was a commotion in the next room, a couple of drunks fighting. It got louder and more agitated until one of them went crashing through a closed window. His fall was broken by the bushes below, but the local militia took over after gravity was finished with him. Two cops beat the hell out of him and took him away in a wheelbarrow. In retaliation for the damage to the window, the hotel manager went out into the street, shouted a loud announcement to all the guests, and summarily locked the communal toilets for the night: when the hotel gets damaged, everyone gets punished. Communism at work! Fortunately, there was a washbasin in the crummy room.

THE 1812 OVERTURE

In the winter of 1812 Napoleon's army made it this far. At the battlefield in Borodino they met two overwhelming forces. The first was the Czar's army under Field Marshal Kutosov, the brilliant defender of Moscow. The second, even more invincible, was the severe Russian winter.

We toured an outdoor museum at Borodino, with statues of the various commanders, French and Russian, poised for battle as they might have been, prepared for victory or death. Strains of Tchaikovsky's 1812 Overture floated out over the green fields, recalling the cannon and devastation, and the eventual victory of Russia over Napoleon. The carcasses of Napoleon's men were scattered all the way back to France. It is said that the red poppies along the way mark the resting places of the hearts of brave French soldiers.

In the twentieth century another colossal European military monstrosity tried to do what Napoleon had failed to accomplish. The Nazi *Wermacht* marched through Poland meeting no effective resistance. Hitler's tanks and guns ground inexorably along Napoleon's route towards Moscow. Before being halted by the Red Army and the Russian winter, the Nazis had advanced almost 1,000 kilometers inside the borders or the USSR. The Germans eventually had no more success than Napoleon, but with devastating twentieth century firepower they destroyed most of what lay between the Polish border and Moscow. By the end of the war more than 25,000,000 Soviet citizens had lost their lives. In 1944 there was not a building or a person left in Mozhaisk or Vyazma, both in Hitler's path. Mozhaisk, the city of flying drunks, and Vyazma, the home of generous bicyclists, were honored by the USSR as "Hero Cities" after the war.

MOSCOW

Our last day on the bicycles was a gray, miserable Moscow day. The closer we got to Moscow, the heavier traffic became. We were sharing the road with thousands of diesel spewing trucks that form a lifeline to Moscow's 10,000,000 people. Pollution made breathing difficult so we tied handkerchiefs over our noses, but that didn't help much. The greenery that had lined our route for so long was replaced by concrete. Long before we got near the Outer Ring Road drab apartment blocks began to dominate the scene. Traffic was bad, cycling was hazardous, and we were afraid of becoming separated from the camper.

We had made arrangements to meet Gennady at the place where we would cross over the Outer Ring Road, and there he was. "You made it. Thank God." We loaded the bicycles into the camper. Gennady joined us as we drove to a hotel owned by the Soviet Sports Committee. After cleaning up we all went to Sarlik's place for a celebration. His apartment was as interesting as Sarlik himself, with odd souvenirs from his travels in the remote regions of Russia. Among the trophies were body parts of animals killed by The Mongol, including a large bear paw, inverted and holding a human skull. Books lined the walls, mostly in Russian, but also several in eastern scripts I couldn't identify. We relaxed and recounted our adventures to Gennady and Dina, Sarlik's wife. We toasted each other with vodka and champagne, and indulged ourselves with sandwiches of black bread, butter and caviar. Fresh strawberries were an unexpected treat. Then we said goodbye to Sarlik. Our adventure together was over, and we didn't know if we would ever meet again.

We stayed at the Sports Committee Hotel for two days. It was a good place to stay because of its location and the fact that it had a guarded parking lot. The hotel, owned by the government, was actually run by the Russian Mafia, whose power base was getting stronger every day, another long and sad story.

While we were in Moscow we arranged meetings with Dmitrii Shparo, the great Arctic adventurer, and his comrade, Feodor Sklokin. It was time to start making arrangements for the next phase of our journey. We were planning to set out from Moscow in 1993 and go to Irkutsk on Lake Baikal, half way across Siberia. Shparo and Sklokin could be helpful. We also got together with an old friend, Dmitrii Khodko, "The Siberian Giant," when we learned that he was in Moscow on business, visiting from his home in Omsk, Siberia. We would be passing that way the next year.

Gennady joined us for dinner at McDonald's our last night in Moscow. The line was three blocks long, but with 40 cash registers it moved quickly. Gennady was downcast. The situation in the USSR was deteriorating rapidly. Crime was getting worse and The Mafia was becoming bolder by the day. The false economy was in turmoil. Gorbachev, with his far-reaching policies, was not in control. Gennady's biggest fear was that there would be open revolution and great loss of life. If it did come, the government could fall into the hands of hard line Stalinists. Gennady's fears were grave and personal because his son, Sasha, who had ridden with me in North America, had recently been called up for his compulsory two-year hitch in the Russian Army. We parted on a somber note.

RETURNING WEST

Early the next morning we were on the way home. It was 1,000 kilometers to the Polish border, and we hoped to get there that night if we could. We stopped in Vyazma to return the borrowed bicycles, thanking our benefactors. We would not have been able to finish our trip without their generosity and trust. Ten Spartak bicyclists escorted us to the highway.

Huey, Sylvia and I took turns driving. In a few hours we were getting low on fuel, so we pulled into a truck stop. We were out of rubles, so buying fuel might be a problem. A youth of about sixteen approached. "Buy souvenirs? Change money?" For $20 we got 500 rubles. He was so elated with his success that he threw in a Russian flag. Those 500 rubles bought gasoline and food for the three of us, enough to get us out of the USSR.

When we got near the border there was a line of cars almost 15 kilometers long waiting to cross into Poland. People in line told us that it would take two days. Vendors had set up food stands along the queue of cars. Police were assigned to the line to keep the peace. One cop came up to our foreign vehicle. He asked for a cigarette, and I gave him a pack of Marlboros. He said, "The line does not apply to foreigners." If we could give him a pack of Marlboros for his commander he would escort us all the way to the border. We passed thousands of cars on the way, expecting to be lynched for cutting the line.

It was late when we got to the border, and it took us only a few minutes and another pack of Marlboros to get through Russian customs. There was a bridge spanning the river between the Russian station and Polish customs on the other side. Cars, trucks and buses were sitting idle in both directions on the bridge, stopped by the inspectors on both ends. We had only a kilometer to go to reach the Polish side.

A young Polish border guard knocked on the door of the camper. He asked if we were German, and we replied that we were American. "The line is very, very long and slow," he said pointedly, watching for my reaction. I figured he wanted a bribe, and I offered him a pack of Marlboros. "I do not smoke, but maybe you have one American dollar for a souvenir?" What the hell, I thought, it's only a buck. I gave him the dollar and watched him walk back across the span.

What he did next was unbelievable. He signaled for the camper to follow him. Slowly he made his way across the bridge to the Polish side, moving the cars, trucks and buses aside as he went, parting the vehicles for us as Moses parted the Red Sea. Before long we were through customs and in Poland. If I had known what he was going to do, I might have given him a lot more than a dollar. I don't approve of bribery, but it is a way of life in much of the world. Any guilt I might have felt about it, or about getting special privileges because I was a foreign tourist, was easily offset by not having to waste hours sweating it out in line.

Sylvia, Huey and I were exhausted. We had driven from dawn until midnight. It was time to get some sleep. We were in familiar Polish territory. Nearby was the Romanian Gypsy camp. Beyond the Gypsy camp, in Terespol, was our favorite whorehouse. Guess where we stayed again that night.

Meeting the head of the Russian Orthodox church in Minsk

Sarlik and Joe stopping at VW camper. The tandem bicycle is still in working order.

Sarlik and Joe within 150 KM of Moscow. Note the borrowed bicycles.

Joe and Sarlik posing in Red Square with the disabled "Magenta Mama" tandem cycle. Note flat tire.

Sarlik the Mongol at home in Moscow with Sylvia and Joe

Gennady Schvets and Joe in front of St. Basil's in Red Square during a previous visit to Moscow.

CHAPTER X

EXOTIC CENTRAL ASIA

Every bush of roses, a feast for the eyes
Grows from the ashes of beauties.
Each blade of grass which we trod on
Grows from hearts filled with emotion only yesterday.
　　– Omar Khayyam

After spending the winter of 1992-1993 at home in California, it was time to get moving again. Thus far logistics, such as food and housing, had been easy enough to find, even in East Germany, Poland, Belarus, and western Russia. But there were sure to be difficulties once we got east of the Urals, into Asia. What situations might we run into where there were no telephones, nothing that we could recognize as a hotel or a food store? What about a medical emergency? The indigenous peoples of Soviet Asia spoke little Russian and no English. With the recent breakup of the Soviet Union the 15 former Soviet Republics were now floundering infant nations, some with rampant crime. I thought about what it would be like riding a bicycle through an area where my bicycle was worth two years' salary. I would have to have the company of someone who knew what he was doing.

A MAJOR DECISION

I called a friend, Feodor Sklokin, in Moscow to ask his opinion. He was a fine athlete, knowledgeable about how to get things done in Russia. He had been on Dmitri Shparo's polar ski expedition from Russia to Canada. He was also one of Russia's top young physicists.

Feodor told me that he was happy to help me, hinting that he might even be willing to join the team. His employer, The Institute of Metallurgical Physics, had been dissolved. One of the tragedies of *perestroika* was the dismantling of great scientific institutes and the loss of the thousands of talented scientists, including Feodor Sklokin.

"You have a decision to make, Joseph, regarding your bicycle route. Would you prefer to go straight east across the steppes of Russia, or would you rather travel south and east by way of Central Asia?" He said that the steppes would be shorter, less mountainous, and the wind would generally be at our backs. We would be in Russia all the way, with familiar Russian food, customs and language—compelling arguments for that route.

"But please understand that this northerly route will be boring. The endless steppes of Russia resemble an interminable Kansas, flat and unchanging fields of grain. Of course for a Russian this is very beautiful, but it will be the same for thousands of kilometers. The southerly route, on the other hand, is exotic."

The juxtaposition of the words "boring" and "exotic" got my attention. Feodor spoke of the five Muslim republics in Central Asia: Tajikistan, Turkmenia, Kirghizia, Uzbekistan and Kazakhstan. To get there we would cycle past the horribly shriveled Aral Sea. Our route, partly along the Silk Road, would not be far from Iran, Afghanistan and China. The people of Central Asia are like no others, he said. They were descendents of Genghis Khan and Tamerlane. There were ancient Islamic cities: Djamboul, Bukhara, Samarkand, Alma Ata and Tashkent. We would cross mountains and deserts. It would be longer and harder, full of adventures that we could not even begin to imagine.

Boring versus exotic? It was a no-brainer. Our route would be through Central Asia.

Feodor would make the arrangements from his home in Moscow. He would find someone who knew local customs and languages. We would need a vehicle to carry our gear and to give us a place to sleep if necessary. We would have to carry a lot of water, food and fuel in remote desert areas.

I called my Canadian friend "Arctic Joe" Womersley. Joe was tough and resourceful. He had grown up on a farm in southern England. As a 15-year-old he talked his way into the fabled Black Watch in WWII, was at the D-Day invasion, and served as a sniper with a sharp eye for bad guys. Arctic Joe agreed to join our team.

ABOUT CENTRAL ASIA

By mid-19th century Britain had pushed through the Middle East, colonizing Afghanistan and India, knocking on the Czar's southern door. To "protect the local people from British colonialism," Russia annexed much of Central Asia (Uzbekistan, Kazakhstan, Turkmenia, Tajikistan and Kirghizia). After the 1918 revolution, these five Central Asian Republics were merged into the Soviet Union. The USSR clamped shut the doors to the outside world in the 1920s, suppressing culture and religion and limiting their contact with the rest of the Islamic world. All but 400 of the 26,000 mosques in Central Asia were closed. Printing the Koran became a criminal offense.

Central Asia is mountainous. The forces that produced the Himalayas also pushed up these more westerly mountains. Imagine the Himalayas extended west in five fingers. The Altai Mountains form the finger from China into eastern Kazakhstan. To the south, the Tian Shan Mountains run into Kirghizia toward Uzbekistan. Further south, the Pamirs go from China into Tajikistan and Uzbekistan. The southernmost finger is the Hindu Kush. Through these mountains were traced the various Silk Roads. In between lie fertile valleys and foothills fought over by pastoral peoples for centuries.

In many ways this is the center of the world. Not very far to the southwest is the Arab world and North Africa. To the south are India, Afghanistan and Pakistan. China and Mongolia are to the east. In the north is

Russia, with access to Slavic and European cultures. No other place on earth is situated so near to such varied and ancient civilizations.

The most culturally rich nation in Central Asia is Uzbekistan, the size of California, with a population of over 20,000,000. Mountain and desert, it is the heart of Central Asia. From Mongolia, Genghis Khan thrust his kingdom westward through Uzbekistan, via Tashkent, Samarkand and Bukhara, as far as the Danube. Trade along the Silk Road brought a transfer of cultures, science and knowledge. 1,000 years ago, while Europe was in the Dark Ages, the library at Bukhara was renowned for its vast collections.

The Silk Road brought spices and oriental goods through the Arab world to Europe. The discovery of America may be laid at the hands of avaricious potentates along the route who extracted tribute here and there, inflating the price of goods en route to Europe. Spices were vital to Europe for the preservation of meat from the annual autumn slaughter. To gain control of the spice trade and bypass Arab middlemen, Europeans sought a route to the east. That led Queen Isabella to tell Signore Columbus, "Go west, young man!" And here we are in America today.

THE ARAL SEA

There is an old Russian curse that goes, *"May you live in interesting times."* As Arctic Joe and I rode our bicycles from Moscow south and east to Central Asia we had no problems. The interesting times would lay ahead of us.

Our bike route took us past the Aral Sea. For millennia the Syr Darya and the Amu Darya rivers ran northwest from the mountains into the low desert where they formed the fourth largest inland body of water in the world, the Aral Sea. A large harvest of fish from the Aral Sea not only fed the people of Central Asia but was also dried in the hot desert sun for shipment north to Russia.

In the 1920s, when Lenin was creating his workers' paradise in Russia, a young American, a professor of agriculture at Tuskegee Institute, had the temerity to wed a white woman. They were beaten, and escaped to New York where they hoped for a better life. But New York was not yet ready for mixed-race marriages, and there was no work for an agriculture professor in New York. Like many intellectuals in the 1920s, they were watching what was taking place in the infant Soviet Union, where all would be treated equally, "from each according to his ability, to each according to his need." They decided to move to The Worker's Paradise.

The agriculture professor was given the immense project of making the deserts of Central Asia bloom, creating a needed cotton industry from scratch. Water was drawn from the Syr Darya and the Amu Darya rivers to irrigate the desert soil. Canals were dug and cottonseed was imported. Cotton bloomed in the desert as it had in the California desert and cotton quickly became a strong part of the Soviet economy. The American professor died young, possibly from injuries suffered in Alabama, and he never got to see the final results of his project.

For millennia there existed a natural balance between waters flowing into the Aral Sea from the Syr Darya and the Amu Darya and evaporation by the hot desert sun. But as increasingly larger quantities of water were withdrawn to irrigate cotton, the level of the Aral Sea fell. Once the process started, it accelerated. Evaporating water was not replaced, salinity increased and the Aral Sea shrank. Today it covers an area of one third and a volume of a tenth of what it was in 1960. The fish died. The fishing industry that fed millions is gone. Rotting hulks of ships sit on a dry seabed, miles from the shore.

Millions of tons of fine powdery soil and salt from 12,000 square miles of exposed sea bottom have become a wind-borne health hazard for hundreds of miles around, with rampant tuberculosis, viral hepatitis and throat cancer. According to the health minister of Uzbekistan, most of the children are weak, vulnerable to infections, and suffer from rickets and anemia. What fresh water remains is contaminated with salt, fertilizers, pesticides and petroleum residues. There is no thought of ever letting the rivers flow free again: that would disrupt King Cotton. And now oil companies are drilling on the exposed seabed.

It is ironic that the Soviet Union doesn't even exist any more. As we cycled along what used to be a seaside highway we couldn't see the pitifully diminished Aral Sea, even with binoculars, and there was no road to take us closer. We were glad to move on; the dust-filled atmosphere was stifling. It was as gloomy as any place on earth.

ALONG THE SILK ROAD: BUKHARA THE BLESSED

A picture comes to mind. Arctic Joe and I are sitting in the shade of a tree, enjoying a 95° F day by a large, ancient stone reflecting pool. A boy is swinging on a rope from the upper branches of a mulberry tree at the edge of the pool. When he swings out far enough he will drop into the refreshing water. The pool, 50 meters square, is in front of the Nadir-Divan mosque, dating back to the 16th century. Our bicycle trip from Moscow had been tedious, and today we are taking a day off to see beautiful Bukhara.

Excavations at Bukhara have turned up evidence of an oasis town 2,500 years ago, in the Persian Empire under Cyrus, Xerxes and Darius. Alexander the Great paused here after conquering Samarkand in 330 B.C. Omar Khayyam was resident in the royal court of Bukhara. Called "Bukhara the Noble," "Bukhara the Blessed" and "Bukhara the Learned," it was an ancient center of learning, a mingling place for Christians, Jews, Muslims, Buddhists and Zoroastrians, at the junction of two major trade routes between Asia and the West. Influences from Asia, the Middle East and Europe melded to produce a flourishing of the arts and sciences.

The strongest influence came in the seventh century, when Umayyad Arabs brought to Bukhara the religion of Islam. In a great battle between Chinese forces and Arabs, the future was determined when the Chinese were repelled. Bukhara converted to Islam and has remained so, even during the dark years of the USSR. Bukhara is one of the holiest cities of the Islamic world. Soviet Muslims, prohibited from going to Mecca, instead made pilgrimages to Bukhara.

We bought pomegranates and struggled with the seeds. A dove cooed and the air smelled of spices. The hot sun was tempered by a gentle breeze off the desert. We watched the boy perform his high dive act a few more times, then joined a local guide to see Bukhara's mosques, palaces, *medrassahs* (religious schools) and historic sites. The clay-adobe-straw-plaster homes shine in the brilliant desert sun. We visited the Jewish quarter, their home since the 14th century. Jews had thrived in Bukhara for centuries, but after the breakup of the USSR an influx of Islamic zealots came from Iran, making life difficult for all infidels. Few Jews remain, and the ancient Jewish quarter is no more.

The next morning we were on our bicycles, headed east into the desert. It was spring, beginning to get hot. Summers are extreme here. The road was good and not very hilly, but there were no shoulders, so we had to cycle on the main roadbed. Traffic was light, with few automobiles and an occasional big truck barreling along. Arctic Joe's stomach was bothering him, so we had to make frequent bush stops. I gave him my small cache of Imodium. It seemed to do the trick, but he was struggling. He wouldn't consider hitching a ride in the bus.

KAHK-RAHMON'S PRIDE AND JOY

I didn't tell you about the bus, did I? In addition to Arctic Joe, Feodor Sklokin and me, we had a 12-passenger bus formerly owned by Aeroflot, and an Uzbek driver named Kahk-Rahmon, who spoke no English. Between his limited Russian and mine, we were able to communicate most of the time. Arctic Joe had difficulty with the name Kahk-Rahmon, so he anglicized it to "Cocker-man," or "The Cocker." Kahk-Rahmon was fiftyish, formal, and quiet and wore the same rumpled brown suit jacket all the time. He was chubby and bald with smiling eyes. His bus was his love. He was forever tinkering with it and could usually be found leaning over the motor, head down and butt up.

To accommodate our bicycles, our gear and our selves he had removed the seats. Because we would go through vast areas where fuel was not available, he installed a big spare fuel tank down the center aisle, piped directly to the main fuel tank. Cocker-man was *not* going to run out of fuel in the desert.

Our routine was straightforward. The bus would hopscotch us, with Joe and me riding our bicycles. Sometimes Feodor rode his bike with us, but for the most part he was content to stay in the bus. We would meet up for lunch, for afternoon tea, and again when it came time to set up camp in the late afternoon. Our daily goal was 100 km.

The second day out of Bukhara started with fine weather as we entered hill country. A sudden downpour forced us to retreat to the bus until it cleared up. The road climbed and fell steeply with blind curves and little room for a passing truck. Our camp that night was pretty typical, in the trees just off the main road. We had stocked up on local produce and fresh meat at a farmers' market in Bukhara. Dinner was pears, apples, Uzbek *lepyoshka* bread and *so-oos,* a stew of fried beef and vegetables. It was hearty fare, but Arctic Joe was still having stomach problems, and his appetite was poor. As hot as it had been in the sun during the day, it was freezing in our tents at night. In the morning we set off for the small mountain city of Shakrisabs.

In the 13th century Genghis Khan ruled an empire that stretched from Hungary to the Pacific, from Burma to Siberia. But his descendants became lax, and rivalries left the empire vulnerable to the forays of local tribes. Amid the chaos in the 14th century rose the greatest Mongol leader of all, Timur (Tamerlane), who rallied the competing factions under his banner and re-established the Mongol empire in history. Timur was born in the village of Shakrisabs.

UZBEK HOSPITALITY

All over Shakrisabs are beautifully carved wooden doors. We asked about this superb craftsmanship and were taken to the shop of a master door carver. He was thrilled to meet his first westerners, overjoyed that we showed interest in his work. His Tadjik family had been door carvers here for 17 generations. He invited us to his home for tea.

In a large upstairs room we sat cross-legged on pillows around a low, square table. The walls were covered in oriental carpeting. Bare light bulbs hung on wires from the ceiling. We had the honor of meeting our host's 74-year-old father, the village patriarch, and the brothers of our host, all dressed in traditional turbans and vertically striped robes. The young men of the family were all away, at war in Afghanistan. Our meeting was friendly and formal, with Kakh-Rahmon as interlocutor.

In the morning we visited a gigantic victory arch erected by Timur. It predated the French look-alike Arc de Triomphe by four centuries. It loomed above us, covered with blue glazed tile, untended and deteriorating, like so much of the USSR. Then we were off toward Samarkand, two days ahead of us, downhill most of the way.

After 100 km we stopped in the late afternoon at a remote village. Arctic Joe and I introduced ourselves to the headman as North American travelers, and formally requested permission to pitch our tents in his village, where we would be safe. The swarthy, solidly built man had a mean-looking scar running down one cheek. He squinted one eye, looked us over for a long minute and finally said in halting Russian, "Absolutely not!" After a slight hesitation he went on, "Tonight you must honor me by staying in my home." He then clapped his hands loudly and vigorously six times. Women came running from all sides as he shouted orders in Uzbek. A girl with a lamb cradled in her left arm approached me, offering the lamb for my inspection. I scratched the lamb's head and smiled. From under her skirts she produced a dagger and slit the throat of our dinner as I tried to hide my shock. Women were scurrying in every direction. There was a feast to prepare.

These people were living off the land, as they always had. Almost everything in this village was made there. Lumber and stone for building came from nearby forests and quarries. They made their own clothing, from shoes to hats. Nothing was purchased except a small electric generator for a few dim light bulbs and a scratchy radio. The men spent their days and nights in the hills with the flocks, keeping them together and protecting them from wolves. Women, children and older men stayed in the village, working at the many chores necessary to keep village life going. Life was hard and basic.

At dinner women scurried in and out with heaping dishes of food, saying nothing. It was a wonderful meal, starting with trays of walnuts, almonds, raisins, baked apricot seeds and several unfamiliar delicacies. A bowl of fresh yogurt was served, then spicy lamb soup. They had heard only Soviet propaganda about the west and they wanted to know what life was really like. Over skewers of succulent *shashlik* served with freshly baked *lepyoshka* bread, we answered their questions honestly and completely. Were people really starving in the streets in America? Did politicians really accept bribes from large corporations as "campaign contributions"? What did the politicians give to corporations in return for those millions of dollars? Throughout the meal fresh carrots, greens, onions and cucumbers were at our fingertips. A traditional rice pilaf was served, then green tea and an assortment of candied fruits and sweets, including halvah. It was a feast fit for visiting royalty, and we were at the table for three and a half hours.

Our host, Nail (Na-eel), was gracious and voluble. This was a Muslim village, so we were a surprised when he produced a bottle of strong home brew for us. When it was finished, another appeared in its place. I asked Nail how old he was. He was born in 1934, my birth year, but he didn't know the month, only "When the grass was turning brown," late summer or early fall. I was born on September 7, 1934. Perhaps, I said, we were both born on the very same day on opposite sides of the world, fated to meet here on this day.

The question of religion came up. Throughout Nail's life the USSR had suppressed his Islamic faith. Now, after three quarters of a century, people were again free to practice their religion, but teachers were scarce. He himself had never been religious, but had a strong sense of Islamic identity. I asked him this question: "If one of your daughters wanted to marry a good Muslim, possibly from another country, willing to pay a high bride price for her, would you give your permission?" His answer was unhesitating and direct. "No, no, no. My daughters will only marry an Uzbek, maybe a Tajik, selected by me, from no more than 100 km from this village. No, that will never change." Here, women eat with women and men eat with men. Men have their work and so do women, and they are very different. A woman may speak only to her father, her brother, her husband or her son, no other man, not in private nor in public. It is their tradition.

Arctic Joe was not well. He tried bravely to regale our host with stories of his exploits, but he was weak and dehydrated, and his situation was getting serious. He had little appetite for dinner. His cautious nibbling caught the eye of our host, who was offended that Joe was not enthusiastically enjoying the feast. Kahk-Rahmon explained Joe's problem. Nail shouted to the women, who produced a bowl of plain, boiled rice. "That," he said, "will plug him up tight. That and the home brew will cure him."

We four sated travelers slept on mats and pillows in Nail's home that night. It rained hard during the night, making it a hazardous, slippery trip in the dark to the trench latrine, 20 yards from the house. Joe made the commute several times before a rooster told us to get up. Joe needed a real cure, and he needed it fast. We were out of Imodium, with no hope of finding more in Uzbekistan, where even aspirin was a rarity. Skinny Joe was losing weight fast, but he insisted on riding. We might have to abort the trip to get him medical attention, and that would not be in Uzbekistan.

SAMARKAND

The next morning we rode towards Samarkand wearing rain slickers in a downpour. We made good time on the downhill trip, but Joe was in bad shape when we reached a hotel where he could rest. He collapsed onto his bed. Fate stepped in, in the person of a doctor with an Italian bicycle racing team, on their way home to Bologna. After examining Joe he gave him the team's remaining supply of Imodium and told him, "Plain boiled rice, si. Milk products, no. Complete rest for one day." We offered to compensate him. "No, no, my friends. I am happy to serve you." The good doctor's medicine worked and Joe remained healthy for the rest of the trip. *Molto grazie, dottore*, wherever you are.

We were still cycling along Alexander the Great's 4th century B.C. route. A focal point of Silk Road trade for 2,500 years, Samarkand stands at the juncture of desert and mountains. Registan Square, the fabled market place, is the heart of the city. A huge and breathtaking blue-tiled mosque and the 17th century Ulug Beg Medrassah dominate the wide square. Entering through a majestic arch facing the square, we saw ancient manuscripts and beautiful miniature book art in this living museum, and visited the tomb of Timur.

Before leaving Samarkand we ate at the Russian Travelers Club. Russians, no longer the ruling class after the breakup of the USSR, were worried about being expelled, along with others who had been "resettled" in Uzbekistan. New nationalism and old resentments were seething.

IN THE TENT OF JABBOR SATOR

As we continued cycling eastward through Central Asia, there was always a range of mountains to the south, bordering with China, some over 14,000 feet. Their north faces, towards us, were snow covered. And there were more mountains to our north. Between these two mountain ranges we rode through lush, grassy valleys. Boys and older men rode through the villages on small donkeys, a stick held upright in the right hand to show authority. Flocks of sheep often joined us on the road. The feeling was one of not really being there, but of watching a movie about times long gone in some exotic place.

Ahead of us was a long stretch of desert, and there were a few camels on the road. Could we ride camels along this part of our route? We heard of a camel herder living on an oasis to the north. Maybe we could arrange a Hertz-Rent-a-Camel deal. Into the desert we flew in the bus, hopes high, visualizing ourselves as Lawrence of Uzbekistan, looking for a camel herder.

Jabbor Sator lived in Nur Ata, the "Shadow of the Father," a holy oasis in the desert. In the middle of the tiny village was a spring-fed pond. It is said that the biblical patriarch Jacob had passed through Nur Ata during a severe drought. In his compassion he struck the ground with his staff and water gushed forth, creating a spring that still flows centuries later.

We entered Jabbor Sator's tent. Jabbor was a large, oily man, wrapped in layers of robes in the heat of the day. He was reclining on a pile of pillows, smoking a hookah, like Star War's Jabba the Hutt. He rose slightly with a big, yellow and brown gap-toothed smile of welcome. Instead of asking for a driver's license and two credit cards he invited us to sit with him and drink sweet green Uzbek tea. We made conversation as Arctic Joe admired Jabbor's wall coverings, elaborate camel's hair blankets that Jabbor's wife had painstakingly made by hand. We were offered *shashlik*, sweets and lemon water, no feast, just a bit of hospitality. No, the blankets were not for sale, said Jabbor, there was too much personal labor in them, from combing of the camels to spinning and weaving the wool. A shrewd and observant businessman, he watched Joe's eyes return again and again to the blankets.

Our talk turned to camels. He said that he did have camels, mostly females, and right now they were pregnant. He was building his herd because he thought that rich tourists would come to ride his fine camels now that the area was opening to foreigners. He could possibly break out four of them for us, he said, one each for Joe and me, one for a guide and a sparc, saddles included. His price would be very high, he said, watching our eyes. I wanted to ask him if it included unlimited mileage.

We asked Jabbor if he would be kind enough to let us see the animals. After some hesitation he summoned a camel boy who took us to the beasts. They were ugly, smelly, dirty and sick looking, perhaps the most miserable looking camels on earth. Joe and I agreed that this was *not* how we wanted to spend the next several days. Jabbor was visibly upset that we had not fallen in love with his beautiful animals. Had he not shown us his hospitality? Mushy-hearted Joe was still eying the blankets. He offered Jabbor a price that would feed the scrawny herd for six months. Jabbor demurred, but gave in when Joe raised the ante. Joe got his blanket, and the camels got a reprieve.

KIM'S KOWBOYS

Wherever we went someone wanted to entertain us with a *programma*, a visit to this or that, the opera, the ballet, a statue of Lenin, an ancient dig or a museum. People were proud to share something of their heritage that had been hidden for three-quarters of a century.

A *programma* could be a nice treat after day's work on the bicycle. It put us in contact with people we would not have met. But sometimes, though, it wasn't easy, after a hard day, to get enthusiastic about a *programma*. Like the day we rode into Dzhizak a few days after leaving Samarkand. It was a chilly day and I had not dressed warmly enough. My knees were frozen and I was glad to be done. I just wanted to fill my belly and get warm, when Feodor announced with a big grin, "We have wonderful *programma* tonight. It is surprise." A *programma!* Oh, great!

We cleaned and stowed the bicycles in the bus, and headed down a rutted track into the mountains. We stopped at a group of a half dozen shacks and a lot of horses. It looked like a wild-west town. "Okay, Feodor, where are we?" He said that we were at a horse station, a place where horses are bred and trained for government geologists who explore the mountains. "And here is your surprise. Tonight for your *programma* you will ride horses." Chilled to the bone on the bike all day and saddle sore, and now he wanted us to ride horses! Mother Nature mercifully intervened for us. The sky opened up and the rain poured down. Thank you, God!

Inside the biggest of the shacks we met the ranch manager. Alexander Kim was a slim, wiry Korean, about 40, born in Uzbekistan. His parents were from the ethnically Korean area of Russia near Vladivostok on the Sea of Japan, close to North Korea. In the 1930s, Stalin got it into his head that these Koreans, who were native-born citizens of Russia, might somehow harbor sympathies for their traditional Japanese enemies. He forcibly relocated 500,000 Koreans,

Russian citizens, to Central Asia, Kim's parents among them. The Korean minority flourished in Uzbekistan, but after the break-up of the USSR, they were worried about their citizenship status. Would they have to leave? Where could they go? Some might be accepted as refugees in Korea, America or Australia. But Kim spoke no Korean, and his wife was Russian. Stalin's paranoia had sent Kim's people to Central Asia more than 50 years ago, and now it looked as though racism might drive them out.

We sat down to dinner with six grizzled horse wranglers. They prepared lamb stew for us, with fresh vegetables and hot bread. Over tea they questioned us about our journey. Not for the first time, we found that we had seen more of the USSR than any of these citizens. I asked if any of these cowpokes knew a game of the Caucasus, a game called *dzhigit*. The cowboys smiled. They told us that they had a champion *dzhigitoch* among them.

In the simplest form of the game, a handkerchief is placed on the ground, tufted up about three inches. Two horsemen gallop toward each other from opposite ends of a field to snatch up the handkerchief. It has to be picked up in the teeth, no hands. In another version, two teams of horsemen face off with the same handkerchief in mind. Offensive and defensive strategies make ice hockey look like a schoolgirl's game. The sport of *dzhigit* makes for some very interesting interactions among the ground, hooves and faces. As I looked around the room, one wide-grinned, toothless, scarred face seemed to have *dzhigit* stomped all over it.

The people of Central Asia, like the neighboring Mongolians, are born to ride. Their short, stocky Mongolian horses are bred for riding, work and for meat, milk and hides. An interesting equine product is a potent brew called *kumiss*, fermented mare's milk. We sampled Kim's moonshine variety. It had the kick of a horse.

THE SCENE OF THE CRIME: SYR DARYA

Our next major goal was the Syr Darya River (pronounced Sear Dar-YAW), one of the two rivers that fed into the Aral Sea. We camped on the river near the main highway. The Syr Darya was big, wide and slow, with marshland on both sides. It was the May Day holiday weekend, fishermen were drowning worms, and hordes of biting insects were feasting on fishermen. It was a pleasant evening and a nice place. It was hard to imagine this peaceful river sucked up by huge pumps a few miles away, to be dumped onto the thirsty roots of millions of cotton plants, even as the Aral Sea died of thirst.

We dined on leftovers from the horse ranch: cold, unrefrigerated lamb stew, left sitting in the hot bus for 24 hours, with apples. Breakfast was the same thing. There was a market, but it was closed for the May Day weekend. We shared my emergency supplies: a jar of peanut butter, a package of granola and a can of sardines, which disappeared in minutes.

CHAMPAGNE TASTES

Finding potable drinking water was a big problem. Joe had already been gut-sick, and we were taking no chances. When we were not sure of the local water supply we always purified it with iodine. It tasted lousy, and we wondered what effect weeks of iodine intake might have on us. Then we made a wonderful discovery. They bottle good champagne in Uzbekistan, and we could buy bubbly by the case for the equivalent of *85 U.S. cents a bottle*. We exchanged U.S. dollars for several cases of champagne and stashed it on top of the fuel tank. Champagne became an integral part of our diet. We planned to leave none of it when we headed home. Have you tried champagne and corn flakes?

We were on the main road between Samarkand and Tashkent, the two biggest cities in Uzbekistan. The foul-smelling exhaust from the cars, trucks and buses was choking us. Air pollution was never a consideration in the USSR. The morning we left the Syr Darya we were blessed with a strong tail wind, and we ran 30 km in an hour. We stopped for a short roadside tea break in mid morning and all hell broke loose. The temperature dropped ten degrees, the wind did an about face and the sky hit us with a hailstorm and cold rain for the next two hours. A group of snotty teenagers thought it would be fun to pelt us with stones from an overpass as we went by. Thankfully none of them were major league pitching prospects.

Kahk-Rahmon had a habit of pulling a pop bottle out from under the dashboard every half hour or so. It was plugged with a wad of paper and filled with a dark, peppery-looking powder. He would pour a dollop of it into his hand and toss it under his tongue, making a sour face. After a while he would open the window and cut loose a mighty wad. You didn't want to be riding behind the bus when that happened. He told us that it was *tabac* mixed with secret ingredients. Arctic Joe, forever teasing our driver, took to calling him "Narco-Mon." Kahk-Rahmon responded by calling Joe a *hoo-lee-gan*.

At first Kahk-Rahmon was stiff and formal. He seemed humorless and didn't seem to like the idea of playing chauffeur to rich foreigners. He warmed up, though, in spite of Joe constantly playing little pranks on him, like Joe's "Pull my finger" routine. Kahk-Rahmon was offended when Joe let out his first blast. Weeks later, when he was comfortable with us, he would grin, finger extended, and say, "Poo-ma finga." The only time he really got mad was when Joe peed on the wheel of his bus. It didn't happen twice.

The license plate on the bus indicated that it was from Samarkand, making us marks for local cops. As in Russia, the *miltsia* in Central Asia set up their private tollbooths, and the bus couldn't leave until our driver paid his *baksheesh*. Kahk-Rahmon hated it, but he had no choice.

Bukhara, Shakrisabs, Samarkand, Dzhizak. We were now in Tashkent, the capitol of Uzbekistan. By some ancient stunt of gerrymandering, Ubekistan's capitol is located in the country's extreme northeast corner on a long, skinny finger of land that should belong to Kazakhstan. In Tashkent there were many Russians and Ukrainians. We saw Kazaks for the first time, and some Kirghiz.

Central Asian ethnic groups each have a distinctive appearance. Over the centuries the rugged mountains had kept the tribes separated. Language differences formed barriers. Some, like the Kirghiz, were clearly Asian, living just across from China. Western Kazaks appeared to be Siberian, while those in the east looked Mongolian. The Tadjiks and Uzbeks had Arabic features. But it wasn't that simple. Faces blended in a continuum, morphing from Arabic in the west, Slavic in the north to Mongolian in the east. You could flip through a stack of photographs of faces and see them change from one ethnicity to another. One way you could tell who was who was by their hats, variously called *kalpak, tyubiteka* or *shlyapka*. A geometric beanie with a fancy Arabic inscription marked an Uzbek. A Kirghiz wore a smallish, conical coolie hat, and so on, like the clothing and colors that differentiate L.A. street gangs.

Tashkent, with a population of over 2,000,000, is the biggest city in Uzbekistan. We had budgeted a day to be tourists. There was an opera house, a circus, an operetta theater and a ballet company. But it was still the long May Day holiday and everything was closed: no *programma* for the tired cyclists!

Joe and I enjoyed a good dinner, a hot bath, a massage and a night in a hotel. Noah's Ark might be a better description. At three a.m. I awoke to a dripping sound. Water from an overflowing bathtub on the floor above was seeping through the ceiling. Hotel management was gone for the night. I moved my bed across the room and went back to sleep, but while I was awake, I got to witness a football game, not in the stadium across the street, but in my own room. Two teams of large, very agile roaches played a complicated running game, scurrying away at sprint speed when the light came on. To keep them under cover I left the light on and wrapped a bandana around my eyes.

We had our *programma* in the morning. Feodor took us to the Chimgan ski resort. It was a gorgeous place, reminiscent of the Alps. Young grass and wild tulips pushed through the melting snow. Nature's beauty contrasted starkly with the unfinished ski resort, skeletal concrete structures left half done, erection cranes abandoned in place. There was no money to complete the project, typical of Soviet inefficiency.

MAX AND CONSTANTINE

At the ski resort we welcomed two volunteers to our traveling circus, Constantine, who would cook for us, and Maxim, who became our official guide. They were from the Sputnik Sports and Travel Club in Tashkent, along for an adventure. Constantine was a 34-year-old Russian, born in Tashkent. He was a strong and handsome man with a ready smile. We hoped that he could cook.

Maxim was an ethnic German whose pacifist ancestors had emigrated centuries ago to avoid serving in the German military. Catherine the Great welcomed them and gave them farmland in the Volga region, where they prospered. In the 1930s, when paranoid Stalin relocated Russia's Koreans, he also moved the Volga Germans to Central Asia, confiscated their farms and plunked them in the desert "where they could not spy for Germany" (Max's people were related to the people we had met in Rugby, North Dakota.) Like the Koreans, the Germans were still in Central Asia many years later, very worried about their status. And as a legacy of the Great Patriotic War, Germans were still despised throughout the former USSR.

Max was a plumber by trade and a skilled carver of wooden miniatures. With straight blond hair and blue eyes his Aryan heritage was

158

obvious. Max wore thick eyeglasses and was intense and introspective. Constantine spoke English with difficulty. Max spoke English with Prussian precision. "I lear-ned eet from a booook."

Constantine set out a picnic table for us in the magnificent mountain setting, *shashlik*, bread, tea and succulent tomatoes, washed down with the Uzbek champagne to toast our new companions. Constantine was a good cook. The next day we planned to reach the border, leave Uzbekistan, and pass through a corner of Kazakhstan to enter Kirghizia.

ENTERING AND LEAVING KAZAKHSTAN

There was a long line at the border. Kazak border guards were being meticulous. Until recently Kazakhstan and Uzbekistan were republics of the USSR; the border then was like that between New York and New Jersey: you just crossed, no fuss. Now no one could cross the border without a full inspection, and all papers had to be in order. Joe and I had *single-entry* (take note!) visas to get into Kazakhstan. Our papers were in order.

The border guards made a thorough search of the bus. They asked Kahk-Rahmon a lot of questions, never finding his bottle of snorting stuff, routinely stamped our visas and sent us on our way. *Oh, no!* The border guard had just stamped our *single entry* Kazakhstan visas. We didn't want that. We were only crossing this corner of Kazakhstan to get into Kirghizia, and we would have to get back into Kazakhstan again after we were done in Kirghizia. Too late; the visas were stamped. We would have to deal with the problem of getting back into Kazakhstan later.

That night we camped in a broad Kazak meadow near what must be the busiest railroad in the world. A long freight train clattered by every few minutes, all with squealing wheels. But we were tired and we slept. It was just cool enough in the tent to be comfortable. The air smelled fresh and clean. In the morning we woke to the sound of bleating sheep close to our camp. Nomadic Kazak herdsmen were on the move. The flock passing us numbered about 500, headed into the mountains for summer grazing.

The traditional Kazak home is a hemispheric felt tent called a *yurt*. When it is time to move the flock, they just roll up the house and take it with them. We passed several *yurta* on the way to the Kirghiz border. I asked Feodor what a *yurt* was like inside. He said that Kazaks were very friendly folks. If I wanted to see the inside, we should knock on a door and introduce ourselves. It sounded pushy, but Feodor assured me that it was quite normal. We went to the framed wooden door of a nearby *yurt* with heavy, grayish-brown felt walls, and no exterior decoration. It smelled of sheep.

We knocked. A middle-aged woman in a floral pattern robe and a turban-like head covering came to the door. Her bright, dark eyes and jet-black hair were Asian, but her features were slightly Slavic. Her name was Baira and she was pleased to have visitors. When we were introduced as American and Canadian travelers, she was over-joyed. In school she had heard of America and Canada, but she had never dreamed of meeting someone from there, especially here in her own home. She immediately invited us in.

The one room *yurt* was about 35 feet in diameter with a domed high ceiling. The large pieces of felt that made up the walls were stretched over thin, supple wooden poles joined at the apex. An area was curtained off with a hanging carpet to create a sleeping area. Across the room was a coal stove covered with steaming pots and kettles. The dirt floor was covered with oriental carpeting. There was no shortage of furnishings, and everything was built for portability. It was colorful, well lit, warm and cozy. It didn't feel like a tent. Two young women, our hostess's daughter and her daughter-in-law, were preparing road meals for the upcoming move. The men were days ahead, moving the flock to the high summering ground. When everything was ready at the *yurt* the women would break down the house and haul it by horseback to join the men.

Baira invited us to sit and have a snack. Feodor, Joe and I sat cross-legged on the carpeted floor. Our hostess hurried across the room and returned with a teapot from which she poured hot, sugary tea. One of the younger women brought us warm bread slices, slathered with freshly churned butter. The atmosphere was relaxed and friendly. We talked for a while, and answered questions about home and family. It is amazing that these women were unafraid to entertain us, strangers, in their home, sharing food with us.

Baira's daughter offered each of us sweet-looking, white balls the size of walnuts. They were made of flour and yogurt, and we had watched her rolling them in the palms of her hands. This was a favorite Kazak food when on the move. I expected something sweet, but when I popped one into my mouth it was the sourest thing I have ever tasted. I forced it down with buttery bread and hot tea. It was time to go. I smiled, thanked these gracious and generous ladies and told them that we had to be on our way to Kirghizia.

Artic Joe Womersley and I were a sight to behold cycling across Central Asia.

A Tadjik and an Uzbek in Bukhara

Kids will be kids everywhere. This young man is leaping into the sacred pool in Bukhara.

The Registan, or town square, Samarkand, Uzbekistan. The Madrassa here was a school for religious education. More recently Madrassas have become terrorist training grounds.

The preferred mode of rural transport is the donkey.

Kahk-Rahmon doing his thing—the daily carburetor adjustment.

Tadjik feast: host, Arctic Joe, Joe Oakes

Headman of Uzbek village: tourist, headman, Feodor Sklokin, Joe Oakes

Dining in the home of the village headman: headman Nail, Cocker-man, Joe Oakes, Artic Joe, Feodor Sklokin.

Jabbor Sator had the sorriest-looking camels in the world.

Mr. Kim—the Korean horse wrangler in Uzbekistan. Stalin forcibly relocated three million ethnic Koreans to Central Asia.

Market scene—Uzbekistan. Not very appetizing—on the road near the Amu Darya.

CHAPTER XI

CENTRAL ASIA, PART TWO: KIRGHIZIA TO IRKUTSK

". . . the bear went over the mountain, to see what he could see. And all that he could see was . . . another mountain, and another mountain, and another mountain . . ."

KIRGHIZIA AND LAKE ISSYK-KUL

The lackadaisical border guards at the Republic of Kirghizia border didn't seem to care if we were foreigners or Martians. They hardly looked at our passports. But they did tell us we would have problems reentering Kazakhstan, with their militant border guards.

Kirghizia is a long, narrow country running east and west, flanked by high mountains on the southern border against China and the northern border with Kazakhstan. The center is a high, arid valley dominated by Lake Issyk-Kul, which bisects the nation. Shortly after entering Kirghizia we came to the capital city, Bishkek. It was a small city with one hotel that seemed acceptable. We took rooms and settled in for the night. No restaurant was open, so we had canned sardines, energy bars and trail mix for supper.

Kahk-Rahmon slept in the bus, as he usually did. In the USSR it was normal when parking your vehicle to remove windshield wipers, mirrors and anything that might disappear in the night. Car parts were hard to find. If our driver didn't stay with the bus, there was no telling what would be left in the morning. At ten p.m. two policemen came to shake him down. Rather than give them money, he satisfied them with a package of M & M's from our cache, a rare treat in Kirghizia. Word got out that Kahk-Rahmon was an easy mark. All night pairs of Bishkek cops kept came, two by two, waking him, hands extended in expectation of M & M's. It was trick or treat night in Bishkek.

We talked about it in the morning. Kahk-Rahmon had gotten little sleep, playing candy store to the cops all night. Max was incensed. "I've been putting up with this crap all my life. Most of the time you just shut up and swallow it. Everyone, not just police, has his hand out for something. The system stinks. And they hit you harder if you are from another city, or if you are a minority." Max's bitterness betrayed a strange twist of fate: blue-eyed blond Aryans, Hitler's Master Race, now the target of discrimination. People accepted corruption as normal. Feodor said that Russian businesses built it into their budgets, comparing it to the huge contributions corporations make to the Democratic and Republican parties.

The air was terrible in Bishkek the next morning, smog that hung in the air like a Los Angeles inversion. Max said there wasn't much to see in Bishkek, so Arctic Joe and I mounted our bikes and headed east, climbing steadily. Every pedal stroke took us to higher, cleaner air. Outside of Bishkek men on horseback wore small, conical coolie hats. No longer were languid donkeys carrying men and boys. The faces were clearly Mongolian. The men were short, sturdily built and at ease on horseback. In this very isolated area no one spoke English, and few spoke much Russian.

We camped on a sandy beach along the south shore of Lake Issyk-Kul, five miles down a rutted track from the main road. To cycle to our campsite we labored through dry, sandy creek beds, washouts and a narrow cut between cliffs. At 6,000 feet above sea level, we could feel the elevation. By the time we got the tents set up it was getting dark and windy. Joe and I were sharing a tent. Initially we had each brought a tent, comfortable enough for one but a little tight for two people. Back at the Syr Darya, however, Joe had generously given his tent to Feodor, whose borrowed Russian Army tent fell apart. The temperature plunged as the sun set. Constantine prepared dinner quickly in the cold and dark, wearing a headlamp and a warm blanket over his shoulders. Dinner was boiled rice with pieces of dried beef, followed by the usual hot, sugary tea. And champagne.

During the night the wind howled down from the mountains. I expected the tent pegs to yank out of the sandy soil, sending the tent into the lake with us in it, but we had hammered them deep. In the morning everything was covered with a blanket of frost. The sun came up over the mountains, bright and warm. It was going to be a glorious day. We decided to take our time and, after a leisurely breakfast, break camp slowly. Once the sun had melted the frost and dried the tents we would be on our way.

At about eight o'clock there was a tumult coming from the trail we had taken in, getting louder and closer. Suddenly a herd of 30 wild horses charged onto the beach, running towards the lake. They saw us camped 50 yards from them and ignored us. For a half hour they frolicked in the lake, drank the brackish water and, as suddenly as they had arrived, they left. A majestic dappled stallion was last to leave. Before disappearing into the mountains, he turned to face us, raised his big head to the sky and gave a vigorous shake of his long mane, as if to say, "Play for a while, but be on your way. This is my turf. I don't want to see you here when I get back." Then he was gone.

There wasn't much flat bicycling around Lake Issyk-Kul. If you weren't going uphill, you were going down, and it was 90 % up. After one long, hard climb we came to a summit marked by a bronze plaque and a monument. "This is the famous Snow Leopard Pass," advised Max. "From here we will go no higher on this road." Below the concrete statue of a snow leopard was Lake Issyk-Kul, blue and peaceful. The 360-degree vista was breathtaking. Across the lake rose high mountains, Kazakhstan beyond them. Behind us more mountains separated Kirghizia and the Kashgar region of China.

We could see at least 100 snowcapped peaks in two parallel lines. There were few trees because of the high desert climate and the overgrazing of livestock. Patches of forest remained beyond grazing range, high in the Tien Shan Mountains, near the Chinese border. It was a captivating place. The day had gone from a cold morning to a warm, dry afternoon.

To us the people in the area were exotic looking, but we were the ones being stared at. Our skin color, facial features, our cycling outfits and our mannerisms marked us as the aliens. Whenever we stopped, children would crowd around, competing to communicate with us in a language we could not understand, getting responses from us in words that made no sense to them. Joe's bike got a flat tire near a village, and we drew a crowd of 50 friendly, curious kids. We set up camp near a pond not far from a village and the kids kept coming until it was time for supper. The only one who could communicate with them was Kahk-Rahmon. His language was similar to theirs, but it was slow going. He was gentle and patient with them. Sometimes he took time to instruct them from his Koran. That might have been the only religious training that these children had ever received. Kahk-Rahmon asked us again that day, for the umpteenth time, why we were doing this. His logic was simple and straightforward. He would have stayed home where he belonged.

One afternoon we finished our ride near a sanatorium by the lake, a rest home for retired union workers, a place called Djety Ogu, in the mountains at 7,000 feet. The residents were Central Asians and Russians, mostly older women. There were rooms available, but no one seemed to know how to go about getting permission for us to stay. We were not on their list, and one must adhere to rules! It took Feodor three hours to work it out with the bureaucrats. Staying in our tents would have been okay, but the prospect of a hot shower seemed a real luxury.

Word of the unusual visitors spread quickly among the elderly residents. While we were waiting for the results of Feodor's negotiations, a dozen elderly women came to get a look at us. They chatted among themselves and decided on a course of action. Since conversation was impossible, they would sing for us. What beautiful songs they sang! They sang sweetly, their smiles big and their hearts full of good will. Joe and I, both cynics, were touched. We reciprocated with an unrehearsed "Clementine" and a round of "I've Been Working on the Railroad." Kermit the Frog and The Croakers would have sounded better, but the ladies appreciated the effort and applauded us vigorously. We broke out a package of our dwindling supply of M & M's to be shared among them.

Feodor must have bribed or shamed someone, because they hustled us into the dining room and fed us heaps of mashed potatoes, gravy, kasha and tea. No meat. It was the best they could do, and it was most welcome. The manager had not yet figured out how to allow us to use their beds, so we took a hike up a wooded canyon, past a murmuring creek. We passed a bush tied with pieces of prayer cloth: There were Buddhists in this area, so close to China. We came to brass marker mounted on a rock face. My Russian was good enough to read that this was the favorite place of Russian Cosmonaut Yuri Gagarin, the first human in space, placed there after his tragic death in a small plane accident. When we got back to the rest home they had a large room for our group, with four beds and a hot shower.

VICTORY DAY

The second largest city in Kirghizia is Przhevalsk on the eastern end of Lake Issyk-Kul. While Bishkek was dirty, smoggy and heavily trafficked, Przhevalsk was clean, with broad tree-lined avenues and none of the ugly tenements so common in the USSR. It had the homey feeling of an American Midwest 1940s town. The name of Przhevalsk was being changed to Kara Kol, meaning Black River. Throughout Central Asia nationalistic pride was asserting itself by hurling out the names imposed by Russian masters. Traditional names were being resurrected.

We arrived on Victory Day, a holiday that commemorates the day the Germans surrendered in WW II. In that war 25,000,000 Soviet citizens lost their lives. Few families had not lost someone. In Przhevalsk there was a Victory Day parade and ceremony where 1,000 people gathered to honor living war veterans and the memory of the deceased. Veterans of the Great War, now old men and women, were called forward and presented with flowers by pretty schoolgirls as a band played patriotic songs. People wished each other a happy holiday, *"S'prazdnikom."* Joe and I, still on our bicycles, were observing the spectacle from the rear. Somehow word reached the officials that Joe was an English veteran of the Great War, a member of the heroic Black Watch. He was brought on stage, publicly praised, hugged and kissed by the prettiest girl of them all and presented with a large bouquet of flowers. With him were aged Soviet Army veterans in their rumpled suits, rows of medals hanging from their chests, while Joe, their comrade in arms, wore his colorful bicycling togs, his outdoor tan in sharp contrast to his white hair. If there was any strangeness, it was easily overcome by the warmth and sincerity of the people of Przhevalsk on that beautiful Victory Day.

Because of Joe's war service we were invited to stay in the former Communist Party elite's mansion. We each had a large room with a full bath. The furnishings were comfortable and everything worked, including a color television, although there was no color TV in the country. The rooms had ornately decorated ten-foot high ceilings and good views of the manicured gardens below. We were served a fine meal in a private dining room, with free flowing wine and vodka. The best part was an oversized bed with a down comforter when we were finally ready to call it a night. Ordinary citizens of Przhevalsk had never seen the inside of this Communist Party palace!

We discussed our visa predicament a local official. He said that we would not be allowed into Kazakhstan without a multiple-entry visa, and we had to go to Kazakhstan to get one, a Catch 22 situation. Joe and I decided on an alternative plan. Since we had to reenter Kazakhstan and couldn't do it legally, we would do it illegally. We were looking at the mountains, and beyond those mountains was Kazakhstan. We were pretty sure that the officious Kazak border guards were not sitting at the top of every snowy pass freezing their officious butts.

THE BEARS WENT OVER THE MOUNTAIN: ILLEGAL ENTRY II

Our Communist Party hosts gave us a big sendoff breakfast. We cycled around the eastern end of Lake Issyk-Kul to the north side. We didn't have a clue about where we would cross the mountain, so we had to search for a pass. We started our search at Karl Marx Collective Farm Number Three, which occupied thousands of acres below the Kazakhstan border. It was not really a farm, more of a cattle ranch, with scrawny livestock eking out a sparse living on the lower slopes. We drove in, bus, bikes and all, and set up camp in a field with views of the lake and the mountains.

While we were pitching the tents two teenage cowboys rode up on horses, bareback and toting AK-47s. They wanted to know our motives regarding their livestock. Kahk-Rahmon welcomed them and asked them to join us for coffee and bread. The shy lads dismounted and joined us around our fire. Eventually we asked them about a pass over the mountain to Kazakhstan. They looked at each other and giggled. "The pass is right up there," said the taller of the two, pointing to a gully, "But nobody can go up there yet. There is snow, and it is very far." They said that they had never crossed, but everybody knew about the pass. It was difficult to tell if they were telling the truth or if they were covering up for drug smugglers' routes across Central Asia into Russia.

Joe offered them M & M's and asked if we could take a short ride on their ponies. We mounted the Mongolian horses bareback and rode about a half mile. Joe grew up with horses and was right at home. I was lucky not to fall. We rode back to the fire and talked some more. The boys were friendly, so we decided to confide in them. We told them that we were going to cross the pass in the morning and offered to hire them if they would bring horses to take us up as far as they could go. They agreed to be there at five-thirty. It looked like things were starting to come together.

On an old Soviet map Max located the ranch and the gully. But as U.S. intelligence knew only too well, the Soviets usually published incorrect maps for "disinformation," reasoning that the less people knew, the better. Max and Feodor tried to match two maps, one of Kazakhstan and one of Kirghizia. They were different scales, but there were enough match points to give us a picture of what was ahead of us.

We had to go north to get into Kazakhstan. The gully would take us to a 12,000-foot pass at the border. About 3,000 vertical feet above our camp, we expected to hit the snow line at 9,000 feet. That meant another 3,000 vertical feet of trudging in snow. The Kazak map showed a creek valley running north, on the other side of the pass. Further north, the creek formed three small lakes a few miles apart before it reached a road spur at 5,000 feet. It looked like a 20-mile hike, all of the uphill portion coming in the first few hours. Joe and I had completed mountain trail runs of 50 miles or more. We felt confident that it would take us no more than eight hours. Max wanted to come with us as our guide. He was young and healthy, and he felt that he could keep up with us. The bus would drive around the long way, cross into Kazakhstan legally and meet us at the road spur late in the afternoon, in time for dinner. We expected to be there before the bus. But first we would go to the snowline with the horses in the morning to take a look before committing ourselves. If it looked too risky we would turn around.

We got up at five and ate breakfast. Following Murphsky's Law, the cowboys failed to show up. We went without them, but starting with a 6,000-foot climb, we would have to move light and fast. We ditched everything but the basics. We carried no flashlights, no extra clothing or food, no backpacks. We each put a bag of trail mix and two energy bars in our pockets. I gave lightweight Mylar emergency blankets to Joe and Max and stuffed one in my parka. Joe pocketed a can of Pepsi he had been hoarding. We were dressed in blue jeans, running shoes, sweatshirts, wool hats, gloves and parkas, insufficient for the mountains, but good enough for a few hours of cold. We would learn to regret our underestimation of what lay ahead.

Feodor joined us up to the snow line at 9,000 feet, where he turned back. From there to the pass it was slow going. The spring snow was wet on this south side of the mountain as we walked. In places there was a crust to walk on, and once in a while there was no snow at all where exposed rocks had been absorbing the warm spring sun. The slope became gradual as we neared the pass. The air was crisp and clear. We looked back south across Kirghizia to the Chinese border. The reflected morning sun danced on the surface of Lake Issyk-Kul below us and again on the snow. In front of us to the north was more snow, and it seemed to stretch out for a long way. We took a moment to enjoy the view before starting what we thought would be a quick descent to the creek bed. Now that the hard part was surely behind us we ate our sparse lunch.

Max took off his parka, sat on it and slid down a short slope to the north, glissading 200 feet down. He turned and indicated that we should do the same. My parka made a good sled. Joe was more conservative and walked down. The Kazakhstan border was not guarded, as we had guessed. We had expected to go downhill quickly, but the mountaintop seemed to stretch on and on in front of us, long and flat. Progress was much more difficult on the north side, protected from the sun by the shadow of the mountain. The snow was deeper and softer and gave little support. I would be walking along on a thin crust, when suddenly one leg would dig a deep posthole in the snow, buried up to my butt, with the other leg splayed clumsily on top of the snow. Every posthole we dug slowed us down, and we plunged a lot of them. We were moving very slowly and not losing enough altitude to get out of the snow. We were cold and wet and we had to get the hell out of there. Max was doing little better than Joe and I, and he was concerned. At two in the afternoon he said he was going ahead to see if he could find a route down. With that our "guide" left us. Arctic Joe and I were on our own.

We followed his tracks north for a while. To our right was a precipitous drop down to a valley, thousands of feet below, where the creek we had seen on the map must be. It would be free of snow. It was going to be a very tough, steep climb down, but that was what we had to do. Once we decided to descend we lost all trace of Max. Clinging to rocks and bushes we slowly inched our way down, often sliding or dropping ten or fifteen feet to the next tenuous handhold. It would have been very easy to fall and break a leg, but we had to get out of the snow, and excess caution was a luxury we could not afford. We heard the creek long before we saw it crashing down the valley.

The last part of the descent was treacherous, and we finished by dropping and scraping down a 50-foot rock face, gathering mud, brush, scrapes and bruises. When we reached the creek it was clogged with boulders and centuries of deadfall trees. There were steep cliffs on both sides of the creek, which was now in full spring flood. We had freed ourselves of the snow, but now we had no place to walk but right down the icy stream, slowly climbing over boulders and over and under fallen trees and branches. It was reassuring that we were still on a northerly track, moving in the right direction. If this were indeed the right creek we would reach the road spur and the bus. Eventually.

The stream widened to the first of the three lakes. That was the good news. The bad news was that we couldn't walk in the stream anymore. The lake was deep, and cliffs rose steeply on the left and right. We had to climb a long way up to work our way around the lake, clinging to the slope. Our clothing was soaked, and we were tired. Our food was gone, but the ice-cold lake slaked our thirst. Halfway around the lake I shouted "Halloo," hoping someone might hear. An answer came from across the lake in front of us, "Halloo." Thankfully, someone was nearby. At five-thirty we reached the end of the lake and there was our hero, Max, as cold and miserable as we were.

We were starting to worry about whether we would make it out alive. We were cold, wet, hungry and headed towards hypothermia, with a long way to go to the road. We had to keep moving. After another hour and a half the icy stream bed took us to the second lake. The west shore of the lake was not bad hiking, and we passed the lake in an hour. It was getting dark and the temperature was dropping fast. The sun had descended behind the mountain, but there was still just barely enough light to allow us to keep moving. Even after the sun was gone, there was a half moon, and we could see enough to go on for a while longer, stumbling over logs and getting smacked in the face with branches.

Then the moon, too, traveling from east to west, was gone behind the big, black ridge to our left. We had been moving constantly for 17 hours. It was pitch black. We could go no further until daylight. When we stopped moving we became very cold. The three of us were shivering.

A GOOD USE FOR MONEY

A single wolf gave a long howl somewhere far behind us, its echo reverberating off the canyon walls. His call went unanswered, but wolves were the least of our problems. We knew that we might freeze to death if we didn't get a fire going. Neither Joe nor I had matches. Thank God Max was a smoker. He had a matchbook with three matches left. In the pitch dark we groped about with numb fingers for kindling. To avoid becoming separated in the dark we kept up a loud voice contact. When we had enough kindling, we cleared a spot, broke up the kindling and piled it like a teepee. We made a wad of Russian rubles and stuffed it into the base of the teepee. Then Max lit one precious match with his trembling fingers and touched it to the money. It caught immediately! The rubles burned fast and hot, and the kindling grabbed the flame. "Finally those damned rubles are good for something," chortled Max.

In the dim light of the flame we gathered more wood and gradually built a fire that was radiating life-renewing heat. When we had enough wood to last the night we erected a drying frame for our wet shoes and clothing. We wrapped ourselves in the thin Mylar blankets and tried to get some sleep near the fire, but it didn't work. The fire was hot, and we were toasting on one side and freezing on the other. We had to keep turning to stay warm. The plastic emergency blankets did a great job of keeping body heat in, but they also kept moisture from escaping, re-soaking our clothing with condensation. We kept telling ourselves that at dawn we would get the hell out of there.

At three in the morning I heard something. Joe raised his head. There it was again, a faint "Halloo." Looking in the direction of the sound I could see a light flickering through the trees. "Halloo," I shouted back. Feodor and Constantine had come with a tent, sleeping bags, and a big pot to boil water. After a couple of cups of very welcome hot tea we stripped down, crawled into the cozy sleeping bags and waited for daylight. At sunrise we were out of there, quickly passing the third lake. At the far end of the lake was our beloved bus. Kahk-Rahmon had a scolding expression on his face. "Why do you do these things?" We ate a big breakfast of eggs, bread, hot tea . . . and grateful champagne toasts.

In retrospect we made three errors in planning our trip across the mountain. The first was that we never even thought about the fact that the snow is *always* deeper on the north side of a mountain in the Northern Hemisphere. A Boy Scout would know that. Our first error was in failing to sit down and think about it. The second error was not knowing where we were going. We should probably have spent more time gathering information in Przhevalsk. We didn't make a real effort. For our third error I will quote Al Pacino in the movie, *The Devil's Advocate*, speaking as Satan, "Vanity is my favorite sin." We were definitely lacking in humility.

ALMA ATAY AND ON

We took a break in Alma Atay, the beautiful capital of Kazakhstan. It was modern and more western than most of Central Asia, with elegant office buildings and hotels. After being so long under the Soviet thumb, the Kazaks were starting to reap the benefits of their enormous mineral wealth. Oil companies were wooing them. Turkish and Korean business interests were making solid investments in infrastructure and industry. The future looked bright, but there were lingering problems. The Soviet nuclear test program had contaminated large areas of the country, and the death rate from radiation-related diseases was high. Half of the devastated Aral Sea is in Kazakhstan. The Soviet Union screwed the Kazaks big time, and the effects will be felt for centuries.

Joe and I took in the pleasures of Alma Atay. We went to a multi-story bathhouse, like a big, modern hotel with a broad variety of luxurious bathing options. One whole floor was devoted to Finnish style sauna. On another floor was a *Vostochnii Banya*, Turkish bath, tiled and steamy, with individual compartments for privacy. We tried a circular arrangement of tiled platforms, each at a different temperature, graduated from cold to quite hot. For an hour a burly, sadistic Siberian masseur worked me over, and I never felt better than when he stopped mauling my wretched and battered body.

Later that evening we ate at a good restaurant. Then we found an obliging convert to capitalism, a ticket scalper, so Joe and I saw a Russian language version of Tosca by the Kazakhstan National Opera Company. We had survived our ordeal and now we pampered ourselves. We deserved and needed it after our almost fatal folly in the mountains. Then we were on our way again, heading east, with Irkutsk in mind.

The rest of the trip was anticlimactic. Long miles finally took us to Irkutsk. No one got sick. We didn't get lost. We did not break any laws by illegally crossing borders. Arctic Joe and I were ready to go home. The champagne was all gone.

A smallish Kazak yurt in the village

Our hostess, Baira, and family outside their yurt. They were ready to follow the herds into higher pastures.

Making really sour yoghurt balls in yurt

Wild horses on the shore of Lake Issyk-Kul, Kirgizia. Beyond the Tien Shan Mountains in the background is China.

These Russian ladies sang for us near Prezhevalsk, Kirgizia

Kirgiz cowboy at Karl Marx Ranch #3

*Joe on borrowed
Kirgiz pony*

Kirgiz cowboy at Karl Marx Ranch #3

Joe postholing in the snow—crossing illegally from Kirgizia to Kazakhstan

Arctic Joe on top of mountain. Our last look at Lake Issyk-Kul and the Tien Shan Mountains before getting bogged down in the deep snow.

It was easier going up.

Kahk-Rahmon did not sleep all night and scolded us when we finally showed up.

CHAPTER XII

THE BERING STRAIT

*"In time the land bridge disappeared, overrun by the seas,
and then Asia and Alaska were separated . . . ."*
— James A. Michener, *Alaska*

The Arctic Circle intersects the International Date Line at sea in the Bering Strait. Here, the extended finger of western Alaska reaches out to the extended finger of easternmost Asia, as do the fingers of God and Man on the ceiling of the Sistine Chapel. This is the only opening between the northern Pacific and the Arctic Oceans, not much more than 50 miles wide, a constriction that generates violent currents as the vast Pacific forces its way northward.

Polar winds rage south from the Artic Ocean. When they come from the northeast, they sweep western Alaska before strafing the Bering Strait. More often the fury of the wind rushes out of eastern Siberia. This vicious wind churns the surface of the Strait like an off-balance washing machine. The icy north wind over the relatively warmer surface of the Strait produces a thick fog, making it a dank, gloomy place.

On the eastern shore of the Bering Strait is the Eskimo village of Cape Wales, the westernmost point of the American continents, situated at the western end of Alaska's Seward Peninsula. Across the Bering Strait, northwest of Cape Wales, is what looks like a mirror image of the Seward Peninsula, Russia's Chukotka Peninsula, the easternmost point of Asia.

Mainland Russia is only 50 miles from the United States mainland, and half-way across the Bering Strait sit two small islands, straddling the International Date Line. Two and a half miles apart, Little Diomede is part of the United States, while Big Diomede (Ratmanova to the Russians) is in Russia. Think about it. An American citizen can sip tea in his home and watch Russian border guards in their outhouse-like shacks on Big Diomede. The border guards (only five in 1994) were on Ratmanova to protect the Motherland from attack by fierce American Eskimos, whom the Russians drove away from their Ratmanova homes more than half a century before. Those miserable, lonely Russian border guards can only look longingly across the narrow gap to imagined luxury.

A PLAN TO CLOSE THE GAP

We had started our world trek long ago in Fairbanks, Alaska, going east across North America, the Atlantic, Europe and Asia. To complete the circumnavigation we had to cross the Bering Strait to get back to Alaska. There were two possibilities. Plan A would be a summer crossing in a small boat, maybe an Eskimo umiak, from Chukotka to Cape Wales, Alaska. Ffity miles in that water would be rough, and it might be a lot more than 50 miles with unfavorable currents or bad weather.

The best route would take us via the Diomedes, a good place to take refuge if things went bad. From the Diomedes it is 25 miles to Cape Wales. Altogether the crossing should take three or four days, except for the very real chance of having to wait for good weather. Only one person had ever swum between the Diomedes. A gifted athlete, Lynne Cox, swam west from Little Diomede to Ratmanova a few years before. No one had yet swum the other way, from Russia to Alaska, Asia to North America. That intrigued me. The more I thought about it, the more I liked it. "Hey, I'm passing that way anyway." Might I possibly become the first person to do it? I am not a world-class swimmer, but I could give it a shot.

Plan B would be a winter crossing. In winter the ice pushes south, into the Bering Strait. Ice usually reaches as far south as the Diomedes, sometimes beyond. A person might walk, snowshoe, ski, or travel by dog sled. An Eskimo named Spike Milligrock made a foot crossing before the Russians closed the border. More recently, "The Bering Bridge" expedition of American Paul Schurke and Dmitrii Shparo, the great Russian Arctic explorer, reunited Eskimo families separated for decades by the closed border, a piece of the Iron Curtain.

What I learned from *National Geographic* magazine and talks with Schurke and Shparo was not encouraging. Even in the coldest winters the ice is unreliable and dangerous, a jumble of massive chunks of ice forced upwards by the shifting ocean. Long, open cracks called leads block passage, and one can suddenly open in front of you. If you fall into the 28° F water, you might die. If you do not freeze to death on the ice or fall into the ocean, plenty of polar bears are out there looking for an easy lunch.

I considered plan A and plan B. Neither would be easy, but paln A sounded better. I decided to take my chances with the water when it wasn't frozen.

COMRADE MONEYGRUBBER

In the fall of 1992 I started working on getting permission to cross the Bering Strait in the Diomedes. I got no encouragement from either Russian or American officials. The Russian visa people told me that Ratmanova was a closed military area. It would take special permission to go there. But they couldn't identify the proper military person to approach with my request, so I called a friend in Moscow.

I will not use real names for reasons that are obvious. My Moscow contact put me in touch with Sasha in the office of the military commander of the Russian Far East. Sasha spoke English and expressed surprise and a little chagrin at getting a phone call from America on his unlisted military telephone. I assured Sasha that I had no sinister purpose, and that I only wanted to swim from Ratmanova to Little Diomede. I needed a favor, a special permit. He expressed his doubts, but he would speak to his boss. He asked me to call back in two days. These calls, I might add, were made midday Moscow time, in the middle of the night at home in California.

When I called two days later Sasha said that his boss, General X, would be happy to help; his organization would be a partner in the expedition of "our dear American friends." He would support us with helicopters and patrol boats. All resources of his command would be available to me. "And it will only cost you $25,000, to be paid in small American bills, $10,000 within one month and the rest on your arrival in Moscow." He also told me that I would have to travel to Ratmanova by way of Moscow and return that way. That route would amount to two trips almost all the way around the world using unreliable Russian transportation just to get there and back. It would take weeks. I told Sasha that I was pleased that the General had been so kind, but that it would require some thought. I thought about being in his clutches. I thought that for $25,000 the bastard would slit my throat and dispose of me in Siberia. I thought about it for three seconds. That was the last time I spoke to him.

I was depressed thinking that I might have to give up my dream after getting so far, but there was no way in hell that I was going to fork over that kind of money to a thief. I mentioned my situation to an Alaskan friend who had a contact in the Russian Far East, the local military commander in Providenya, near the Bering Strait, Colonel Z. Two weeks later my Alaskan friend called to tell me that Colonel Z would do the job for $10,000, helicopters and all, and I would not have to travel in and out of Moscow. The price was coming down, the conditions were getting better, but it was still expensive and distasteful. There had to be a better way.

BUT I CAN SKI, CAN'T I?

My luck seemed to take a turn for the better when I got a call from Dmitrii Shparo in Moscow, inviting me to participate in an interesting project. He and a Canadian partner were going to drive an SUV from London to New York, going the long way around. After emerging from the new Channel Tunnel they would drive across Europe and Asia to the Bering Strait, where they would cross the ice to Alaska, then drive to New York. Their automaker client wanted to claim that his vehicle was the first to be driven from London to New York. My job would be to ski ahead of the SUV in the Strait, boring test holes in the ice to make sure that it was thick and strong enough to support the SUV. It fit in with my requirement that I not use a motorized vehicle as part of my trek. And I would not have to bribe any crooked Russian officers.

I got to work immediately. It was late 1992, and we planned to make the crossing in February of 1993. I spent weekends on cross-country skis in the Sierra Nevada. Shparo's Canadian counterpart contacted American manufacturers for the arctic gear we needed and had it sent to my home to avoid paying Canadian duties. In January 1993 we were ready to take off for Siberia.

Then I got a call from the Canadian, whom I had started calling Doctor No-No. We never met, but conversations with him felt like he was pulling tensely on the phone line. His focus, as it should be, was solely on his project. He didn't care about my plans or how they might intersect with his. Dr. No-No told me that I would not be able to ski. I would have to drive a heavy Russian vehicle called a Buran, a cross between a tractor and a snow mobile. They wanted me in front using the heavy contraption to test the ice. Guess who would be first to find thin ice . . . the hard way! I told him that I would not be going on his snowmobile excursion, and that he could shove the Buran where the snow doesn't fall.

The expedition went ahead and they did not succeed. I heard that there are several Burans decorating the bottom of the Bering Strait. Thankfully, I am not down there with them.

HELLO, OPERATOR?

Then I remembered a story Don Logan in Fairbanks had told me when we were getting ready to set out from Fairbanks to New York long ago. Don and his girlfriend had made an unauthorized kayak trip across the Bering Strait and were stopped in Russian waters near Big Diomede. They were arrested for being in Russian waters illegally. Their kayaks were confiscated and they were sent home on a U.S. Coast Guard cutter. The Russians were polite and treated them well, not a horrible experience. My evil little mind started churning up an insidious plot. I could enter into Russian waters illegally and take my chances on not getting arrested.

I needed help to pull it off. Whom do you call when you need help and don't know the number? You call the telephone *information operator*! I phoned the information number for the State of Alaska, 1 907 555 1212. I wasn't sure what to ask, so I just told the operator what I wanted to do, putting myself in her hands. She was intrigued with the idea of swimming in the Diomedes and suggested that I call the Diomede Native Corporation and gave me the number. Progress!

I dialed the Diomede number and reached a receptionist who, though she offered only one- or two-word answers to my questions, seemed helpful. Finally I asked her if she could recommend a guide with a boat to take me to Big Diomede and escort me as I swam back. "My father." *Would you please repeat that?* "My father,

Moses Milligrock. He knows these waters better than anybody." She gave me his number. Moses, by the way, is a cousin of Spike Milligrock, who had made the crossing from Siberia to Alaska on foot in the 1930s.

When I phoned Moses Milligrock, I got a woman I couldn't understand at all, speaking in an Eskimo language. It was winter and I imagined the wind blowing at gale force, with snow flying through the chinks in an igloo, an igloo that happened to be equipped with a telephone. Finally, I convinced her to get Moses for me. My conversation with him was as direct as with his daughter. I asked for his help. He said that it could be complicated, but he would help. I got his P.O. address and sent him a list of questions.

In a couple of weeks I got a reply from Moses. He answered my questions about currents, weather, housing, and so forth. I called him and we laid out a plan. For compensation, Moses asked that I bring two cases of fresh fruit with me, soft fruits that they never get in the arctic, no apples or pears. That sounded a whole lot better than $25,000 or $10,000.

I wanted a reliable partner with me as I swam, so I telephoned Ted Epstein. Ted had shown toughness and endurance during our long trek across Siberia, and it didn't take him long to say yes. We both understood that no one had ever swum from Russia to Alaska and that this swim might be extremely difficult. We would swim one at a time, one of us life-guarding as the other swam.

A SHINING EXAMPLE

Lynne Cox is a world-class athlete. As a teenager she had set the record for the fastest swim across the English Channel, nine hours and 36 minutes. That time has been bettered, but not by much. On August 8, 1987, at Little Diomede, 30-year-old Cox entered the 43° F water, as cold as an icy highball. She was accompanied by two walrus-skin Eskimo umiaks, a press contingent and British physiologist Bill Keatinge, an expert on hypothermia. In her stomach was a thermo-sensitive electronic transmitter, which allowed the scientist to monitor her core temperature as she swam. If it fell too low, she would be in mortal danger.

The distance to Big Diomede from Little Diomede is 2.7 miles. Big Diomede had been off limits to westerners since 1948 when Ratmanova's Diomede Eskimos had been forced by the USSR to leave. It was a major diplomatic coup for Cox that, after many months of frustrating effort, she finally got Russian permission for her swim, a harbinger of the spirit of *glasnost* soon to come.

As she skillfully knifed her way through the frigid water on her east-to-west swim, she was pushed north by currents that made her swim longer and more difficult. After an hour, upwellings from the much colder bottom dropped the water temperature to 38° F and the surface became agitated. The closer she got to Ratmanova, the harder it became. Her last 50 yards, fighting an adverse current, took an eternity. At last, she touched shore on Russian soil after two hours and five minutes, depleted and very cold. Cox was quoted in *People* magazine as saying, "It was the riskiest, most frightening, most difficult thing I've ever done." I thought about those words as I got ready for my swim.

Lynne Cox is particularly well suited for long, cold-water swims: 5' 6" and 207 pounds, with 40 percent body fat, excellent for survival in cold water. Most people become hypothermic in 45° F water in 12 minutes and die in 20 minutes. Lynne was prepared. She had trained for weeks in the 54° F waters of Norton Sound near Nome. She had the low heart rate of a marathon runner and wore no wet suit or grease to protect her. Lynne Cox completed her historic first as purely as one can. No one has duplicated her feat, and she deserves her place in the International Swimming Hall of Fame.

Ted and I had no illusions about our ability. We were not in a league with Lynne Cox: she was a super-star and we were minor leaguers. If we were to succeed in our swim, if we were even going to survive, we needed to take extra precautions. Ted and I were both long distance runners, at home on mountain trails. Our percentage of body fat was low. We needed warm wetsuits, including head, hand and foot covering. Besides thermal protection, the wetsuits would give us buoyancy.

I did my homework about the Diomedes, using the resources of the U.S. Navy, the Coast Guard, the State of Alaska, and the National Oceanic and Astronomical Administration. A chart of the channel showed an underwater ridge ten feet below the surface near the shortest route, thus the cold upwellings that Lynne Cox had experienced. Maps showed that the two islands were parallel on the south ends, but the bigger Russian island extended three miles further north. Little Diomede is two by two miles, and Ratmanova is roughly five by two. Topographical maps indicated that both islands consisted of steep cliffs jutting up from the sea, with little flat land. The only flat place on Little Diomede was where the tiny village Inalik was located, home to 130 Diomede Eskimos. We learned that the prevailing current runs from the south to the north, bending to the northeast as it passes the Diomedes. That also shed light on the difficulty of Lynne Cox's swim a few years before: she had had to fight the current. The information regarding the currents was extremely valuable because it would allow us to make some critical decisions about our route.

Moses, Ted and I agreed on a date in July for the attempt. The cycle of the moon would be right for the tides we wanted.

Part of our preparation was to gain weight, by eating more and running less. Oh, the agony! I wanted to gain 20 pounds by July or explode trying. I increased my swim workouts to six a week, three of them in the cold ocean without a wetsuit. Late winter ocean temperatures in Northern California were in the low 50s. I did my swim training in San Francisco's Aquatic Park at the South End Club and in Santa Cruz at Natural Bridges State Beach. My Santa Cruz route was 300 yards off shore, back and forth, several half-mile round trips. There are sea otters, seals and sea lions in the area, and that means that there are great white sharks. A hundred times, brushing against a piece of kelp, I was sure I had met a shark that wasn't there.

GETTING THERE: THE FUN PART

Ted and I got together in Seattle for a flight to Anchorage. We had time before our connection to Nome, so we went to a restaurant for lunch before leaving civilization. Hovering over us in the lobby was a mean-looking, eight-foot tall stuffed polar bear, ready to pounce. The plaque at his feet said that he had been taken near the Diomedes. Now I had more food for nightmares, and I was the food. The flight to Nome was via Kotzebue, above the Arctic Circle. Total travel time, home to Nome, was over twelve hours.

We didn't have much time to spend in Nome, so we took a stroll around town. You could almost smell gold in the air. In 1898 prospectors found it on the beach where it had accumulated over millennia. Back then no excavation was required. Today the easy pickings are long gone. There are still mining operations outside town, gigantic pieces of equipment gouging huge bites into the earth.

There are souvenir shops and drinking establishments in Nome. We had dinner at Fat Freddie's and found a room for the night. Before sacking out, we made a pilgrimage to the wooden arch that marks the finish line of the 1,049-mile-long Iditarod Trail Dog Sled Race*, a classic among endurance contests. I felt that I would be back at that arch some day.

197

The final leg of any trip to a remote part of Alaska is usually by bush plane. On Sunday, July 18, 1994, Baker Aviation took us on a four-seater aircraft from Nome to Cape Wales, along with a frisky, airsick malamute puppy and a load of cargo. I sat in the co-pilot's seat, and Ted shared the rear seat with the puppy. We made a couple of stops en route to Cape Wales, getting a chance to see the western part of the Seward Peninsula. Over Shishmareff we saw polar bear skins drying on racks—very large, even from the air.

About 200 Eskimos lived in Cape Wales, further west than anyone on either American continent. There was a small store, but the hours were very limited, and they didn't have much to sell anyway. What they did carry was pricey and geared to the needs of the native people. In Nome we could have chowed down at any of several eateries. In Wales there were homes, a church, the store, an airstrip, the town hall and a "washateria," complete with a pay shower and a coin-op telephone: no restaurant. We bought rock-hard pilot bread, peanut butter and a gallon of reconstituted milk. We had brought with us fresh fruit, raisins, energy bars and trail mix. We would survive. Ted and I had lived through Siberia and the Pinocchio Gang. It could be worse.

Our sleeping quarters were: worse, that is. Uncle Pete, who operated the washateria, had a cousin who had moved away years before, shuttering his house all that time. Pete wanted $40 apiece for us to spend the night in the smelly, moldy hovel. We didn't have much choice, but Ted The Negotiator bargained with him to lower the price to $20 each, linen for Ted included. Getting to sleep with the sun shining can be frustrating. Here's a trick: cover your eyes. A bandana knotted around your head will do the job very nicely.

The U.S. Postal Service delivers mail once a week to Little Diomede. In the winter a small plane lands on the ice outside the village. In the summer there is no ice, so delivery is by helicopter to a small pad at the water's edge near the village. Our plan was to catch the next helicopter out to Little Diomede Island. The Postal Service contractor was scheduled to make deliveries every Monday, but weather conditions on Diomede often made that impossible. It had been foggy two weeks before our arrival. There was a pile of Diomede mail waiting in Cape Wales. It might be a problem for us to get onto the helicopter to Little Diomede.

We went to the washateria to telephone Evergreen Helicopter Services, the Postal Service contractor. Eric told us that he would be there that afternoon. Because of the volume of mail, he would make multiple runs to the island. He assured us that we would be on Diomede that day. Our luck was phenomenal. A German kayak group had recently been stranded at Cape Wales for two weeks waiting for a break in the weather. The last thing we wanted was to spend weeks waiting in Uncle Pete's palatial digs.

Ted and I took a hike along the sandy beach that faced the Bering Straits. We could see the Diomedes jutting up out of the sea in the distance. The beach was clean, and the water, cold though it was, looked inviting. Outside the village we were assailed by the foul odor of the decaying bodies of several walruses. Walrus is a traditional food source in this area. They are big, meaty, easy prey and tasty, but these marine mammals are protected by federal law. An exception is made for subsistence hunting by indigenous people. So why would good walrus meat be left to rot on the beach? A closer look showed that they had all been decapitated to remove the tusks. Because of the ban on elephant ivory, the demand for walrus ivory had risen dramatically. With high unemployment, a big tusker walrus was more than dinner, and a few individuals in the area were slaughtering walruses just to sell their tusks.

Except for jewelry made from tusks as a byproduct of subsistence hunting, trade in walrus ivory was then, and still is, illegal. But there is a network of crooks that buys ivory from the Eskimos, ships it to Siberia, then on to China to be carved into expensive trinkets for milady. The Alaskan coastline is huge. The small number of federal agents policing the area was spread thin and not able to do much to help the beleaguered walrus, whose only sin is to have a magnificent set of teeth.

Ted and I went up Cape Wales Mountain, 2,000 feet above the sea, to get a better look at the Diomedes. Before landing at Wales, our bush pilot had detoured a few miles onto the Strait to give us our first sighting. From the airplane the islands stood one behind the other and looked like one island, the smaller one in the foreground blending into the bigger one behind, but from the top of Cape Wales Mountain we could clearly see that there were two islands and then Siberia, 50 miles away. We were on the North American continent with a clear view of the tip of Asia. It looked amazingly close.

On the mountain we saw plenty of reindeer sign: hoof prints, hair, scat and a few antlers. With long days and a lot of moisture, wildflowers were everywhere. We saw an arctic fox, a couple of marmots and several hares. Ted spotted a herd of reindeer far away in the next valley. On the south side of the mountain we looked down on "Tin Can City," a U.S. Army encampment from WWII. The soldiers had been there because Japanese had invaded American territory in the Aleutians. It was called "Tin Can City" because the heaps of food tins left there by the Army were still there 50 years later. Human tracks last a long time in the fragile Arctic.

We hurried down the mountain, not wanting to miss the helicopter. It was waiting, but there was a small problem. There was room for only two passengers. Besides Ted and me an Eskimo woman was returning her sick infant niece to the baby's mother on Diomede. We could not all go. Ted The Negotiator worked out a compromise. The woman would stay in Wales and Ted would carry the infant to Diomede on his lap. The kid was a screamer. Poor Ted! On the bush plane to Wales he had shared his seat an airsick malamute puppy. Now he had to nursemaid a yowling infant. The pilot told Ted not to worry, "They always calm down as soon as I start the motor." Uh, huh!

THE DIOMEDES

It is a short hop from Wales to Little Diomede. The village is in the middle of the west shore of the island, facing the Russian island. As we got closer, the island took shape. Cliffs that from the mainland seemed to jut straight up out of the sea appeared from up close to plunge down into the cold, dark water. As we rounded the north end of the island and moved south, we could see current lines on the surface as the sea flowed north between the Diomedes.

That view from the chopper was worth its weight in gold. It gave us information on the direction and strength of the currents. Now that we had actually seen the currents, we knew where they were and how to use them. We had scheduled this swim to coincide with the greatest tide swings and the strongest currents of the month. We were not looking for a day when the currents would be gentle: we wanted strong those currents working for us, river-like currents to help us during the swim.

The pilot knew why we were there. Word gets around fast in the Arctic. He made his approach long and slow for us, going all the way south so we could get a good look at both islands. Knowing what the south end of Big Diomede looked like was critical to our plan. Eric may have strayed *just a little bit* into Russian airspace for us, but there were no MIGs or ground-to-air missiles to worry about, just a few lonely border guards marooned in the extreme reaches of Siberia.

Living in Diomede village were 130 people, the only people besides the Russian border guards in a circle 50 miles in diameter. The entire village is half the size of a football field, pushing 100 vertical feet up the mountain because there is no other place for houses. A small store sits near the water. Saint Patrick's Catholic Church is on the south end of town and the school (18 students, three teachers) is on the north end. There is little space between buildings, but there is all the space in the world behind the village. But that space is so steep that you can't build on it. To the north and south are sheer cliffs, and after that hundreds of miles of open sea. Precipitous footpaths traverse the hillsides going north, south and straight up. Out front, to the west, Big Diomede is in plain sight.

Since 1981 I have directed many swimmers in the "impossible" swim from Alcatraz, through the cold, choppy and swift waters of San Francisco Bay. The distance between Alcatraz and the mainland is about half the distance between the Diomedes. The water in San Francisco Bay is 20 degrees warmer. Would my experience be of any use here?

GRANDPA MOSES

Eric eased the chopper onto a 25-foot-square pad of steel plate balanced on a pile of boulders five feet above the high water line. This was "Inalik International Airport," Alaska. Inalik is the Eskimo name for the village on Little Diomede. Ted looked around frantically until he found an anxious looking mother willing to unburden him of the still-screaming child in his arms. In the crowd at the helipad was a white-haired short man with a craggy face. It had to be Moses Milligrock. I dragged my duffel down and Moses took my hand with a powerful grip. "Welcome to Diomede, Joe." He was about 75 years old, built like a halfback, low to the ground, solid as a fire hydrant. His face was wrinkled from years of laughing and doing battle with the elements. Moses looked the part of a wise village elder.

In the old days the Diomede Band of Eskimos had a reputation for ferocity. They would cross the ice or open sea to raid villages in both Asia and Alaska. I could picture a young Moses and his cohorts chasing the men of a village into the hills and running off with the women and whatever they could stash in their kayaks. Rumor had it that Moses had obtained his first five wives that way. Today the Diomede Band is a gentle and friendly group. We were told that no one would ever be allowed to go hungry on Diomede, and we saw an example of that. While we were waiting in Wales we came across a poor unfortunate, possibly homeless or mentally ill. He had gotten to Wales and wanted to go on to Russia via Diomede. He may have been homeless, but he had money. He claimed to be a sergeant in the Russian Border Guards. He spoke no Russian, embarrassed when he learned that I did. He was about as Russian as apple pie on the Fourth of July. He admitted that his home was in affluent Burlingame, California, and that the lawyer handling his inheritance had suggested that he "return to his real home in Russia." When he got to Diomede he was going to signal the Russian Border Guards and they would bring him home. The helicopter took him to Diomede on an extra run. Once there, he just sat on the rocks near the helipad looking out at Russia, waiting for his escort. The Russians never came, of course, but the villagers did. They sensed his illness and quietly brought him food. He was still sitting there days later when Ted and I left Diomede.

Moses introduced us to Patrick Omiak, who would be our pilot for the crossing. Patrick, Moses and a young boy would go with us to Russia and guide us back. Patrick was an intelligent and sensitive man. Like most of his generation of Eskimos he hadn't finished high school. His self-education combined with some schooling at the Jesuits at Holy Cross Academy had produced a man with broad knowledge. Patrick and Moses were elders passing on the traditions of their people to following generations. A culture that took countless generations to hone is worth saving.

Patrick was 57 at the time, with the energy of a 25-year-old. We watched him as he created a piece of walrus ivory jewelry by hand, drilling a hole the traditional way by using a bone-and-thong bow wrapped around a handmade drill bit. One end of the drill bit bored the hole in the ivory while the other end was pressed against a fixture held in his teeth, applying pressure to the drill with his head as he sawed the bow back and forth to rotate the drill. He could have used an electric drill, but Patrick preferred the old way. It took time, but the result was a beautiful piece, truly handmade.

Patrick told me about a problem related to our swim and to the traditions of his people. There is very little greenery on Little Diomede, but for a few weeks every summer there is an explosive growth of grass on the island. When the grass ripens the women climb the narrow trails to gather it by hand. They haul heavy bundles back to the village, where it is preserved in barrels of seal oil. It is the only source of vegetation in their diet. In the old days, they gathered grass on Big Diomede until Russia closed the border. They longed to be free to go back and forth between their two islands, to be allowed to return to the other half of their home. But that was in the hands of Moscow, and they did not want to anger their Russian neighbors. They would need to be careful regarding Big Diomede if they wanted to regain access to their traditional lands. And that included our swim.

Patrick, Ted and I sat at the Omiak kitchen table to work out the details. There were two of us swimmers, but only one boat. It is very difficult for two swimmers to stay together in the sea. More important, we needed to have one of us in the boat in case the swimmer in the water got in trouble. Eskimos do not learn to swim because the water is always too cold. We would both be safer if we played lifeguard for each other. The question was, who would swim first? Ted suggested flipping a coin. Patrick flipped. I called it right and chose to swim first. After my swim we would go back to the Russian side for Ted's turn.

Before leaving California, Moses had sent me sketches of both islands, showing the best places to enter the water, with arrows detailing the movement of the water. The current was from the southwest, headed north-northeast at two and a half to three knots. We had a boat and a crew. Everything was ready. We looked at the water. The day was clear, the sun was bright and the water was calm. We might never again get as good a day. Moses said, "Get ready to swim." A few minutes later we were at the launch site by the helicopter pad. It took me ten minutes to get into my wetsuit and we were off, with most of the village looking on. It was circus day on Diomede. Moses was in the boat with his video camera at the ready.

We did <u>not</u> have permission to enter Russian waters. Because what we were doing was illegal, and because it could be harmful to the Eskimos' aspirations for free access to Big Diomede, I will switch over to "*What might have happened.*" What you will read below is neither a confession nor an admission of guilt on my part, nor that of Ted Epstein nor any of the Diomede Eskimos. You could put splinters under my fingernails and I wouldn't tell.

THE SWIM: "WHAT <u>MIGHT HAVE HAPPENED</u>"; ILLEGAL ENTRIES III, IV

Let's pretend that we are in a small boat on July 19, 1994, and have just crossed from Little Diomede to Big Diomede, Ratmanova. In the boat are the Eskimos, Ted and I. We have with us a case of fresh fruit, an extremely rare treat in the far north, especially for the border guards on Ratmanova. The three-mile crossing to the south end of Ratmanova was smooth and fast. As we moved south and west the current was just what we wanted. We measured the temperature of the water, 39° F on top, a little colder below the surface. As we neared

Big Diomede I put on my insulated hood, taking care not to bunch it up where the bottom flap goes inside the neck of the wetsuit. On went my booties and gloves, each tucked neatly into the sleeves and legs of the wetsuit. I tugged my sleeves up so there would be slack in the elbows and shoulders for swimming flexibility. Last to go on were my goggles. Ted smeared lanolin onto the exposed areas of my face. I was ready, and I was scared to death.

When we got to a small rock pile on the south side of Ratmanova, we looked up and waved to the border guard observing us from 1,000 feet above. We pointed to the carton of fruit and shouted, *"Malinky podarky iz vashy Amerikansky druzhay,"* Russian for "Small gifts from your American friends." The curious guard had an Asian face, possibly a Yakut. He would not shoot Americans for merely trespassing. That would create a big international incident, and he would surely be punished. He would climb down to the beach especially slowly and see me "fall" into the water as I tried to get back to the boat. Would he notice that I was wearing a wetsuit? Would he care? He might wave goodbye to us as he ravished the first banana he had ever tasted, watching the crazy *Amerikanitz* swim away. He might also choose not to notice when Ted did the same thing later. It could happen, couldn't it?

I said a silent prayer and rolled backwards into the water by the boat. Patrick, James and Ted looked down at me expectantly. Moses had his video camera rolling. The neoprene wetsuit, boots, hood and gloves were insulating me, but my bare face felt like it had been slammed into a block of chopped ice. Even knowing that the shock was coming didn't help because I could think of nothing but the intense pain in my face, like 100 ice-cream headaches.

Get moving, Joe! I gave the thumbs up sign and turned away from the boat, starting to swim with long, smooth crawl strokes. The wetsuit gave me flotation, keeping my body high in the water, lowering friction as I swam. A trickle of ice water made its way from my neck down into my chest. I could handle that. It would eventually warm up in the wetsuit. As I swam, the pain in my face was easing up. I was exhilarated, highly energized, on cloud nine, now that I was finally in the water after so many months of preparation.

I had a swim routine to keep my mind occupied: count ten breaths on the right side, then ten breaths on the left side. After 20 cycles of that I would do breaststroke for 100 strokes, and then 100 strokes on my back. My counting mantra kept me from thinking about the cold. It was a good formula, and it was working well, except that every time I changed body position for a different swim stroke the Ice Man would send a new trickle into my wetsuit someplace.

We were making good progress. My stroke rate was good, and the cold water did not feel as bad as I had anticipated. My cold water training and my wetsuit were paying off. Every tenth breath I raised my head to check my direction and to see where the current was moving me. We had started on a southerly course to get into the north-by-northwest current and kept on a southerly heading for 200 meters. Then we shifted to a southeast bearing, fixing on a large rock in the sea, south of Little Diomede. To swim in a straight line in the open sea, a swimmer has to sight on a target. My first target was that large rock. Then, as I was pushed north by the current, I sighted on a streak of snow in the cliff near the south end of the island. The snow streak was easy to see, white against the black cliff, long, high and vertical. I could make it out with a quick head raise without missing a stroke.

BIG COMPANY

I was about halfway across and had probably crossed the International Date Line into American waters. I had swum from "tomorrow," Tuesday, July 20, 1994 (Russian time) back to today, Monday, July 19, 1994, on the Alaskan side. My stroke was steady and my formula was working. I raised my left arm to stroke, brought it down and lowered my face into the water and felt a heaving motion below me, a pressure wave. Underneath me something very big and dark, spotted with barnacles, was crossing from my right to my left, six feet below me. I was astounded. My arms and legs kept stroking automatically, but I couldn't take my eyes off this thing that kept coming and coming. I was too fascinated to be afraid. It looked close enough for me to reach down and touch it. *This is as close as I will ever be to a whale. I want to hear it sing, to hum, to somehow communicate with me, please, please.* Then there was another pressure wave as it gracefully undulated its massive flukes and . . . it was gone.

The entire thing took only a few seconds, very long seconds. I was so completely captivated by what was below me that I forgot to breathe. I raised my head for air and turned to the boat, 20 yards away. They were gabbing and had missed it completely. Some observers! Moses' video camera was dangling by his side. My very own whale visit and nobody knew about it but me! There was a warm sensation where I had peed in my wetsuit.

As I got closer to Little Diomede I noted that the island was moving fast to my right, and that my favorite snow patch was now far to the right. With the current rushing me past the island, there was no single reference point that I could fix on to hold a steady course. I decided use the sun for direction. It was about 30 degrees above the horizon and at two o'clock to my course. If I kept breathing on my right side I could fix my course on the sun and not worry about any other target. I would stay on that line until I hit the island.

I did a personal inventory. Did I have any physical problems, aches or pains? Nothing out of the ordinary. My shoulders were aching, but that was normal. My face didn't hurt much any more. Was my gear performing well? Except for the trickles of icy water, flawlessly. Was I getting hypothermic? No, I was a bit cold, but fine. Was I fatigued? I was tiring, but less than I had expected, and I was almost through with my swim. Everything was going better than planned. For the first time, I felt confident that I would make it.

After an hour and two minutes I pulled myself through swaying kelp and squeezed between two large boulders at the base of a cliff a few hundred yards south of the village. We were around a bend and out of sight of Inalik, but I knew that several pairs of binoculars had followed my swim. I climbed unsteadily onto a rock, turned to the boat, raised my arms in triumph, and we all gave a victory whoop. My swim was over. It had not been the ferocious monster that I had feared.

It was a very significant link in my around-the-world journey. I had made it all the way back to Alaska. I felt 50 pounds lighter, despite the 20 pounds I had gained for the swim.

TED SWIMS FROM RUSSIA

I climbed into the boat for the short trip to Inalik. Now it was Ted's turn. He seemed uncomfortable, and he said that he had been chilly sitting in the boat, even in his wetsuit. Ted had not put on much body fat in preparation for his swim. His training at home, far from the sea, had been very different from mine. Ted was not a fast swimmer, but he had great endurance. The previous year he had completed a 40-kilometer swim in Mexico. In Siberia he had shown that he could run all day. Now we would see if King Neptune would accept his training effort as an acceptable tribute of respect for the sea.

Ted took his time getting ready. When we finally left the village he was wearing a layer of lanolin, a layer of plastic film, a wetsuit, another layer of film and a second wetsuit. He carried three pairs of goggles, a nose clip and a snorkel. He was wearing two hoods, boots, gloves and an added piece of insulation around his neck. He also had a 15-foot tether, which, because of his poor eyesight, he wanted tied to the boat with the other end attached to his right leg. The Eskimo kids on the beach followed his every move.

We went back across the International Date Line to "tomorrow." Conditions were still great. That day, by the way, the temperature in Nome reached a record 79 degrees, warmer than Los Angeles. When Ted dropped into the current his tether got snarled up. He waited while we untangled it. When we got it free, it became wrapped around his legs. The tether was a bad idea. I unfastened it and chucked the damned thing. He swam much better without it.

Ted was having trouble with his snorkel and his goggles. The waves were getting into his snorkel, rendering it useless. His goggles kept fogging up. Finally, he gave us his snorkel and cleaned his goggles. From then on he swam like a fish. Ted had a problem holding a straight line, partly because of his vision and partly because, as a pool-swimmer, he had not developed open water navigating skills. (We had neglected to tell the Eskimos to paint a line on the bottom of the ocean for us.) To keep him on course we had to shout instructions to him, "More to the right . . . a little to the left." We wanted with all our hearts for him to make it, and we took every stroke with him.

And Ted kept plugging away until he reached shore north of the village, near the north end of the island. If he had been in that northerly current much longer he might have missed the island altogether: next stop, the North Pole. He was bone-weary, chilled, and his calves and thighs were cramping. We were elated and proud of Ted. His victory was a win for all of us. His swim took over two hours, about as long as Lynne Cox had taken in the other direction.

Ted's swim was more difficult because of a lack of specificity in his preparation, and he might have benefited by adding some bulk to

210

his slim runner's frame. The important thing is that he made it. Few have even tried. (Mimi Hughes from Tennessee later swam the other way in July of 1997 in a wetsuit. I believe that she, Lynne Cox, Ted and I are the only ones ever to have attempted Diomede swims.)

If anyone asks you, that is what might have happened that day. Tell them that you do not know if we entered Russia illegally, then crossed the border into the USA illegally. Say that you cannot confirm or deny that a small team of unarmed Americans made an amphibious invasion of Russia that day. Tell them that you heard that there is only one copy of the video, and it is not for sale. Offer them a banana.

(Lest there be any doubt, Ted and I *did* swim from Russia to Alaska that day.)

DRUMS IN THE ARCTIC: AN INVITATION TO THE BALL

After the swims Evelyn Omiak whipped up a great dinner for us: baked chicken, mashed potatoes, vegetables, fresh baked bread, cookies and coffee. You can bet that we were hungry, and this meal went down like a kid down a water slide. It is extraordinary when you consider what Evelyn had to do to round up the food 1,000 miles from the nearest supermarket and 25 miles from the mainland.

The Omiak house is higher up the slope than most, towards the south end of the village. Moses came up to the Omiak house to invite us to a celebration in the Big Room. The Big Room is large enough for all the villagers to gather, located down the hill from the Omiak's home and across the village. Before going down, Ted borrowed the Omiak's telephone to call home with the good news. His wife relayed it to the Associated Press, and it made the newspapers from Anchorage to Key West, *"Two men swim from Russia to Alaska."* We were having our 15 minutes of fame.

Moses had told us that the village would perform Eskimo traditional celebration dances in our honor. "Come to the Big Room in an hour." I thought about the *programmas* in Russia and Central Asia, but this was truly an honor. Ted was not feeling well and needed to rest. On the narrow trail that took us to the Big Room I had to get past a large, loud husky fiercely defending his turf. He strained at his leash, looking very mean. But he was tethered more tightly than Ted had been. Giving him wide berth, I remembered that these animals were known to face down polar bears, often with the bear turning tail. Very few of these magnificent dogs remained in rural Alaska; they were being replaced by snowmobiles.

At one end of the Big Room Moses, Patrick and another elder sat cross-legged on the floor. In front of them were thin, flat drums, two feet in diameter. The circular frame was wood, and the surface was made from the stomach of a female walrus. The wooden drumsticks were three feet long. A handle attached to the drumhead gave it the shape of a large frying pan.

The music started. Drumsticks slapped the surface, hitting both rims and the membrane. The harder the slap, the louder the membrane resounded. By striking the membrane in different places they could make a range of tones, and striking the wooden rim made a slapping sound. The rhythm changed with the activity being described in the story dance, each finishing with a crescendo.

There were three groups of dancers. First to perform were the young women and girls. Their style was similar to a hula, with graceful hand gestures and arm movements and lower body swaying, staying in one place. They told ancient tales of family and love. Then the young men danced with ferocity, punctuated with violent foot stamping, tales of the hunt and battles with long-ago enemies. Some of the dances involved both the men and the women, dancing separately to the same music, doing very different things. The third group consisted of the mature women of the village, who performed in the sitting position with great grace and dignity. Throughout the dances the drummers chanted in deep, throaty voices, sometimes soft, sometimes loud, befitting the mood of the story.

We went to bed tired and happy. Tall Ted got the short bed, and I put my sleeping bag on the floor. Bandana wrapped around my eyes to block out the bright midnight sun, I slept satisfied. In the morning Evelyn Omiak rustled up pancakes and murres' eggs. Young Pat had gathered the eggs that morning. Speckled blue green, they were four inches long. Pat told me that there might be a chick inside, saying that would be even better. Lucky for me and for the chick, it was just a large, green, fishy-tasting egg.

After breakfast I hiked along the steep trail to the north end of the island. The rugged trail cut in and out along the rocky cliffs, about 50 stories above the sea. Every step of the way I came upon nesting auklets and murres, gurgling and cooing, staring at me. They were all around me and leaped from the cliff only when I got too close. Swarms of them would take off, clumsily jumping out to the sea en mass, an unruly gang creating a din as they reluctantly gave up their perches. I would walk another few steps and another gang would spring away.

I worked my way along the narrow path to the northern tip of the island, being careful in places where the cliff fell hundreds of feet straight down. To my right I could see Cape Wales, Alaska, USA. To my left was Cape Dezhnev, Chukotka, Russia. They were about 50 miles apart, and they looked pretty much the same to me. They were identical in climate, similar in topography and in isolation, and the people were related. The difference was purely political. People in Moscow and Washington had said, "We on this side of the line are different from you. Stay off our side." The Eskimos, suddenly split up into Russians and Americans, know that the differences are artificial and arbitrary. Because of the border they have been deprived of traditional hunting grounds, freedom of movement, families and land.

If compassion and logic ruled, this place would belong to them, not to Moscow or Washington.

Ted The Responsible was listening to the radio. There was a weather system coming our way that might strand us on Diomede. Heavy winds and fog were due the next day. Ted approached every boat owner on the island to take us to Cape Wales, to no avail. Evelyn made supper for us, but Ted was not up for it. He was focused on getting us back to Wales.

After dinner Ted was cheerful. He had found a man who would take us to the mainland. We would leave in two hours and would arrive in Wales about one in the morning. We were packed and ready to go, so Moses invited me to come to the Big Room for the weekly Bingo Game while we waited. Ted stayed with the umiak as the owner readied it for the voyage.

SIMPLE PLEASURES

At least 50 people showed up for the bingo game, catching up on the latest scuttlebutt, young people and old. Everyone was having fun, making conversation, not taking the low stakes game seriously, with the expected shouts of joy from the winners and groans from the rest. I mentioned to a young man seated next to me that I had seen no liquor in Diomede or in Wales. He said with pride that it was a matter of local choice, and that most of the villages had opted for a policy of no alcohol at all, with heavy penalties for violators. There had been serious problems in the past, he said. They confronted the problem head on and solved it. I didn't see one drunk, derelict or homeless Eskimo in Wales or Diomede. There were plenty in Anchorage and Fairbanks, where local option encourages the sale of booze.

After bingo I joined Ted at the boat. It was late, but there was still plenty of light. The boat was ready. We bade goodbye to Moses and Patrick, thanking them for making this unique adventure possible. As we left, Patrick handed me the piece of antique walrus ivory that he had been working on. It was three inches by one inch, flat and thin, with a scrimshaw design he had made for me. Etched in black against the yellowed ancient ivory were drawings of Big Diomede on the left, Little Diomede on the right, spanned by the large ball of the setting sun. Above the islands were a Russian flag and an American flag. Below the islands was the sea, and in the sea was a dotted line going from the south end of Big Diomede to the village of Inalik—our swim route. That piece of ivory will always be one of my most treasured possessions.

A VIOLENT TRIP TO CAPE WALES

The boat taking us to Wales was a modern version of a traditional Eskimo umiak, a large, open boat with high gunwales, very stable. It was a broad-beamed boat that rode high in the water. But instead of being made from walrus hides, it was aluminum. As we started, the water between the Diomedes was quiet, but the wind was building in the north. Using the wind and a sheet of plastic for a pusher sail, our pilot took us south past the cliffs with the wind at our back. We sailed around the bottom of Little Diomede and turned east into her southern lee, where the wind and sea were calm. Not for long.

As we came out of the wind shadow of the island, we knew that this was not going to be a picnic. The north wind was blowing up five-foot rollers, timed at about every 15 seconds or so, coming at our port side as we moved east. The boat rolled with every wave, taking water on the port side. We bailed as fast as we could. David, our pilot, got out more plastic sheeting, and we rigged it up with sticks reaching two feet above the port gunwale to keep the sea out. It was marginally effective, but we had to keep bailing. The north wind on the plastic sheets was pushing the boat to starboard, making it necessary to crab to the north. To keep her from heeling we kept our weight on the port side. We were cold and wet, but too preoccupied to worry about being cast into the sea.

We beached the boat at Cape Wales at four in the morning, very cold, very wet and very tired. We climbed into the shallow, icy water, shoes and trousers thoroughly soaked, and dragged the boat across the shingle out of the reach of the waves.

We had no place to go. We wandered around and found that the door to the washateria was open. We dragged ourselves in, took 25-cent hot showers, stripped down, put our wet things in the dryer and bedded down underneath the clothes-folding tables. We were asleep in the blink of an eye. It didn't last long. At seven a.m. Uncle Pete showed up and rousted us from his washateria. I felt like a derelict being chased from a park bench by the cops.

It was time to move on anyway. Ted had work waiting for him back home, and I had to make arrangements to continue the rest of my journey. We located a bush plane and boogied.

I spent a lot of time practicing cross-country skiing for a trip that never happened.

Joe trained all winter at Aquatic Park in San Francisco – sometimes in a thick wetsuit and often without it.

Downtown Cape Wales

Wet Eskimo girl wading in cold Bering Strait in Cape Wales

Uncle Pete's luxury cabin

Coming in by helicopter, the north end of Little Diomede in the foreground, Big Diomede in the background, the current lines are visible.

The village in Little Diomede, seen from the helicopter

An umiak under construction on Little Diomede

Danny and Patrick Omiak and Moses Milligrock on his radio. Little Diomede in background.

Swimming toward Little Diomede

It was about here that I met my whale. Note the swell.

Touching the shore at Little Diomede

Elders Patrick, Moses and Peter supply the music.

Kids dancing in the big room.

CHAPTER XIII

THE IDITAROD TRAIL

Were you ever out in the Great Alone, when the moon was awful clear,
And the icy mountains hemmed you in with a silence you could almost
hear;
With only the sound of a timber wolf . . . ."
— Robert Service

THE HOWLING

I thought of Robert Service's words as the chorus of howls built up from that first very soft yip, adding voices one by one, until it reached a full-throated vocalization of the entire pack, some thirty beasts calling out in a primeval unison. It soared to the moon as one voice, but I could clearly make out each individual animal. Every night they would send up this howl around midnight, lasting no more than a few minutes. Then, complete stillness, the profound Arctic silence of being far away from the comforts of family, home and friends.

Every night I woke to that howling, excited at the sound of it, thankful for being awakened by it, half wanting to join them in their spontaneous *a capella* paeon to creation. The haunting sound of a howling pack pierces straight into your guts. It connects you with something you can sense but can't even begin to verbalize, a restlessness deep, deep inside.

But these weren't wolves howling. They were our sled dogs, four teams of them, the closest thing to wolves, and they were staked just outside our tiny BLM cabin on the Iditarod Trail. We were cozy in our winter sleeping bags inside the hut, but it was 30 degrees below outside where the dogs were.

THE FAR, FAR WEST

Flying west from Anchorage had given me a good look at western Alaska. Not far from Anchorage were hundreds of frozen ponds, their surface a different white from the surrounding snow. Further west came a range of rough, craggy mountains, jammed against one another, sharp black knife-edges jutting steeply upwards, dumping deep snow into the valleys below.

The sun never gets high in the Arctic winter, and sunsets can last for hours. This sunset hogged most of the horizon. To the left it started as a thin, gray-blue ribbon, working slowly into violet, blended to rose, and at the very center a screaming fiery red, topped by strata of even more intense red, yellow, yellow green, and finally at the top softening into baby blue below the black sky. To the right the spectrum reversed itself back to the same powdery gray blue.

As the 707 moved further west, the mountains fell away to flatlands cut up by solid rivers, then another splattering of frozen ponds. More mountains, these looking as though Mother Nature had run a rake from west to east, with wide open wind tunnels between, followed by the nursery of the brawling wind, the Bering Sea, wearing its own coat of ice below us near the shore. Where the land runs gently to the frozen sea, both land and sea are coated with a thin layer of snow. From 30,000 feet it is difficult to know where the sea ends and the land begins, except for the many rat-tail creeks, darker and pointing to the sea. Just offshore on the open ice of the Bering Sea were transient contours you will never see on a map, jumbles of ice piled high, erected by wind, tides and currents. In between were openings in the ice that looked like rivers. My heart was in my mouth as I contemplated having to face those open leads in the days to come. Then I strained, pressing my forehead against the cold, plastic window, trying hard to see something else. Was one of those slightly off-color ice mounds a polar bear? Something in my psyche has always given me the feeling that I might one day meet my demise in the company of a large bear, and it could very well happen on the ice.

The plane touched down in frigid Nome. I, with my California tan and inadequate parka, stepped out, looking for a man named Jerry Austin.

This leg of my journey would carry me hundreds of miles east along the Iditarod Trail from Nome, on the Bering Sea, to Kaltag, where the Iditarod Trail crosses the Yukon River. There were two reasons why I was doing this leg of my journey by dog sled. Because western Alaska is largely marshy, boot-sucking, gooey muskeg in the summer, it is impossible to cross by bicycle or on foot when the weather is good and the permafrost is mushy. Listening to my boots making a *schluuurping* sound as I made very slow headway did not sound like fun. Then there is the "Alaskan Air Force," mosquitoes like helicopter gun ships and deer flies that maneuver like an F15 and hit hard and fast. If I must donate pints of my precious red body fluid, my choice is to give it to the Red Cross.

The alternative to traversing western Alaska in summer is traversing it in winter. It can be done on cross-country skis or by dog sled. A dog sled trip would take less time than skiing, and there is a well-traveled route, the Iditarod Trail.

AN EPIDEMIC

In the winter of 1925 a diphtheria epidemic grabbed hold of western Alaska. People in Nome were dying, and it was getting worse. The nearest diphtheria serum was 1,000 miles to the east, and it was impossible to get it to Nome by air or sea. A heroic Finnish-American named Leonhard Seppala organized a relay of dog mushers to carry the serum to Nome, a hazardous journey of over 1,000 miles. They struggled through deep snow, rugged backcountry, over mountains, past wolves and bears, and across a frozen arm of the Bering Sea in

Arctic temperatures, arriving in Nome in time to save many lives. Their route came to be known as the Iditarod Trail.

In 1973 Joe Redington, Sr., organized a dog sled race along the Iditarod Trail to honor these mushers, following their route 1,049 miles to Nome. The winner took 20 days, averaging 50 miles a day. The Iditarod race has become a major event in Alaska. Lightweight sleds and polymeric clothing have introduced a high-tech element. Today's dogs are bred for speed and endurance from generations of successful Iditarod dogs. The fastest teams cover 100 miles a day, with the winner earning $50,000, plus sponsorships and appearances.

But the fact that the race has gone big time cannot change the nature of the route itself, the very essence of the Alaskan bush: deep snow, a ferocious and unpredictable north wind, extreme cold and miles of unstable sea ice. You might meet a belligerent moose, a pack of hungry wolves, a grizzly looking for breakfast, or a polar bear that has wandered south on the ice. The Iditarod, the "Last Great Race," is a mirror of old Alaska. And nothing will stop the real Alaskans, the full-bearded, rugged backcountry men in their woolen long-johns, from jumping in every year to give the Iditarod, their race, their very best. It is in their nature to do so.

AN IDITAROD LEGEND

One of those rock-hard men is Jerry Austin, an Iditarod legend. Jerry grew up in Seattle and went to Alaska after college. He found hard work, a good woman and a life in the remote village of Saint Michael, where the Yukon River spills into the Bering Sea. Jerry and Clara, a Yupik Eskimo, are now grandparents. When the sea ice recedes in the summer, they barge life-sustaining fuel oil to the coastal communities in western Alaska, and they operate a fish camp.

In 1976 Jerry decided to give the Iditarod Trail Dog Sled Race a try and came back 13 times to get it right, often finishing in the top ten. He has retired from racing, but the Iditarod still owns a hunk of him. Clara is scholarly-looking, like a librarian, while Jerry looks like a bearded wag. He may look kind of average, but there is a heap of fire in his belly. A couple of years ago he got the idea that there might be folks who would like to try mushing on the Iditarod Trail, people who couldn't make a full commitment of time and resources. He was right, and I was one of those people, and that is how I came to be in Nome in the winter of 1997. I was there to travel in the reverse direction on the Iditarod Trail, from Nome to Kaltag after the racers finished in Nome, moving me closer to my goal, Fairbanks.

Jerry makes it easy for you. He supplies everything from a team of seven top-notch, Iditarod-trained sled dogs to the Arctic clothing you will need. He arranges places to stay and food to eat. There is no hotel or restaurant en route, so finding a bed and grub is critical. Even more critical is a competent Alaskan trail guide. Jerry does that job himself. It is one thing for an experienced outdoorsman to take care of himself in the wilderness, but it is much more challenging to break in greenhorns. Jerry relishes the challenge. With all he does, you still have to drive the sled and team yourself.

Dog mushing was not in my bag of tricks. I had heard about the Iditarod Trail, always spoken of in the most respectful tones, and I wanted to try it. Now here we were, four sleds and a snowmobile, in the Great Alone, many miles from anything. We had set out on the trail from Nome the day after the Iditarod Race awards banquet, having listened to all 45 finishers give thank-you speeches with appropriately feigned humility.

The high point of the awards banquet was sitting next to 91-year-old Norman Vaughn, who had gone with Admiral Byrd to the South Pole three quarters of a century before. Byrd named Mount Vaughn in the Antarctic for Norman, who performed the amazing feat of climbing that mountain at 80. During World War II he made daring rescues of flyers stranded in the Arctic. In 1943 President Roosevelt summoned him from his home in Massachusetts. A bomber had crash-landed in a remote part of Greenland, and the entire crew was in danger. What also concerned the military was the fact that the bomber was carrying our top-secret experimental radar. If the Germans reached it first, it would be a major intelligence disaster. Vaughn and his crew, using teams of Greenland huskies, rescued every member of the flight crew before the Germans arrived.

Before setting out on the trail, Jerry invited me to the wedding of his daughter Dena to Glenn Shears. They had grown up together in Saint Michael, Alaska. Dena was a student at the University of Alaska, Fairbanks. Glenn was 6' 3" inches tall, strong and quick-witted, with a ready smile. Their kids will have good genes. The wedding was a modest affair with family and a few friends in a Nome apartment. One of the people at the wedding was Larry Weas. We looked at each other for a while wondering where we had met. We had last seen each other at Fort Devens, Massachusetts, in the US Army in 1955, and this was 1997. In 1955 we were both younger than today's bride and groom, and here we were 42 years later in Nome, Alaska. After the wedding Dena went home and Glenn packed his bags. He was joining us on the trail.

MUSHING UNIVERSITY

After dinner Jerry took us outside of Nome to a big field where he had his dogs stashed. He gave us a talk on mushology before we boarded the sleds. He told us there were only four things to learn.

First, the dogs' total vocabulary consists of four words. Anything beyond those words will confuse the dogs. *"Hike"* means "Go." *"Gee"* means "Go right." *"Haw"* means "Go left." And *"Whoa"* means just that, sometimes shouted in panic at full volume. Jerry stressed that the dogs were not linguists and that they know only those four words of people-talk. I would relearn that lesson soon enough.

The second thing we had to learn is where we would spend the day, all day, every day. There are two runners under the sled. They extend 18" back from the carriage of the sled. The runners are two inches wide and two feet apart. We would have to stand all day on those two runners, one foot on each 18" x 2" runner. For variety we might step on the brake, which was between the runners. Our hands, at least one of them, must *always* clutch the handlebar in front of us at waist level.

The third thing Jerry said was that we must *never* fall off the sled. Sled dogs love to run, and running is a lot easier without my 200 pounds of blubber and boots. It can get very lonely on the trail when your dogs are gone. Jerry stressed that if we did somehow manage to fall off the runners, we were to hang onto that handlebar for dear life while being dragged across the tundra screaming "WHOOOOOA!" at maximum decibels in a tone that would remind the dogs about who was supposed to be in command.

Related to thing three was thing four. Each sled is equipped with two heavy steel hooks that function as anchors. When the sled is stopped for any reason, stomp the anchors deep into the snow to keep the dogs from running off. If not anchored, the team will be gone in very short order. That, too, we would have demonstrated under battlefield conditions.

My half hour of mushing training completed, I was ready for the trail. On a bright and sunny morning we set out from Nome, the mercury trying unsuccessfully to reach −10° F. The goal for the first day was a tiny wilderness cabin 50 miles east. This was the day I learned that you do not *drive* a team of sled dogs, you *accompany* them, and you communicate with them only through the lead dog, a large, aggressive, intelligent alpha male with a will of his own. He is in charge; he listens to your commands, makes sure that the other dogs are working together, and sets the direction and pace. My lead dog, Diamond, knew exactly what to do and where to go. Diamond was a professional. This is what he did for a living. My team (I should say *Diamond's* team) covered the 50 miles in five hours, at ten miles an hour that first day. That is faster than the top human marathon runners. And the dogs were pulling a load of 350 pounds.

Each dog has a different job to do. The lead dogs set the direction and speed. They get an assist doing that from the second pair, the "swing dogs," who are ready to react fast enough to turn the following dogs as Diamond moves left or right. The most hazardous job on a team is that of the "wheel dog." My wheel dog was Rebar, a big beast, strong as steel, hitched up immediately in front of the sled. The other dogs were tied one behind another, on alternate sides. Rebar was last, right up against a 350-pound payload. Where his butt went, the sled had to follow. I was on the other side of the handlebars behind Rebar.

It didn't take long for the competence of the team to calm me. As I gained confidence in our ability to work as a team, I began to relax and enjoy the situation and to put my trust in the dogs. Diamond always knew exactly where to go. Harnessed next to and behind Diamond was the second lead dog, a bitch named June. Paired behind the lead dogs were Whitey and Knik, two strong three year olds, then Flash running without a partner, and at the back were Foxie and Rebar.

ON THE TRAIL

Our first few days out of Nome on the Iditarod Trail took us east, sometimes on land on the southern shore of the Seward Peninsula, sometimes out on the ice parallel to the shore. The people who live along this coast are Yupik Eskimos. Further north are Inupiaq Eskimos, and in the interior of Alaska are Athabaskan Indians. The three groups live in different areas, so interaction is minimal in this huge and sparsely populated land. As we moved along the coast, we spent our nights with Yupik families. In White Mountain we stayed with the Grays: B.J., Tom and their three children Hannah, fifteen; Travis, eleven; and Hunter, nine. We saw a photo of a 600-pound grizzly that Travis killed when he was nine. They fed us a fine meal, gave us warm beds, and the use of their outdoor hot tub: water temperature 100° F, air temperature – 43° F.

Earlier in the day, as we headed into White Mountain, all four teams took a wrong turn up the Fish River and we had to double back on a narrow trail. The dogs were tired, confused and upset. A two-team melee broke out as one team passed too close to another going in opposite directions. That meant 14 dogs were going at each other, snarling, barking and biting, half a ton of thrashing muscle entangled. It was frightening as we struggled to separate the two teams. Luckily, no dog was injured, nor were we. It is important to keep the teams separated from each other because as soon as they get within lunging range, a lethal gang war will erupt.

These dogs are not pets; they are semi-wild animals that will not shrink from tearing each other to pieces. Order and status are of great importance to them. When hitching them up, it is critical not to pair a male next to another male, nor a female beside another female. They will fight, and the fights are very serious. When staking them down for the night the same is true: no dogs of the same gender are placed next to each other. The chains are about six feet long, so lots of ground is needed for a big team. Even the order in which they are hitched to the sled in the morning is important. The lead dog must be hitched to the sled before the rest of the animals, in his proper place, then working backwards, dog by dog to the wheel dog. When unhitching at the end of the day, it is done in reverse order. The lead dog wants to be the first into the harness and the last one out of it. If you do not follow protocol, they will let you know.

Sled dogs have only two states of being. Either they are running or they are tied down. They prefer running. After their morning meal, as soon as they see the hitches being readied, they bark excitedly. They want to *go*, and once they get going, they do not want to stop. They will run all day long with only a short snack break. During that 15-minute break they will get a half-pound chunk of solid frozen salmon, bones and all. They wolf that fishy ice cube down and are raring to go again. These lean, mean running machines eat two full hot meals a day, in the morning and again in the evening. Each meal consists of a thick stew of fatty lamb pieces and fish. They consume 3,500 calories a day, 50% more than an active adult human. They get no water except in the stew. They seem never to drink at all, until you catch on to their secret. It puzzled me for a while as I watched one dog after another biting at the snow as they ran along. If we passed close to a snow bank, that was what they bit; otherwise chunks of snow or ice were snatched from the ground at ten miles an hour.

I was intrigued by the dogs' insensitivity towards one another when toilet time came around. When that happened, and it happened often, the affected dog just got dragged along by the rest of the team, squatting all the way, never complaining, but pooping as fast as possible. June, our female lead dog, seemed to squat and get dragged a lot.

Our human diet on the trail closely followed the basic Alaska food pyramid: fat, sugar, grease, meat, butter, salt and alcohol. We packed in a lot of bacon, sausage, steaks, caribou burgers, salmon, desserts, candy and trail mix, and we washed it all down with whiskey in the evening. It wasn't what I would eat at home, but then again we never see 40 below at home. We ate only *after* we had fed the dogs.

Getting started in the morning after feeding the dogs took some time. After breakfast we took care of our toilet needs before getting bundled up. It takes a long time to get undressed and dressed again with all the layers and zippers, so you want to avoid doing that on the trail. You do not eat between breakfast and dinner except for the trail mix in your pocket, not easy to get at wearing both gloves and over-mittens, jouncing along at ten miles an hour. Unlike the dogs, we had to have water, and we each carried a thermos. It would be scalding hot in the morning and reach a drinkable temperature after a couple of hours.

The sleds are usually spaced far apart, and it can be lonely on the trail. I am talkative. I like to chat, and I like to sing. One bright morning I was feeling really good, so I thought that I might entertain the entire Arctic world with my rendition of *Clementine*. Almost immediately the dogs screeched to a complete halt. Diamond cocked his big, black head back at me and gave me a stern look that said very clearly, "What the heck is *going on* back there?" Then I remembered: they knew only four words, and *cavern* and *canyon* were not among them. Chastened by Diamond, from that moment on I would use only the agreed upon four words, and only when the situation called for it.

LEARNING TO FLY

When the trail is smooth and flat you can almost take a nap, put in cruise control, and let the dogs take over, but it was definitely not like that leaving White Mountain. After an easy climb of about 1,000 feet, we crested the hill and started down the other side. Norton Sound was in front of us and to the right 1,000 feet below. The trail shot down the mountain with dwarf willows on both sides, making rapid switchbacks with five-foot moguls every few yards. The dogs were running full bore. I was getting whip-cracked left and right, bounced up and down and going airborne over the moguls, all at the same time while careering down the mountain. This was a real test for me. What you *must* do when descending a steep hill is slam on the brake, a steel bar between the runners, by jamming it into the snow with your entire weight to slow the sled down. Otherwise the sled will overtake and run over the dogs. The braking is right when there is enough tension on the traces so the dogs can pull lightly and string out.

Rebar was worried. So was I. Hanging on to the handlebar for dear life with both hands, my left foot light on the runner, my right foot bearing my full mass on the brake, I kept my knees bent, my eyes frantically darting around. Snow thrown up into my face made it hard to see. Shifting my weight into each switchback, knees flexed to cushion the slamming jolt that followed each mogul, and keeping pressure on the brake to keep the traces taut, the bottom was approaching very fast. All at once the contours of that bottom became all too clear. It was a narrow creek bed with a bank that dropped 20 feet straight down to a frozen creek at the bottom.

The dogs were going hell bent for leather, and I couldn't stop them. I would probably kill half of the dogs if I ditched, and I would get busted up pretty badly myself. The last few yards before the bank I put everything I had onto the brake, bent my knees deep, ready to take air as we flew over the rim. Down the bank we plunged, the trailing ends of the runners slicing into the face of the bank as we dropped. SLAM! The sled banged onto solid ice at the bottom. The jolt hammered every joint in my body. It was a miracle that the sled stayed upright, I stayed on, and nothing broke. In less than a second the dogs were across the ice and clawing their way up the steep bank on the other side. I knew what I had to do and jumped off the sled to push from behind, relieving them of hauling my own weight up the slope, and gave them a push when it was most needed. I never let loose my death grip on the handlebars, having no desire to climb up that hill alone. When we reached a flat place on top Diamond cocked his head back at me and gave me a look that said, "Welcome to the team, tenderfoot."

At times Diamond exhibited a snotty, know-it-all attitude, like a few teenagers I have known. Yes, he was competent, and, yes, he was indispensable. The problem is that he knew it, and he knew that I knew it. There were times when he took on the mindset of a union shop steward, ready to make all the unreasonable demands he could. He communicated his feelings by head position, facial expression, body language and sometimes with his voice, making himself quite clear without words. Tearing down that hill outside White Mountain, he had tested me.

There is purity on the tundra, where everything is reduced to raw basics. There is no sound but the constant *shooosh* of the sled runners as they glide along the surface, the sound varying with the consistency of the snow: soft snow, corn snow, ice or packed snow. Sometimes it sounds like a distant jet plane echoing off walls that aren't there, sometimes like a leak in an inner tube. The team made no sound at all when running, plugging along in silence hour after hour, with not even a grunt.

There are no smells. Everything is under a frozen blanket of snow. The only smell is from our own team, but we are moving fast, leaving it behind us. There is little color but white, which in varying shades and intensities covers almost everything. What occasionally pierces through the snow, like a wind-scoured rock or a willow, is dark, and that only accentuates the pervasive whiteness. The soft, warm colors of the dogs are a relief, but the garish colors of our modern clothing shock the eye.

On the sixth day, still running east along the southern shore of the Seward Peninsula, we were hit by a fierce wind from the north. It had not been extremely cold until then, but on this day the wind clobbered us like an 18-wheeler, rising to gale force as the temperature plunged, with a wind chill of –50° F. We had taken a necessary rest day in Elim in the hut of an Athabaskan hunter named Tommy Kourshekeff. Today we were on the frozen sea, headed for Koyuk, and the wind was punishing us for taking a day off. Because it was blowing from the left, it was shoving the sled to the right, making life hell for the team, and for Rebar in particular. The dogs' protective fur was being parted by the wind, brutally chilling their left flanks.

Ice picks of chilling air found tiny openings in my protective clothing, too. They pierced where the three or four last teeth of a zipper that had not been done all the way up. They worked into the opening between my balaclava and my parka hood and pulled so hard that I had to grip the left side of the hood in my teeth to keep it on my head. Because of the constant wind, my entire left side had become much colder than my right. My left cheek, where the draft worked around my goggles, lost sensation, and my left ear was tingly under the hood and balaclava. This was not just bitter cold; it was agony.

As we rounded a headland I thought we must be close to the day's finish. No such luck. In front of us the sea bent far to the north. We changed our heading from across the wind to facing directly into it. The dogs were suffering. The protection of that thick coat of fur loses effectiveness in a strong wind. On days like this they want to dig a hole in the snow and wait out the weather. The teams put their heads down and squeezed closer as they pulled into the wind. Diamond closed the distance between our team and the pack in front of us so he could tuck into their lee. We were four yards behind them now instead of the usual 100 yards. Very slowly, as the distant hills took form in front of us, so did the town. Eventually there came the shape of a large building, then a fuel tank on a hill, and finally homes. The wind fell off suddenly as we entered the wind shadow of the hill in front of us. It was like being transported to Hawaii.

We ran up the river into this remote Yupik village to the greetings of the local dogs: "Welcome to Koyuk. Now leave." The dogs in all of the villages we visited were territorial, and this was no different. In Koyuk we stayed with the Hannon family in a log home that they had built for themselves. When I say that they built the house, that means that they went 20 miles up-river, found a stand of trees, felled them, rafted them down the river to Koyuk, set up a sawmill, and built the house. Bob, a large man, guides hunting trips, and over the years his clients have bagged three of the ten largest grizzly bears ever taken anywhere, including the biggest in the record books. I no longer hunt and I do not own a gun, but his stories could have kept me up all night. But tomorrow was a big day. We were going to venture far from land onto the frozen sea, crossing Norton Sound to the village of Shaktoolik, the most dangerous section of the Iditarod Trail.

A PRINCESS

Our party consisted of four dog teams and a snowmobile driven by Jerry's new son-in-law, Glenn. Jerry drove the lead team and I was second. The other two were a husband and wife from the Midwest, the Princess and her consort. They should never have been on this trip. From the first day on the trail, nothing was good enough for them. The food was not up to their standards: she wanted to be served vegetarian cuisine. The pit toilets at the Bureau of Land Management huts were too smelly, so they chose to relieve themselves wherever it was convenient. The sleeping accommodations offered by our hosts were not up their Ritz quality levels. They would lose or misplace things and suggest that they were being robbed. Worst of all, neither of them seemed to give a damn about the dogs in their charge. When it came time to hitch, unhitch or feed the dogs, they did a disappearing act. They were not having fun, their egos were not being massaged, and they did not to want to be there. If there had been a way out of there, I would gladly have paid the bus fare to be rid of them.

One day, after losing control of her team several times, the Princess had a screaming fit in the middle of nowhere, announcing that she would not go another step. Glenn, the gentle giant, asked her if she wanted him to leave the dogs with her, or did she wish to die alone? After half an hour of hysterics, she came around. Her husband was not much better. Too often he let the team run off the track, once falling so far behind that we had to send a posse back for him. Once, he left his hitched-up team alone with no anchors while he took a stroll. The dogs took the hint and left. It took Jerry and Glenn an hour to round them up. They are not bad people, but they did not belong on a wilderness trip, expecting to be waited on hand and foot. If you want pampering, try Club Med.

CROSSING THE FROZEN SEA

From Koyuk to Shaktoolik it's about 50 miles across the frozen sea. In March the sea ice is about five feet thick, but the constant up and down movement of the tides, the circulation of the currents, and the relentless push of the north wind combine to fracture the ice. It piles up high, putting enormous weight on the surface, crazing it like dried mud, with open water in between. I could never tell if the ice was strong enough to support our weight, but Diamond could. Running along, his sixth sense told him to veer a bit to the left or the right to avoid a troublesome spot. He knew that when we hit thin ice, *he,* the lead dog was going to be the first to get dunked.

The sky was a broad expanse of brilliant blue, and the weather was sunny and cold, with a steady north wind. But today it was at our back, pushing us along, making it easier for the team. The wind raised zephyrs of powdery snow, small clouds that moved along beside us, low on the ice. We were sailing south at 14 miles an hour. Halfway across the ice we came to a large rock jutting up from the sea, where we stopped at a shelter to rest and build a fire. Because we were running with the wind we didn't feel the cold until we stopped. Jerry said that we were at Cape Denby, where a treasure trove of artifacts had been unearthed, thousands of years old. This might have been the first place where immigrants from Asia settled thousands of years ago. Glenn climbed to the top of the cape and shouted that there was a polar bear sniffing around out on the ice. I could feel the hairs bristling on the back of my neck. Time to get moving.

With 20 miles to go, one of Jerry's dogs came up lame. Jerry's sled was carrying the heaviest load and moving slowly, so he put the lame dog on his sled and borrowed Flash from my team to help. Whitey was limping perceptibly. Sharp ice crystals had abraded his right front paw, so I put a protective booties on all the dogs. Dogs hate booties and try to tear them off, but they are necessary to protect the dogs' feet.

We turned from south to east for the last mile into Shaktoolik. The north wind, which had been at our backs, was battering our flank again, but we were close to our goal and could handle it for another mile. Our hosts in Shaktoolik were Savetlik family. We tend to think of Eskimos as exotic foreigners, but they are more American than the rest of us. They were in America before we got off the Mayflower, the slave ships or the immigrant boats.

The dogs always knew when you were making a midnight trip to the outhouse. They would be curled in a tight circle in the snow, head in the middle, tail over the head. When you left the hut their heads would go up, pairs of eyes following you all the way to the throne. On the return trip those same pairs of eyes were still watching. We never worried about wild animals coming into camp, because 30 dogs would give us plenty of warning. No sane animal wanted to

240

tangle with a dog pack. Just the same, Jerry and Glenn kept loaded rifles ready day and night in case a bear or a moose got stupid.

A midnight trip to the outhouse in the frigid Arctic night was never much pleasure. There was the business of having to put on your warm clothing in the dark. The trip through the snow to "where the hell is it" might be an adventure in itself when you are using a different one every night. Of course, if you wandered away from camp, there was always the possibility of a nocturnal encounter with a prowling bear, a pack of wolves or a moose. Of the three, the moose is responsible for the most damage in Alaska. They are huge, unpredictable and aggressive. That gigantic rack can do a lot of mischief.

But a nocturnal loo call can have its beautiful side. Comet Hale-Bopp was making its transit across our heavens while I was making my transit across western Alaska. I had seen Hale-Bopp in California, and it was very impressive, but that same skyball took on a whole new personality up north. It seemed 100 times brighter and bigger, with a sharp tail, a full aura and no question about where it was going. It was there night after night, moving a bit to the left every night.

One night early in our trek we had been treated to a full lunar eclipse. Around midnight a huge full moon reflecting off the dazzling white snow lit up the world with brightness coming from everywhere at once. All of a sudden the shadow of the earth took a love bite out of the left side of the moon, and the reddish penumbra eased slowly to the right. Dirty red at first, the shadow slowly darkened the moon until it was all black, a barely visible disk. In the complete blackness every star became a brighter light, and there were thousands of them. Then the moon inched its way out of the earth's shadow, and soon enough it was noon at midnight again.

On our last day along the shore of the Bering Sea we traveled further south, from Shaktoolik to Unalakleet, covering varied terrain. We moved inland two miles, then straight south, rather than the longer route over the ice. For several hours we went up and down rolling hills, forested with dwarf willow trees, some of those hills very steep. At the bottom of every descent there was always a frozen stream, a few of them big enough to be rivers, and there was always a climb back up on the other side.

The trail crossed a place on a downhill where water had broken through the icy surface of a creek, flooding and refreezing on the trail, building a thick ice sheet slanting steeply to the left into the trees. My sled skidded sharply to the left and flipped onto its side. I struggled to keep my grip on the handlebar as I was dragged along. It took Diamond a few seconds to respond to my roaring "WHOA," but the damage was done. Dragged along the ground, my left hand kept a firm grip on the handle bar as the combination of the bar, my fist and my cranium mowed down a row of willows with two-inch thick trunks. As I lay sprawled across the trail, pain shot from the top joints of three fingers, my head felt like it had been pole-axed, and my mitten and wristwatch were in the snow someplace.

The next sled was coming down the narrow trail at me fast, and I expected to be creamed. The driver managed to stop his team inches from me. We dug my mitten from the snow and the watch was inside it. After a quick determination that I would probably not die on the spot, I removed my wedding ring before the swelling started and we moved on. We were still far from Unalakleet, and there was no time to waste with trivialities like a few broken fingers.

The last miles into Unalakleet were anticlimactic. We whizzed south at 20 mph, the wind again behind us. The icy surface made it tough going. It was slick, footing was bad, and ice needles were tearing up the dogs' feet. We stopped three times to put booties on bloody paws. The dogs are tough, and they will continue to run, even with sore feet. A little blood on the snow isn't easy to see at full speed, but Jerry knew what he was doing and made sure that we tended to the animals' feet. When we finished our day's run, I got help un-hitching and feeding the dogs, jammed my swollen hand into a soft snow bank and took a couple of aspirins. The net damage was a goose egg on my head, a badly bruised hand, three sprained fingers and a torn watchband.

There used to be a military base in Unalakleet, but they packed up and left, taking jobs with them. There is an abandoned airstrip, radar antennae and derelict military gear. An airplane fuselage has been creatively rebuilt to house the town offices. Larger than most villages, Unalakleet has a native cooperative store, a lodge, a restaurant and a community center. We had a Tex-Mex dinner at the home of Vance and Leona Grishkowsky, émigrés from North Dakota. We watched the Academy Awards on a big screen TV, and I beat every-one at backgammon (playing with my one good hand), only to be called a predator by The Princess.

Often at sea I have watched the last seconds of a sunset hoping to see a rare phenomenon. Under the right conditions there is a bright green flash of light, lasting an instant, just as the sun blinks below the horizon. I have watched for it and missed it so many times that I began to think it was a hoax. I got another chance in Unalakleet. The sun was brilliant setting over the Bering Sea to the southwest. We sat at the big picture window in the Grishkowskys' living room and watched as the trailing edge of the sinking sun became very wide and thin. Quickly it squared itself into a long, red rectangle and split into two thin rectangles, one above the other. The lower rectangle sank below the horizon and the second one was left hanging there above the horizon for a few seconds. All of a sudden it changed to lime green and instantly was gone. I had finally seen my green flash! It was a good way to turn our backs to the Bering Sea. Tomorrow we were heading inland.

OVERLAND

The next morning, after feeding the dogs, we went south along the shore for a half mile, then hooked left inland up the Unalakleet River. Millennia ago this was the course the Yukon River took to the sea. Over several centuries the ground lifted and the Yukon made a southerly detour of 400 miles. The Unalakleet River Valley is the best route from the Bering Sea to the Yukon River. The first few miles were smooth and flat. As we moved away from the sea and into the protection of hills and forest, we were more sheltered from the wind.

We had been told that this would be the loveliest and the most interesting part of our journey. Before noon Jerry pointed to what looked like a line of ants on a hillside in the distance. He handed me his binoculars, and I counted 70 caribou moving along a trail high above the valley. Then 45 minutes later we stopped at the crest of another hill. A mile away we could see what looked like a herd of buffalo. They were musk oxen, and there aren't many of them left. What a rare treat!

Jerry put Glenn and the snowmobile in the lead, and he told us to stay in close formation in this stretch of forest. We did not want to surprise a belligerent moose or tempt a hungry bear. Glenn had a gun ready, and so did Jerry, who brought up the rear. We came across the remains of what a pack of wolves had left of a large-boned animal, and I asked Glenn what he thought it was. "No, Glenn, I don't think it's a giraffe. I'm not that dumb." We climbed steadily, parallel to the north flank of Old Woman Mountain until we reached a BLM hut in a clearing. The Federal government wastes a lot of money, but this hut was a treat that this taxpayer was glad to see. A little tight for six travelers, the log cabin was well cared-for. There was a big woodpile and a wood stove for cooking and heating. It is traditional for people who use these remote facilities to treat them with care, to leave them neat, and to make sure that there is enough wood for the next cold traveler. Lives have been saved, and the harshness of the Arctic has been softened by following these simple courtesies.

Clara Austin had joined us in Unalakleet and would travel with us to the Kaltag. Jerry fried some tasty caribou burgers for supper, along with canned corn and Tang. It was hardly a typical meal: almost no fat. This would be our last night on the trail, and it was going to be literally all down hill from here. We were all in good voice, lubricated with a bit of John Barleycorn. We went through *Clementine, Row Your Boat, Old MacDonald* (the Alaska version), *The Death of Dan McGrew* and more, and I recited a few technicolor limericks. We played charades for a while and were getting ready to hit the hay when the howling started, loud and clear, a lot of voices.

The dogs were tied up just outside the cabin, but the howling was coming from the trees to the north and south of us, and it sounded close. It was much louder than what we had heard before. Our dogs did not join in. They were very quiet. I don't know if their silence was out of respect for the wolves on Old Woman Mountain or out of fear. Maybe both.

In the morning I went to the creek with Glenn to cut ice to melt for breakfast water. We carried axes to chop the ice, but he had his carbine slung over his shoulder. Halfway down to the creek, Glenn put out his arm to stop me. He carefully scanned the area. In the thin layer of new snow he pointed out fresh wolf tracks, many of them less than 50 yards from our cabin.

KALTAG

From the cabin at Old Woman Mountain it was a magnificent ride down to Kaltag. In the distance to the left was a string of snow-covered mountains about 10,000 feet high. We passed through a forest of spruce and aspen. The snow was deep and covered everything that would hold it, but the trees had shaken off enough snow to patch some green into this glaringly white world. Ahead of us, as far as the eye could see in this crisp, clear air, the land fell off as it flattened toward the horizon. We were moving into the long, broad valley of the Yukon River.

As we closed in on Kaltag and the Yukon River, where this part of my journey would end, I asked Jerry if I could borrow the team and continue on the ice up the Yukon River, maybe to the town of Nulato, or even further. Every mile I logged up the Yukon would bring me that much closer to Fairbanks, where I had started out so long ago. It was early spring, and the ice was still thick and strong. Jerry explained that the problem was not in the long stretches of river where the ice was thick but in a hundred or more places where small rivers and creeks join the Yukon and the in-flow erodes the ice from below, invisible from the surface. A musher daring spring ice not only puts his team at risk but also stands a good chance of being pulled under the ice by the swift current, maybe to wash up hundreds of miles downstream. Bad idea.

The last five miles into Kaltag were flat and easy. Just before the village was an airstrip where I could catch a bush plane to Anchorage, Fairbanks or Nome, homeward bound. It was getting dark when we got into the Athabaskan village of Kaltag. Jerry got us a place on a rise 90 yards from the Yukon. We tied down the dogs, fed them and got ready for dinner. From the upstairs bedroom I could see the wide expanse of the Yukon. It turns south near here after 1,000 miles of wandering west. Below my window the dogs were all curled up, bellies full, turned in for the night

At dinner Jerry told us that the snowmobile had broken a rod coming down the mountain, and a local man was welding it back together while we ate. That's how things get done in the Arctic: people make do. We joked a little and reminisced about the trip. Clara would drive my team from Kaltag to Saint Michael. Jerry made a call to get me a bush flight to Anchorage in the morning. I packed my gear in my big REI duffel and hit the sack.

At 1:27 a.m. I heard the howling for the last time. I got up and looked out the window. The dogs were all curled up, howling from inside their cozy snow burrows. Except for Diamond. He was standing tall, head high in the air, facing my window, and his voice was bigger and his howl lasted longer than the rest. I slept content.

I do not think I will ever mush again. I will never see Diamond, June, Rebar or the others. They were a good team. *We* were a good team. Sometimes I wake in the middle of the night and think I hear the howling. I know it isn't there, but I can hear it. It's inside me. It will never go away.

MEMO FROM: DIAMOND, LEAD DOG
TO: JERRY AUSTIN

Dear Boss:

I have a complaint, and I want you to hear me out. I've been running for you, let's see now, seven times six people years, 42 years. How often have I given you trouble? Yeah, there was the time I disappeared for two weeks. I had fun, but I came back, didn't I? I'm a good and loyal lead dog. I've paid my dues, come up through the ranks. I've been with you through some hard times, like the time we went through the ice on the Yukon River during the Iditarod Race because you got too smart for your britches. I've broken new dogs for you a dozen times. So hear me out, please.

Bringing greenhorns to ride the trail with us is, well, not too good of an idea. They come up here not knowing a willow tree from a fire hydrant. They are poorly dressed and haven't the slightest idea of what real cold is. They fall a lot, and God! That singing! Most of them have never seen a real sled dog, let alone been part of a team. And then you expect me to break them in along the trail. It's hard, stressful work, Jerry, and I don't like it.

Take that Joe guy for instance. I didn't have to look at him to know that he was scared to death. We dogs can smell fear, you know. He came up here with his California tan and that macho attitude of his, but he didn't know squat. The first few days out he was gripping the handlebars so tight that I thought he'd get splinters right through his mittens. We took it real easy on him, gave him a chance to get his sled legs. Okay, we did play crack-the-whip with him a few times, and there was that one time when we scared the poop out of him on that hill outside of White Mountain, but that was all in good fun, wasn't it? I have to admit that he improved after that.

And that, Jerry, brings me to my point. I do a great job of breaking in these greenhorns, bringing them up to speed, and what do you do? Just when they start to show a little bit of promise, just when they are learning teamwork, just when I start to become attached to them, you send them away. That just doesn't make dog sense to me.

What are you, some kind of an insensitive animal?

> *Your Faithful Lead Dog,*
> *Diamond*

Setting out from Nome with "Diamond's Team." No singing, please.

Booties protect "Whitey's" feet from sharp ice crystals.

Diamond telling the world he wants to get started.

Joe at the "Old Woman Cabin" near where we saw musk oxen, wolf and grizzly sign.

Ten of us stayed and slept in this BLM cabin. Several nights were spent in village homes along the route.

How about a hot tub at forty below?

CHAPTER XIV

THE MIGHTY YUKON

Up a lazy river by the old mill run,
That lazy, hazy river in the noonday sun,
Linger in the shade of an old oak tree,
Throw away your troubles, dream a dream with me.
    – The Mills Brothers, 1952

SAVAGES ON THE BEACH

The tall, dark-skinned man moved across the rocky beach toward me. He looked like an Indian, but his expression was odd: he was trying to look mean and funny at the same time. As he extended his big hand to me he said, a bad boy grin on his face. "Hi. I'm Peter and this is Darryl. We are fierce, savage Athabaskan Indians. We read about you guys in the Fairbanks *Daily News-Min* a couple of weeks ago. You made good time coming down river from Fairbanks. Welcome to Kaltag!" I thanked Peter for his welcome and said a silent prayer of thanksgiving that we had made it to Kaltag, and that my nine-year-long quest had at last come to an end.

This was the end of the last act. Two weeks earlier we had left Fairbanks bound for Kaltag, the last 500 miles of the circumnavigation. Kaltag was where my Iditarod dogsled trip had ended the previous year. It was now the summer of 1998, nine years after Gennadi Schvets and I had nervously mounted our tandem bicycle, going the other way, from Fairbanks to New York.

How the world had changed in those years! The Berlin Wall came down before we went through Germany. The Soviet Union intact when we started, no longer existed. And the population of the Earth had increased by a significant fraction of a billion, among them my three youngest grandchildren.

It was long past time for this project to come to an end. I was now in my 65th year and my energy reserves weren't what they were back when I began this circumnavigation, which was beginning to feel more and more like a career. After the Iditarod trip I was looking for excuses to slack off, postpone leaving home again, but there was that nasty little voice inside that kept whispering *quitter, wimp, weenie.* There was no way I could give it up having come this far. I started this, and I was going to finish it, come hell or high water.

High water? There is a network of rivers connecting Fairbanks to Kaltag. The small Chena River runs right through the back yards of Fairbanks. At Nenana it joins the Tanana River, which winds north to the village of Tanana. There the Tanana River is swallowed up by the Yukon, and the Yukon continues on to the Bering Sea, en route passing through Kaltag like a Greyhound bus.

There was a wee technical problem with my following these rivers to close my loop. My circumnavigation had been from west to east. If I continued in that direction, I would have to go *up* the river, fighting the current for 500 miles. Screw that! Even if I were capable of that kind of effort, it would take months. The sensible alternative was to go in the opposite direction, down the rivers, going with the flow all the way. Hell, it was *my* trip and my rules. If I wanted to do the last 500 miles of my circumnavigation backward, so be it. I forgave my reversal by imagining myself drifting gently down the river, the warm sun beating down on me, a book in one hand and a cool drink in the other, birds floating gently overhead, the smell of spruce, a multi-sensual symphony of the humming of the river. Nice dream if you can get it. Reality, of course, was something else.

BEASTS, HUMAN AND OTHERWISE

What about the mosquitoes and the bears? Alaska's mosquitoes are legendary, but I knew one good thing about them: after the first frost, the mosquitoes evaporate. The few that remain are so sluggish that you can count to ten before swatting them while they are trying to figure out why they landed on you in the first place. Along the Yukon the first frosty nights come in late August or September.

But the bears are still very active through September, gorging on whatever they can find (like me, maybe?) to carry them through their long winter's nap. Everyone said, "Bring a gun, Joe, a big gun that will take down an 800-pound grizzly." I didn't *want* to take down a bear. I didn't want to see a bear that close, and I didn't want to carry a gun. When Uncle Sam sent me home after Korea, I didn't want to play with guns any more. But there would be plenty of bears along the Yukon. We would need protection.

Research led me to a river rat named Sam Beverlin in Anchorage. Sam makes his living guiding tourists on river trips in Alaska. I called Sam in the spring of 1998 and regaled him with wondrous tales of my circumnavigation. I told him that I wanted to complete the circle by kayak from Fairbanks to Kaltag, with him right next to me. I told him that I did not want a confrontation with a big bear. Sam laughed. "Only a moron wants to meet a grizzly bear. The solution is knowing how to stay away from them—and how to keep them away from you." Yes, he said, there were lots of bears along the rivers, and, yes, he did carry a big gun for emergencies. "Unfortunately, Joe, I have a family to feed, and as much as I would like to join you, my river guiding season doesn't end until Labor Day, and I'm fully booked up until then." I told Sam that my trip could wait until the tourists were gone, along with the mosquitoes. Sam agreed to join me. We would start in Fairbanks on September 3.

SASQUATCH AND THE BLUE BANANA

My friend John Warren expressed interest. John is a strong paddler and an experienced outdoorsman with a lot of camping savvy. We have been friends for 20 years and have shared many adventures. He is easy-going and intelligent and has an analytical approach to solving problems. His normally serious demeanor is tempered by a droll, British sense of humor. But poor John has these big, ugly feet that leave tracks like Bigfoot. There are very few people I would rather have along with me on a trip like this than our own Sasquatch.

In June Arctic Joe Womersley called me from his farm on Prince Edward Island. We had not been together since our near-suicidal crossing of the mountains from Kirghizia into Kazakhstan. As we talked about my upcoming Yukon River trip, I could sense his interest building. He had to be on Baffin Island in July, but after that . . . "Would you like to join us, Joe?" I asked. I didn't have to ask twice. If trouble were iron, Joe would be a magnet, especially when we are together. He is a witty raconteur, resourceful and adaptable. Our team was coming together.

Sam Beverlin uses big rafts in his river guiding business. They are comfortable and stable and can haul a lot of gear, but they lack the mobility of a kayak. Sitting in a raft all day for weeks didn't sound appealing to me. I wanted mobility and more activity. That called for a kayak. But flying a kayak to Alaska from California would be expensive. Renting one in Alaska was impossible, and returning it to Fairbanks from Kaltag would not be easy.

I wanted a kayak that I could carry with me on an airplane, something I could take apart and put into a duffel bag, but big enough when assembled. There were collapsible kayaks, but most of them were flimsy, easily pierced by an underwater branch or a rock. Our success and maybe my life might depend on this boat. And a beached boat might be an attractive chew toy for a bear or a wolf at night.

The criteria, a collapsible and tough boat, with a large carrying capacity, were met in a boat called SOAR ("Something On A River"). It can be paddled canoe or kayak style, but it is neither, and although it is built like a narrow raft, it is much more mobile. Wider than a kayak, with five inflatable sections, it is 14 feet long and easily carries two paddlers and a heavy load, and it is just short of bulletproof. At 60 pounds, it packs into a duffel bag.

John and I borrowed one to see how it performed. Our trial run was on the Russian River, north of San Francisco. We worked for 20 minutes trying to get it inflated, but it kept collapsing with a loud *pfffft*. A twelve-year-old boy who was watching approached us respectfully. "Maybe it would work if you tried the valve this way, mister." Duh! We pumped it up in no time, looked at each other, and burst out laughing at our own ineptitude. The rest of the trial, and another trial in San Francisco Bay the next week, went well. We had found what we were looking for. We christened her the *Blue Banana*. John and I would paddle the Blue Banana with Sam and Arctic Joe in a raft.

GETTING STARTED

Sasquatch, Arctic Joe, Blue Banana and I arrived in Fairbanks on September 2. To placate the Water Spirits, we did a ritual swim in the frigid Chena River. Someone saw us and, thinking that we were committing mass suicide or just plain nuts, called the police. An explanation and a promise never to do it again placated the cops. A young reporter from the Fairbanks *Daily News-Miner* showed up to cover the cult suicide. When I asked him if he knew Kelly Bostian, the young cub reporter who had interviewed Gennady and me when we started in Fairbanks in 1990, he said "Sure I know him. Kelly is my boss, the managing editor." It *had* been a long time.

Sam showed up the next morning. Instead of the burly, rough-and-tumble guy I had imagined, he turned out to be serious, intelligent and careful, and he was trim and fit. He made it clear that we were the greenhorns and he was the expert. We had no problem with that. That settled, we were off, headed for Kaltag.

The Chena is a backyard river. It meanders behind the beautiful homes on the west side of Fairbanks, ranging from massive log mansions to an authentic replica of Tara. We were paddling right past those homes, close on both sides. Fairbanks is not a big city, though, and before long forest replaced the riverfront homes. Civilization fell away fast as the Chena merged into the much larger Tanana.

Winter was coming, and the birds knew it. Along the Tanana the sky was full of Canada geese, ducks, noisy sandhill cranes, and an occasional pair of trumpeter swans, headed south, wondering why, I suppose, we were paddling north. We were *supposed* to be headed north, but the unruly Tanana River has a mind of its own. It twists and turns like a rattlesnake on a conga line. For every mile we gained north toward the Yukon, we had to paddle three miles in every other direction as the river looped and turned. Coming into the village of Nenana we could see the big black bridge, our landmark, less than a mile ahead of us, maybe ten minutes away. NOT! As we got close, the Tanana took a nasty detour to the left, taking us on a wide loop for an hour before we got to the bridge.

Just as frustrating as the loops and turns were the many channels and islands forever being built up and torn down by the river. Because of constant erosion there are no reliable charts, so we often had to guess which of two or three channels to take. Most would eventually end up in the same place, but some would break up into tiny rivulets and sloughs too small to navigate, forcing us to backtrack. That's where Sam came in. His advice was, "Read the water. If you look carefully, the river will tell you which way to go." We learned that shallow, sloping banks meant that silt was being deposited there; that meant slow water. Frequently a fast current could be seen eating away at the opposite bank. On the outside of a curve the current was usually faster than on the inside; the middle of the river was best for long, straight stretches of water. We watched for hidden underwater hazards by scanning the surface ahead for boil-ups. Most, but not all, of the dangerous snags were along the banks. *Pay attention!* Sam was molding us into passable river rats.

We each had assigned chores when we settled down to camp. My job was to set up the dining fly and the tents. Sam did the cooking, and Sasquatch did the hauling. Arctic Joe's job was building a blazing fire. He gathered wood and always had a conflagration going in ten minutes with only one match, even in the rain. His other assignment was making clean water. We did not trust the river water, so Joe would pump our daily ration of water through a manual filter as we drifted along during the day.

Because Joe was in charge of both fire and water, it also fell upon him to maintain our supply of firewater. In our first three evenings on the river we depleted our supply of one bottle each of bourbon, brandy and scotch. The villages along the river were "dry," but Joe always managed somehow to find hooch. Sasquatch, an engineer by trade, was our navigator. Using a GPS he was able to tell us within a few meters just where we were and how far to the next village or feature on the map. We were paddling long, hard days, and his navigation reports were a big morale booster.

Except for the sound of the river, it was quiet. We could hear an approaching flock of birds miles before we saw them. All along the banks we saw evidence of beavers, including chewed stumps lining the banks and their oversized lodges crowding the edge of the river. Almost daily we saw busy Mr. Beaver himself swimming towards his lodge, our arrival disturbing his work. Before diving, he would give a loud "Who-needs-you?" THWACK! with his tail and he was gone. If beaver hats ever come back into fashion, I'll know where to look.

The edge of the river was usually lined with a row of short alders, looking like busy elves, crowded together, pushing and shoving. Behind the alders were birches and aspen, golden leaves resisting falling to the ground before a long winter's sleep. In the background were spruces—tall, black and somber. The spruces never sleep, standing a stolid vigil high above the river. In the tops of the spruces were eagles' nests, and we were often treated to the sight of an eagle fishing in the river. Always far in the background stood the mountains, most not yet fully coated with their heavy wintry white gowns. At Nenana we got a rare and wonderful hundred-mile view of Mount McKinley, massive and white, standing clearly above the rest of the world.

On our last day on the Tanana a huge bull moose ambled out to the end of a finger of land a quarter mile ahead of us. He eyed us warily as we drifted quietly towards him, and he seemed to be evaluating distance and timing. After full consideration, he decided that this was the time and the place for him to swim across the Tanana, rafters be damned. Deliberately he entered the water, gradually wetting his pie-plate hooves, his long, skinny legs, then his belly. Finally, all but his head and massive rack was submerged as he confidently made his half-mile crossing just in front of us, getting bigger and bigger as we drifted closer. Just as we passed, he leaped gracefully up the steep bank, hurdling fallen trees as he climbed, shook himself like an 800-pound puppy, and gave us a look that said, "I could easily sink your puny boats and toss you into the woods." What Mr. Moose did not know was that it was the start of moose hunting season, and while we were not after the rack and haunches of this magnificent animal, others were. Watch your arrogance, Moosie, or you'll end up as burgers and a hat rack in a bar in Anchorage. A glorious way to conclude our float down the Tanana.

THE MIGHTY YUKON

After a week on the Chena and Tanana Rivers we found ourselves on something much bigger. The Yukon River flows 2,000 miles through Canada and Alaska before dumping into the Bering Sea. We were at our halfway point, and the nature of our relationship with the water was about to change dramatically. A dozen rivers the size of the Tanana flow into the Yukon. Wider than a mile across with no loops and few turns, there were plenty of silted islands, some requiring us to make a left-right decision. Because the river was so wide, the banks were further away and everything seemed motionless, even though the Yukon was moving faster than the Tanana. In mid-river the sky appeared to be enormous.

From the middle of the Yukon we could see very little life along the banks. We still had the company of eagles and, increasingly, ravens and gulls. The migratory birds were now gone. This was prime bear country, so we tried to find campsites on islands far from the riverbank. An encounter with a hungry grizzly was not on the "to do" list, and Sam had the only gun. Even on islands we often found bear or wolf tracks near our camps. Late one night Arctic Joe and I heard a snorting and snuffling outside the thin walls of our tent. Neither of us dared to make a nature call that night. In the morning there were clear signs that we had been visited by a pack of wolves. Sam showed us where one of them had peed on our tent, a foot from Joe's head. Arctic Joe built his night fires bigger after that.

From time to time we saw fish wheels along the riverbank. A cross between a water mill and a Ferris wheel, fish wheels are powered by the flow of the river. Salmon get trapped in the rotating wheel and slide into a big box as the wheel turns. The operator needs only to show up from time to time to empty his box of fish. On a good day a wheel can trap hundreds of fish. John and I stopped at a fish wheel to talk to the operators, two young men, a local and an immigrant from Germany. The fishing this year, they said, was terrible because of El Nino. They were getting only a few hundred a day, maybe a ton, hardly enough to feed their sled dogs over the winter. We bartered a six-pack of Arctic Joe's beer for a big male salmon and a female full of tasty roe, 25 pounds of salmon. Sam would not let me clean the fish anywhere near where we stopped for lunch. "That smell will sure as hell bring bears." He made me clean them in knee-deep water so the remains would be carried down river, far from our camp. Suddenly he shouted, "Get in the boat. Let's get the hell out of here. Leave the fish." We were not 50 yards out when a grizzly sow came out of the woods with her cub.

The weather was generally sunny and cool, with a few days that were rainy, foggy, windy or all three. On bad days we just plugged along quietly. Sometimes the weather would make a complete change as the day passed on the river. Our spirits were high, and we were averaging 35 to 40 miles a day.

There were a dozen villages along our route, each with a population of 200 to 300, mostly Athabaskan Indians. I suspect that, except for Fairbanks, the entire population along 500 miles of river was less than the street I grew up on in New York City. Occasionally we would stop at a village for some conversation, or at a particularly interesting site, like the Bone Yard, where woolly mammoth bones jut from the sandy cliff face every year as the spring floods expose them. Mostly, we just put in long, hard days paddling, usually ten to twelve hours a day.

On a good day, paddling was fun, but not all days were good. On the morning of September 16 we were getting so near that we could almost smell Kaltag, like horses getting close to the barn. We had only 30 miles to go. We broke camp and were on the river by 7:30 a.m. The weather was decent, and we expected to be there by mid afternoon.

At 8:30 a strong headwind was building up out of the west, coming off the Bering Sea, only 100 miles away. With the wind came heavy rain. The wind was pushing big waves at us, making paddling very difficult. We decided to tie the boats in a line to "draft" each other and lessen the effect of the worsening wind and waves. We were working hard without letup, making very little progress. By two in the afternoon we had gone less than ten miles, averaging one and a half miles per hour. As hard as we were pushing, going with the current, the wind and the waves were pushing harder into our faces. At one point I watched a tree up on the bank moving faster than we were. *We were going backwards!* The Yukon was pummeling us. We were beaten. We gave up and pulled ashore.

I guess I looked pretty miserable because Arctic Joe gave me one of his bad-boy looks and said, "What the hell did you expect, you sniveling wimp. We are within pissing distance of the Bering Strait and Siberia, and a couple of hundred miles south of the frigging Arctic Circle. The birds did not fly south for nothing. Get over it." At times like these it is good to have friends. Setting up the tents in heavy wind and horizontal rain took forever, and we were soaked by the time Joe got a roaring fire going. We had our final camp meal and were in bed before the sun set.

Mother Nature called off her wind the next day. She had shown us who was in charge. Now, done with her lesson, she would permit us passage. By noon we were in the good hands of the "Kaltag savages." We had completed our 500 miles from Fairbanks, and we were dog-tired. I was ready for it to be over, not just this paddling trip, but the whole, long journey around the world. And, finally, it was.

How does the saying go? "Be careful what you wish for. You might get it."

The Tanana joins the Yukon here, where a moose crossed the river in front of us.

Sam Beverlin setting up camp on an island in the Yukon River.

*We rigged a sail from a ground cloth when the wind was right –
not often.*

*I am complimenting Artic Joe, on the left, on his fire-making skills.
Note the drying rack.*

FINITO!

POSTSCRIPT

My lifelong dream came true. Was I satisfied with the way
turned out? How could I not be? Now that it is over, though, it
clear that what took place was very different from what I had e
pected.

Reflecting on my adventures, the border escapades were not suc
big problems after all. At least they were not life threatening. Had
known in the beginning that I would face a hurricane at sea, get lo
in the mountains of Central Asia (while sneaking illegally into Kaz
khstan), see temperatures as low as −40° F in Alaska, be at the merc
of crooks in Russia, and . . . well, you read the book. The questio
I was about to ask is this: Would I have started this if I knew what
was getting into? The answer is *probably*. Next question: Am I glad
did it? The answer is an unqualified *yes*. But I am much happier th
it is over.

In retrospect, I didn't really know what I was getting into, exce
that it would be difficult, adventurous, and costly, and it would tal
a long time. My estimate of the hardships, duration and financi
costs were far too low, but some of the adventures that came o
way exceeded my wildest expectations. The fact is that moving alor
step by step, one day at a time, I never really thought much abou
finishing. My focus was on the present, the next step, the next mil
A string of days brought completion to another leg. The total of th
separate links created a chain forged around the world.

Alcoholics Anonymous founder Bill Wilson counseled "one da
at a time." Alan Firth taught me that small steps and minutes joi
together to form hours, days, weeks, years, miles, continents, and f
nally our whole small planet. This journey was not a single big even
just a lot of small ones strung together, one step at a time.

Sometimes I am overwhelmed by what happened to my friends and to me. When I visited Boris at the Soviet Consulate in San Francisco in 1982 I could not have imagined getting lost in the mountains between Kirghizia and Kazakhstan, enduring a hurricane in the Atlantic, swimming from Big Diomede to Little Diomede, or bicycling through Central Asia. Nor, for that matter, did I have any training in sailing, dog mushing or kayaking. There is no doubt in my mind that we were extremely lucky. On the other hand an employer named Saul Silverstein once told me "you make your own luck." If you do the preparation, chances for success will be greater. Saul was right, of course, but that doesn't take into account the kindness of the people we met nor for the fickleness of Mother Nature, who, mercifully, never really showed us her darkest side.

Something like postpartum depression came upon me as the end of the circumnavigation approached. The dream of a lifetime was ending, and where was I? Ten years older, less capable of taking on another big challenge, and psychically sapped. I didn't expect the world to come flocking to my door to heap adulation on me, and it didn't. But I wondered if maybe I should wear a sign that said, "Hey, I *really did* do a non-motorized circumnavigation of the earth, *and you didn't.*"

That, of course, would be arrogant, and here is why: when you come down to it, it was really no big deal. I spent my time doing what I wanted to do. Others do different things, some of immense value to humanity. My personal frivolity did nothing to advance world peace, find a cure for a disease, or help a child in trouble. It was self-indulgence, but I do not regret it.

I have completely and deliberately eliminated any discussion of a side trip we made, illegally and rashly, across the Tien Shan Mountains into China. The southern borders of Kazakhstan and Kirghizia face the troubled Moslem areas of China, home of the persecuted

Uygur minority. At the time of this writing the USA is holding Uygur prisoners at Guantanamo. The problem facing the USA is that if we repatriate them to China, they will face immediate execution. For a similar reason my discussion of our legally questionable travels and our route through the extreme Far East of Russia is eliminated. The peoples of that area, including the Chukchi, are very different from their ethnic Russian masters in Moscow. Their internal passports reflect those differences, and they are not considered to be "Russians." They are the subject of many Russian ethnic jokes. Much more serious is the fact that if I named the villages through which we passed, I am quite certain that today's version of the KGB would extract a large pound of flesh from them. I hope that you will understand and bear with my reasons for limiting that information.

I would like to return to Russia some day to visit the wonderful Russians who were so kind to me. We will sip tea and reminisce. And maybe have a vodka or two.

I learned that Dorothy was right: *"There's no place like home. There's no place like home. There's no place like home."* The sound you hear is my heels clicking together three times.

ACKNOWLEDGEMENTS

So many people to acknowledge and thank for being part of this worldwide adventure!!! Several very special individuals were my companions and partners in fun, danger and hardship. Seymour Blinderman and Gennady and Alexander Schvets were my workmates and playmates from Fairbanks to New York. Ted Epstein was with me in Siberia and the Bering Straits. Ger Wijenberg allowed me to shanghai him as a partner at the last minute to cycle across England. Alan and Mary Firth were with me all the way across England, France, Belgium, Holland and West Germany. They comforted, fed and encouraged me when Murphsky's Laws were getting me down.

In the USSR I had the support of "Sarlik the Mongol," Feodor Sklokin and Dmitrii Shparo. I will never forget the interaction between Arctic Joe Womersley and Kahk Rahmon in Central Asia, or how Joe and I damned near "bought the farm" in the mountains. Jerry Austin and his dogs, especially Diamond, my star and my lead dog, helped me to survive the Iditarod Trail. John Warren has always been a faithful friend, and his paddling and navigational abilities on the Yukon River were indispensable. Sam Beverlin made the Yukon trip possible, and Arctic Joe kept me from taking it too seriously. To Back Room Bicycle Gnomes, who can be found all over the world: *Know ye that ye are needed and appreciated.* Keep up your good work.

I will even say thanks to the nefarious Pinocchio Gang. Without them I might never have gotten off my duff. In this time of the murderous Russian Mafia, may the Pinocchios' petty avarices not do them in. There is a place in this world for Runyonesque characters.

Dick Powell at the Bicycle Outfitter in Los Altos, California, helped me to become a cyclist. Mary Crowley at Ocean Voyages in

Sausalito got me onto a boat to sail across the Atlantic. My light-weight, inflatable kayak for the Yukon came from SOAR in California. REI Coop gave me a break on gear. My body maintenance was at the capable hands of Dr. David Vik, D.C. Santana was kind enough to lend me *Magenta Mama*.

For inspiration, friendship, patience and encouragement, I thank my friends at the DSE Running Club, the South End Club, the Bay Area Sea Kayakers and the inimitable SF Hash House Harriers, if they are sober enough to read this.

Always there for me was my dearest Sylvia. She drove the VW support vehicle across Europe to Moscow, edited my initial writing and helped in too many ways to list here. She constantly gave of her time, her resources and her energy, and as a reward was too often abandoned as I luxuriated in places like Siberia or Alaska. I would not be much without her. On August 31, 2007, we celebrated our 50th anniversary together. What endurance that woman has!

Special thanks to Sylvia's college friend of more than 35 years, Linda Diehl DeLia, who edited and patiently project-managed this baby into existence. John Morris-Reihl designed the book's insides as well as the cover and brought his special brand of quiet artistic grace to the project.